Praise for *Patients Beyond Borders*

"The $20 billion-a-year global medical-tourism market finally has a guidebook of its own. With medical tourism now growing at 15 percent annually . . . this tome couldn't be more timely." —*Travel + Leisure*

"*Patients Beyond Borders* tells how to plan and budget for medical care abroad and how to find the best doctors and hospitals." —*AARP Bulletin*

"The bible for the potential surgical traveler." —The Milken Institute

"Over the years Josef Woodman and the Patients Beyond Borders publications have become the 'gold standard' for advice and counsel on the expanding world of global healthcare travel. I have found Josef's observations and insights to be of immense value for both prospective patients as well as for those of us operating hospitals caring for large numbers of international patients."
—Mack Banner, CEO, Bumrungrad International Hospital

"Headed around the world for some cheaper medical care? Follow these rules."
—*Outside Magazine*

"*Patients Beyond Borders* is a landmark series of consumer guides to international medical travel that has helped thousands of patients plan successful health travel journeys abroad." —*U.S. News & World Report*

"Woodman suggests a $6,000 rule: if your procedure would cost more than $6,000 in the United States, you would likely save money—possibly more than $1,000—by traveling to a foreign hospital, including all other costs."
—NPR (National Public Radio)

"I have read and am impressed by this book."

—Arthur Frommer

"A useful new book on this topic."

—*The Savvy Senior*

"If you're considering medical travel, your first stop should be the book *Patients Beyond Borders.*"

—*Tulsa World*

"*Patients Beyond Borders*'s author lends advice to patients considering travel overseas for medical care."

—Oprah.com

"While AMA guidelines have established a foundation, additional steps will be needed to set appropriate quality standards that extend from pre-operation care to post-discharge and followup. Accreditation and oversight by neutral overseers—JCI, Patients Beyond Borders, and others—will be important."

—Deloitte Center for Health Solutions

"*Patients Beyond Borders*, the best-selling consumer reference for international health travel . . . is a leading advocate of affordable, high-quality medical care for healthcare consumers worldwide."

—AARP Life@50+

"The [*Patients Beyond Borders*] website lists and recommends accredited medical facilities around the world that have met strict international standards."

—*New York Daily News*

"Woodman's father is not alone in looking abroad for a medical overhaul. After all, if the American healthcare system is not completely broken, it is certainly dysfunctional. As baby boomers age into more medical problems with spotty coverage and would prefer not to deplete their retirement savings, they are looking at all available options."

—*Financial Times*

"A must read for those considering medical tourism."

—ABC News

"A practical guide to planning a medical trip."

—*Washington Post*

What Patients Are Saying about
Their Medical Travel Experiences

"The help has been wonderful, and when you are a nervous person like I am, and you get such attention with many of your cares taken on by other people, that's definitely more important than anything. You can be sure when I go home the standard of care and attention I had in this hospital will be a topic of conversation over many a glass of red wine."

—Ian H., Australia
(traveled to Malaysia for heart surgery)

"I am considering elective surgery, and this was a great compendium of information scattered all over the internet."

—Amy T., United States

"I spent a lot of time on the internet trying to research this topic on my own and looking for certain procedures (mainly dental and cosmetic surgery). I wound up getting dental work done in Mexico at a facility reviewed in this book and am happy with my experience. I recommend this book to anyone even remotely considering foreign medical travel."

—K. Williamson, United States
(traveled to Mexico for reconstructive dental surgery)

"I am very pleased with the success of my treatment. As most of my spine is much more stable, the chest pain is almost completely gone. Should other parts of my poor spine start to flare up, I will have no hesitation in returning."

—Robert W., United Kingdom
(traveled to South Korea for complex spinal surgery)

"And the operation itself? Well, as I am writing this, it was obviously a success, perhaps due in part to my overall health condition, but in greater part due to the superb competence and expertise of my doctors, to whom I owe my life. "

—Conor M., Ireland
(a diplomat who traveled to South Korea for heart surgery)

Patients Beyond Borders®

Everybody's Guide to Affordable,
World-Class Medical Travel

Third Edition

Josef Woodman

HEALTHY TRAVEL MEDIA

patientsbeyondborders.com

Patients Beyond Borders:
Everybody's Guide to Affordable, World-Class Medical Travel
Third Edition

Copyright © 2015 by Josef Woodman

ISBN: 13: 978-0-9903154-0-7

COVER ART AND PAGE DESIGN: *Anne Winslow*
COPYEDITING: *Wendell Anderson, NorthStar Writing & Editing*
PROOFREADING AND FACT-CHECKING: *Barbara Resch*
TYPESETTING: *Copperline Book Services*
INDEX: *Madge Walls*
DISTRIBUTION: *Publishers Group West*

Printed in the USA

Healthy Travel Media
PO Box 17057
Chapel Hill, NC 27516
+1 919 924.0636 (GMT-5)
info@patientsbeyondborders.com
patientsbeyondborders.com

To all the dedicated healthcare workers around the world

Foreword

By Jeremy Abbate, *Scientific American Worldview*

MY PERSONAL JOURNEY into the world of medical travel began with what seemed, at the time, a wholly unrelated professional endeavor. As the publishing director for *Scientific American Worldview*, I had been working on a project tasked with assessing the many facets of a particular country's "innovation climate"—those factors that indicated a nation was poised for increased output of both research and commercial science products.

In the course of producing this special edition, one of my lead editors suggested that in addition to the obvious metrics that would imply a nation's sound capabilities in producing scientific innovation (strong intellectual property protection, an educated workforce, support of research and infrastructure, etc.), we should also include data regarding trends in medical tourism. Medical tourism? I was initially confused by the proposed link. What, I had wondered, does a nation's knowledge economy and its success at commercializing research have in common with the increasing number of patients traveling to foreign lands for medical care?

It did not take much explaining to convince me of what in hindsight is an obvious connection—one quite emblematic of that globalized, interdisciplinary ecosystem we like to call our "flattened world." While medical tourism obviously begins as a personal—often emotionally fraught—decision, the trend has, indeed, larger collective implications. The more a country builds up its healthcare and medical infrastructure to accommodate the needs of a growing international patient base, the more it drives further opportunities.

A modernized, innovative infrastructure attracts more qualified doctors and other allied health workers who, in turn, will collaborate in other ways to form new creative alliances. Regions with cutting-edge facilities can participate in and host more important clinical trials, creating new relationships with international biopharmaceutical or medical device companies, and sharing in more international ventures through these associations. Revenue generated from healthcare services can be used to support other areas of basic research, and thus fuel more local scientific discovery. Businesses that complement the health sector can flourish and create additional economic and social opportunities for a country's citizenry.

In short, what appeared to me at first an unrelated enterprise to the larger network of global progress, was, of course, quite interconnected. But let's get back to that discussion with my editor. His preferred source of medical tourism data to be included in our project was *Patients Beyond Borders,* a resource that was familiar to me, but was about to become much more so in the months following.

It just so happened that at about the same time I was finishing my multi-country innovation outlook project, I was beginning a new collaboration with the health ministry of a Southeast Asian nation and required even more background knowledge on the topic of medical travel. This new undertaking involved my participation in a series of high-level events, travel to many different public and private hospitals, as well as the creation of new content surrounding some of the major issues in the medical tourism arena. It was then I discovered why so many have turned to *Patients Beyond Borders* for the most up-to-date, well-researched, authoritative, and accessible information available. Insightful, wonderfully written, and just as practical as it is intellectually rigorous, this series offers an essential road map to a significant and continually evolving global landscape.

Much has been researched and covered in the media on medical tourism in the past few years. It is now a topic of critical concern, both for those in developed nations where healthcare costs have skyrocketed, as well as for governments and private facilities in emerging nations that struggle to best balance opportunities in serving the growing international demand for quality, economically feasible care, and the mandate of serving their citizenry's health.

Those who would characterize medical tourism as merely a business or "industry" are doing a disservice to the motivations, passions, and professional wherewithal of its core stakeholders. Medical tourism, or in a vernacular I feel more aptly suits the enterprise, *health travel,* is simply the necessary consequence of the same globalizing trends affecting so many of the products and services we consume: the natural evolution of bringing more choice, cheaper access, and better value to those who need it most.

When I toured state-of-the-art medical facilities in Malaysia, spoke to surgeons from Thailand, India, Singapore, and Brazil, or interviewed patients who had nervously boarded a plane to some exotic location only to find utter relief at the sight of a caring, friendly, and proficient team awaiting their arrival, I saw the deeply human side of health, the universal instinct to seek or provide comfort. Indeed, a transaction far transcending culture, country, or class.

Most of us in the developed world hold dear the concepts of personal choice and the democratization of knowledge, so that it serves the many, not merely the rarified few. In this sense, the seeking of health solutions beyond one's own national boundaries can be seen as part of the broader *patient empowerment* movement, in which the locus of control begins to shift from provider to health seeker.

The picture of this changing landscape broadens even further when we consider the potential solutions that mobile health and telemedicine offer for a flatter wellness world. Remote diagnostics, robotic surgery, wireless tools, and sophisticated apps swing the pendulum toward more egalitarian access and democratized health. Indeed, health "traveling" in the future may be just as metaphoric as it is real for a patient seeking global options.

Predictions, of course, are only as good as the data we employ to inform them. And while the complicated world of globalized wellness continues its evolving path, with all of the attendant policy debates, national priority concerns, and economic calculus considerations still to come, sound data are the most relevant currency in our quest to understand both present and future. And for those seeking medical and health solutions now, or those wanting to discover options within the larger, international arena in the not too distant future, there is no better source of sound data and information than *Patients Beyond Borders*. Thank goodness that such a complicated system of roads has such a superior map.

Jeremy A. Abbate
Publishing Director
Scientific American Worldview
New York, New York

Introduction

Beginnings

Despite all that has changed since the first edition of *Patients Beyond Borders* hit the bookstore shelves in 2007, I still think back to what started it all: when my father, age 72 at the time (post-Medicare but pre-Obamacare), announced he was heading off to Mexico for extensive dental work. I well remember my first reaction upon hearing his plans: a mixture of bewilderment and fear, then resignation, knowing that despite my protestations, he was going anyway.

In spite of my concerns—some of them quite real—I was pleased to report a happy ending. Dad and his wife, Alinda, selected a US-trained dentist in Puerto Vallarta and spent around US$14,000, which included two weeks touring the Pacific coast. They returned tanned and smiling, Dad with new pearly whites and Alinda with an impromptu skin resurfacing.

Now as then, those same procedures would have cost them $31,000 in the US.

After his treatment, when I told the story of my father's trip, most friends responded with the same shock and disbelief that I had felt initially. Then, when I explained the quality of care and the savings, more often than not those same folks followed me out the door, asking for Dad's email address. I even had an airport customs agent abandon his post and follow me to the boarding gate, seeking additional information for his son who, he had just learned, required heart surgery.

Not long afterward, I developed an infected root canal and found myself following my father's example. My research led me abroad for extraction and implant work. Although pleasantly surprised at the quality of care, the prices, and the all-around good experience of the trip, I nonetheless made a number of mistakes, creating unnecessary difficulties and discomforts for myself. Had I done some simple things differently, my trip would have been more successful and more economical.

In seeking additional data on medical travel, I found no reliable source of information. It seemed everybody had something to sell or a political axe to grind. Available books, magazine articles, and newspaper reports were more like tourists' brochures than health travel references.

Thus, the idea for *Patients Beyond Borders* was born: a well-researched guide, written in plain English, that would offer an impartial look at contemporary medical travel while helping prospective patients ask the right questions and make informed choices.

Nearly a decade later, *Patients Beyond Borders* is now in its third edition, along with a robust website of the same name. So very much has changed, largely to the advantage of the discerning healthcare consumer. Patients now have access to hundreds—not merely a handful—of high-quality, US-accredited international hospitals and clinics. Trustworthy sources of information—print, online, and mobile—help patients research vital information and make better-informed purchase decisions.

The number of medical tourists has increased nearly tenfold in the eight years since the first edition of this book, to some 11 million patients now crossing borders worldwide each year. More than one million are North Americans, and the overwhelming majority returns happily to tell about it—with some savings in the bank to show for their efforts. If it's true there's safety in numbers, then most who have had doubts in the past can take comfort in the successes of past pioneering patients.

As we contemplate our options in an overburdened, post-Obamacare US healthcare environment, nearly all of us will eventually find ourselves seeking alternatives to costly or heavily triaged treatments, either for ourselves or for our loved ones. America is in the midst of a tectonic shift in global healthcare services: government investment, industry partnerships, and increased media attention have spawned a new industry—medical tourism—bringing with it a host of encouraging new choices, ranging from dental care and cosmetic surgery to some of the more costly procedures, such as hip replacement and heart surgery.

Those patients who take the time to become informed about our changing healthcare world will be pleasantly surprised by a smorgasbord of affordable, high-quality, American-accredited medical options abroad. Those who do not may find themselves grappling with an ungainly, prohibitively expensive healthcare system and a growing limitation of choice.

Who Travels for Healthcare?

There is no single type of health traveler. In researching and writing *Patients Beyond Borders* I talked with wealthy women from Beverly Hills who, despite their affluence, prefer the quality of treatment and attention they receive in Costa Rica or Thailand to medical care California-style. I met a hardworking couple from Wisconsin who, facing the prospect of refinancing their home for a $65,000 hip operation here in the US, headed to India instead. I interviewed a Vietnam vet who had wearied of long waits and red tape. He said bon voyage to this country's ever-deteriorating healthcare system and headed overseas for treatment.

In fact, as the global population ages, I increasingly encounter individuals who have opted to pull up stakes altogether, to settle into lifestyles less expensive, perhaps less encumbered. It's no accident that some of the leading retirement destinations—Mexico, Costa Rica, Malaysia, Thailand, to name a few—are also healthcare hubs renown for high-quality medical care.

From these patients' experiences, and many more like them, you will learn when and how health travel abroad might meet your medical and financial needs. And you will become a more informed healthcare consumer—both here and abroad—for yourself and for your family and friends.

Patient Experiences: Margaret S. and Doug S.

Margaret S., a patient from Santa Ana, California, was quoted us$6,600 for a tooth extraction, two implants, and two crowns. Restorative dental work is not covered by most health plans. Margaret found herself among the estimated 125 million Americans without dental coverage. Through a friend, she learned about Escazú, Costa Rica, known for its excellent dental and cosmetic surgery clinics. Margaret got the same treatment in Costa Rica for $2,600. Her dentist was a US-trained oral surgeon who used state-of-the-art instrumentation and top-quality materials. Add in airfare, lodging, meals, and other travel costs, and this savvy global patient came out way ahead.

Doug S., a small-business owner from Wisconsin, journeyed with his wife, Anne, to Chennai, India, for a double hip resurfacing procedure that would have cost more than $55,000 in the US. The total bill—including travel for him and his wife, lodging, meals, and two-week recuperation in a five-star beach hotel—was $14,000. "We were treated like royalty," said Doug, "and I'm riding a bicycle for the first time in six years. We could not have afforded this operation in the US." ■

You Deserve an Impartial Perspective

The growing phenomenon of medical tourism, or international health travel, has received a good deal of wide-eyed attention of late. While one newspaper or organization giddily touts the fun-'n-sun side of treatment abroad, another issues dire warnings about filthy hospitals, shady treatment practices, and procedures gone bad. As with most things in life, the truth lies somewhere in between.

In short, I have found the term *medical tourism* something of a misnomer, often leading patients to emphasize the recreational more than the clinical in their quest for healthcare abroad. Unlike much of the hype that surrounds contemporary health travel, *Patients Beyond Borders* focuses more on your health than on your travel preferences. Thus, throughout this book, you'll see few references to the terms *medical tourism* or *health tourism*. In the same way business travelers do not normally consider themselves leisure tourists, you'll likely begin to think more of your medical welfare than nights spent in Margaritaville when planning your medical journey.

My research, including countless facility visits and interviews, has convinced me that with diligence, perseverance, and good information, patients considering traveling abroad for treatment have legitimate, safe choices, not to mention an opportunity to save thousands of dollars when compared to the same treatment in the US. In speaking with hundreds of patients who have returned from successful treatment overseas and who have provided overwhelmingly positive feedback, I was persuaded to write this impartial, scrutinizing guide to becoming an informed international patient. I designed this book to help readers reach their own conclusions about whether and when to seek treatment abroad.

What Exactly Is Medical Tourism?

In 2014 more than one million Americans packed their bags and headed overseas for nearly every imaginable type of medical treatment: weight loss surgery in Mexico, heart valve replacements in Thailand, hip resurfacing in India, proton therapy in Korea, fertility treatments in Israel, facelifts in Hungary, restorative dentistry in Mexico.

At the time of this writing, at least 50 countries cater to the international health traveler, with some 12 million patients visiting hospitals and clinics each year in countries other than their own.

If the notion of complex medical procedures in far-flung lands seems intimidating, don't feel alone. That's why I wrote this book, drawing from the varied experiences of hundreds of patients who, for dozens of reasons, have beaten a well-worn path to successful treatments abroad.

Global Healthcare: A World in Flux

On a recent visit to one of Seoul, South Korea's most prominent international hospitals, the CEO insisted on showing me a prostate surgery performed by a doctor sitting at a robotics device 30 feet away from the patient. The implications were clear: one day soon, we'll see top doctors and surgeons in South Korea and Thailand performing everything from health checkups to heart surgeries in Turkey and the US. We'll see patients in Dubai with wireless-enabled pacemakers monitored by healthcare facilities in India. Just as we can go online to search, price-shop, and purchase books, appliances, real estate, and financial instruments, rising transparency in healthcare, coupled with new "plug and play" approaches to treatment, will allow greater consumer options regarding our medical treatments as well.

We are also at long last seeing a shift in focus in the healthcare world, one from hospitals as "fix-it" shops for the sick to a more preventive approach, particularly around obesity, tobacco, and other poor lifestyle behaviors that spawn a host of serious and often chronic medical conditions. Leading medical facilities are increasingly adding wellness centers, complementary and integrative medicine (CAM), executive health screenings, and a host of preventive programs aimed at keeping people well rather than merely treating the sick.

In brief, we're in the midst of vast and exciting changes in the way we think about and purchase medical services. Medical tourism is an important component of a new international healthcare ecosystem, where not only geographic but research, technology, and patient access walls are coming down, to the great benefit of you, the enlightened healthcare consumer. Any patient who is not merely a passive "follower of doctor's orders" will recognize and take advantage of these profound clinical and social changes, to great and lasting benefit. ∎

Why Go Abroad for Medical Care?

Cost savings. Most people like to get the most for their money. The single biggest reason Americans travel to other countries for medical treatment is the opportunity to save money. Depending upon the country and type of treatment, uninsured and underinsured patients, as well as those seeking elective care, can realize 15–85 percent savings over the cost of treatment in the US.

The quest for cost savings is not a strictly US phenomenon. While Americans are crossing borders—by plane, auto, and sometimes on foot—into Mexico for dental and cosmetic treatments, Germans, Swiss, and Austrians head to Hungary, Poland, and the Czech Republic for treatments not covered by government-sponsored health plans. Similarly, patients from the UK fly to India to take advantage of savings up to 90 percent over prices of elective procedures at home.

As Gen Xers become senior boomers and as baby boomers live even longer than expected, costs of healthcare and prescriptions now devour nearly 30 percent of retirement and pre-retirement incomes. With increasing options in top-quality treatments at deep discounts overseas, informed patients are finding creative alternatives abroad. As one successful health traveler put it, "I took out my credit card instead of a second mortgage on my home."

Quality and price disparities occur within national borders as well. As the internet increasingly allows patients to search and compare healthcare costs and quality, "domestic medical travel" is on the rise, whereby a patient in rural northern Thailand might travel to Bangkok, one of Thailand's two main destinations for high-quality specialized care. Similarly, in the United States, corporations such as Lowe's, PepsiCo, and Walmart have entered into agreements with facilities such as the Cleveland Clinic and Johns Hopkins to offer the highest caliber treatment to those willing to travel beyond their backyards for care.

Typical Procedures: Comparative Costs

Procedure	US Cost	Costa Rica	India	Malaysia	Mexico	Singapore	South Korea	Thailand
Average savings		45–65%	65–90%	60–80%	40–60%	25–40%	30–45%	50–75%
Coronary artery bypass graft (CABG)	$88,000	$31,500	$14,400	$20,800	$37,800	$54,500	$29,000	$23,000
Valve replacement with bypass	$85,000	$29,000	$11,900	$18,500	$34,000	$49,000	$33,000	$22,000
Hip replacement	$33,000	$14,500	$8,000	$12,500	$11,500	$21,400	$15,500	$16,500
Knee replacement	$34,000	$9,500	$7,500	$12,500	$12,800	$19,200	$15,000	$11,500
Spinal fusion	$41,000	$17,000	$9,500	$17,900	$22,500	$27,800	$18,000	$16,000
IVF cycle, excluding medication	$15,000	NA	$3,300	$7,200	$7,800	$9,450	$7,500	$6,500
Gastric bypass	$18,000	$11,200	$6,800	$8,200	$13,800	$13,500	$12,500	$12,000
Four-implant porcelain bridge	$23,000	$9,500	$7,200	$7,800	$8,500	$12,000	$10,500	$10,500
Implant-supported dentures (upper and lower)	$10,500	$4,400	$3,500	$3,800	$4,200	$6,400	$5,800	$3,900
Full facelift	$12,500	$4,500	$3,500	$5,500	$5,250	$8,750	$5,900	$5,300
Rhinoplasty	$6,200	$3,400	$2,800	$3,600	$2,800	$4,750	$4,700	$4,300

The above costs are for treatment (except as noted), including the hospital stay in a private, single-bed room. Airfare and lodging costs are governed by individual preferences. To compute a ballpark estimate of total costs, add $5,000 for you and a companion, figuring coach airfare and hotel rooms averaging $150 per night. For example, a hip replacement in Bangkok, Thailand, would cost about $21,500, for an estimated savings of at least $11,500 compared to the US price.

Better quality care. Each year millions of patients with little or no access to quality diagnostics and treatment in their own countries travel for quality medical treatment, usually to a contiguous or nearby nation known for excellent healthcare. For example, approximately 600,000 Indonesians travel to Malaysia and Singapore annually for access to general care as well as more complex treatments not yet available to the country's 240 million citizens. More than 100,000 Russian patients head to Turkey, Israel, and the US. Affluent Middle Easterners travel to the US, Thailand, and Malaysia; mainland Chinese to Taiwan and Singapore. The list goes on. One day in our distant futures, our global healthcare infrastructure will hopefully improve to make this type of medical travel unnecessary; for now, however, it is a part of the culture for millions and contributes vastly to the growth of the international healthcare sector.

Improved patient experience. Seasoned health travelers know that facilities, instrumentation, and customer service in treatment centers abroad often equal or exceed those found in their homelands. Government and private stakeholders in countries such as Mexico, Costa Rica, India, Malaysia, and Thailand have poured billions of dollars into improving their healthcare systems, which are now aggressively catering to the international health traveler. VIP waiting lounges, deluxe hospital suites, and recuperation resorts are common amenities, along with free transportation to and from airports, low-cost meal plans for companions, and discounted hotels affiliated with the hospital.

Moreover, physicians and staff in treatment centers abroad are often far more accessible than their US counterparts. "My surgeon gave me his mobile phone number, and I spoke directly with him at least a dozen times during my stay," said David P., who traveled to Bangkok for a heart valve replacement.

Excluded treatments. Even the most robust public and private health insurance plans exclude a variety of conditions and treatments. You, the policyholder, must pay these expenses out of pocket. Although health insurance policies vary according to the underwriter and individual, your plan probably excludes an array of treatments, such as cosmetic surgeries, dental care, vision treatments, reproductive/infertility procedures, some non-emergency cardiovascular and orthopedic surgeries, weight loss programs, substance abuse rehabilitation, and prosthetics, to name only a few.

Rich or cash-challenged, young or not-so-young, heavily or only lightly insured— folks who get sick or desire a treatment (even one recommended by their physician) often find their insurance will not cover it. Despite the many new benefits of healthcare reform, tummy tucks and a new set of teeth are not among the covered treatments. More than 70 percent of American health travelers hit the road for elective treatments. In countries such as Costa Rica, Singapore, UAE, and Thailand, this trend has spawned entire industries offering excellent treatment and ancillary facilities at costs far lower than US prices.

Specialty treatments. Patients seeking cutting-edge options may find some procedures and prescriptions are unavailable or prohibited at home. Perhaps a regulatory agency has specifically disallowed a treatment or drug, or perhaps it is still in the clinical trials stage or only recently approved. Such treatments are often offered abroad. In the US, certain types of stem cell and regenerative therapies are still not approved for treatment of cancer; Americans now can choose quality facilities as nearby as the Bahamas or as far away as Singapore. Similarly, Canadian patients with multiple sclerosis travel to Mexico and India for CCSVI treatments not yet allowed in Canada.

Shorter waiting periods. For decades thousands of Canadian and British subscribers to universal healthcare plans have endured waits as long as two years for established procedures. "Some of us die before we get to the operating table," commented one exasperated patient who journeyed to India for an open-heart procedure.

Here in the US, wait times are a growing problem, particularly as resources for specialty care become increasingly burdened under the new healthcare reform legislation. Some patients determine it is better to pay out of pocket to get out of pain or to halt a deteriorating condition than to suffer the anxiety and frustration of waiting for a far-future appointment and other medical uncertainties.

More inpatient friendly. As health insurance companies apply increasing pressure on hospitals to process patients as quickly as possible, outpatient procedures are becoming the norm. These days, hospitals in countries such as the US and UK are under pressure to move patients out of costly inpatient beds sooner than later, often not allowing sufficient time for basic recovery. Medical travelers will welcome the flexibility at the best hospitals abroad, where they are often encouraged to spend extra time in the hospital post-procedure. Staff-to-patient ratios are usually lower abroad, as are hospital-borne infection rates.

The lure of the new and different. Although traveling abroad for medical care can be challenging, many patients welcome the chance to blaze a trail, and they find the creature comforts often offered abroad a welcome relief from the sterile, impersonal hospital environments so often encountered at home. For others simply being in a new and interesting culture lends distraction to an otherwise worrisome, tedious process. And getting away from the myriad obligations of home and professional life can, for some, yield healthful effects at a stressful time.

What's more, travel, particularly international travel, can be a life-changing experience. You might be humbled by the limousine ride from Indira Gandhi International Airport to a hotel in central New Delhi; or struck by the simple, elegant graciousness of professionals and ordinary people in Thailand; or wowed by the beauty of the mountain range outside a dental office window in Mexico. As one veteran medical traveler put it, "I brought back far more from this trip than a new set of teeth."

Who Should Read *Patients Beyond Borders*?

You'll benefit from reading this book if:

- you are an un-insured or under-insured individual who wishes to explore less-expensive options for a treatment often covered by health insurance
- you are one of tens of millions without a dental plan and wish to take advantage of the full range of affordable dental procedures in other countries
- you wish to save money on an elective treatment (such as cosmetic surgery, in vitro fertilization, or dental implants) not normally covered by health insurance policies
- you are considering one of many treatments either not offered or not approved in your country
- you feel a friend or family member might benefit from learning more about health travel, yet that person might lack the confidence or focus to launch an inquiry
- you plan to join a family member or friend for treatment abroad

What *Patients Beyond Borders* Will (and Will Not) Do for You

Patients Beyond Borders is not a guide to medical diagnosis and treatment. It does not provide medical advice on specific treatments or caregiver referrals.

Your condition, diagnosis, treatment options, and travel preferences are unique. Only you—in consultation with your physician and loved ones—can determine the best course of action. Should you decide to investigate traveling abroad for treatment, we provide you with the resources and tools necessary to become an informed medical traveler so that you will have the best possible travel experience and treatment your money can buy.

Our job is to:

- help you become a knowledgeable, confident health traveler
- assist you in planning and budgeting your trip and treatment
- provide you with up-to-date information about the most popular, widely used treatment centers
- make your in-country visit as comfortable and hassle free as possible
- provide tips for a successful medical travel experience before, during, and after treatment

Your job is to:

- consult with your local doctors to ensure you've reached a satisfactory diagnosis and recommended course of treatment
- decide, based on your research and the material featured in this book, whether you wish to travel abroad for treatment
- select a travel destination, treatment center, and physician based on the information you find in this book and elsewhere

It's a truism: every journey begins with the first step. Health travel is no exception. Once you've made that first move toward learning more, you'll find that your friends, family, this book, and a trusty internet connection will speed you on your way.

How to Use This Book

Before you dive into Part Two, "The Most-Traveled Healthcare Destinations," you'll want to carefully read Part One, "How to Become a Savvy, Informed Medical Traveler." It provides you the basic resources and tools you will need to do your research and make an informed decision.

Chapter One, "What Am I Getting Into? Some Quick Answers for Savvy Health Travelers," addresses the questions and concerns most often voiced by patients (and their loved ones) considering a medical journey abroad.

Chapter Two, "Planning and Budgeting Your Health Travel Journey," walks you through the financial basics of a medical trip and gives you the tools you need to prepare an estimated budget. Our "*Patients Beyond Borders* Budget Planner" helps you determine specific cost savings and avoid financial surprises.

Chapter Three, "The Twelvefold Path to Enlightened Health Travel Planning," helps you design your trip step by step. The chapter provides data and advice culled from interviews with hundreds of patients and treatment centers. You'll learn how to separate the chaff quickly to find the right clinics, determine physician accreditation, narrow your destination choices, choose the right companion, and more.

Chapter Four, "While You're There," provides valuable information on what to expect from your treatment center and physician, plus general tips for dealing with local cultures, language barriers, and more. A section on communicating while on the road includes pointers on using cell phones and computers to communicate with physicians in-country, as well as loved ones back home.

Chapter Five, "Home Again, Home Again," helps you get settled in post-treatment, offering practical advice on working with your hometown doctor, shaking off the "post-treatment blues," coping with discomforts and complications, and getting back on your feet.

Chapter Six, "Dos and Don'ts for the Smart Health Traveler," helps you avoid common speed bumps and potholes on the health travel road.

Chapter Seven, "Checklists for a Successful Health Journey," helps you track important details as you plan your health travel.

Part Two, "The Most Traveled Healthcare Destinations," features hundreds of destinations in 20 countries, with up-to-date information on hospitals and clinics, specialties, accreditation, recovery centers and recuperation resorts, transportation, communication, and more. You'll use the information in this section to get a good idea about where to travel for your particular procedure and what to expect for the costs of common treatments.

Part Three, "Resources and References," provides additional sources of medical travel information and helpful links, plus a glossary of commonly used medical terms.

As you work your way through decision making and subsequent planning, remember that you are following in the footsteps of millions of health travelers who have made the journey before you. The overwhelming majority has returned home successfully treated, with money to spare in their savings accounts.

Still, the process, particularly in the early planning, can be daunting, frustrating, even a little scary. That's normal, and most health travelers we interviewed experienced the "Big Fear" at one time or another. Healthcare abroad is not for everyone, and part of being a smart consumer is evaluating all the impartial data available before making an informed decision. If you accomplish that in reading *Patients Beyond Borders*, we will have achieved our mission.

Let's get started.

How to Become a Savvy, Informed Medical Traveler

CHAPTER ONE

What Am I Getting Into?
Some Quick Answers
for Savvy Health Travelers

Is Healthcare Overseas Safe?

Interestingly, the friends and family members of patients considering healthcare abroad ask this question more often than do the patients themselves. In fact, at least one friend or family member is virtually guaranteed to balk at the thought of your heading overseas for treatment. Most of these concerns are unfounded. They usually arise either from a lack of knowledge or from cultural myopia.

Although no medical procedure is 100 percent risk free anywhere in the world, the best hospitals and clinics abroad maintain health and procedural standards equal to, or higher than, those you might encounter in the US or your own country. The leading hospitals abroad are accredited by one of several renowned international accreditation institutions, including the US-based Joint Commission International. (For more information on hospital accreditation and safety standards, see Chapter Two, "Planning and Budgeting Your Health Travel Journey.")

It is not hard to find overseas physicians, dentists, and surgeons who received their medical training and degrees at first-rate medical schools in the US, the UK, Canada, Switzerland, or Germany. All the countries listed in *Patients Beyond Borders* enforce strict governmental and private standards for healthcare, hospital, and clinic certification.

Finally, many hospitals, particularly the larger institutions in South Asia and Southeast Asia, boast lower morbidity rates than in the US, particularly when it comes to complex cardiac and orthopedic surgeries, for which success rates higher than 98.5 percent are the norm.

A Briefing on International Accreditation

When you walk into a hospital or clinic in the US, chances are good it's accredited, meaning that it complies with standards and "good practices" set by an independent accreditation agency. A general rule of thumb for a global patient, particularly if you're planning on major surgery, is to first seek out internationally accredited facilities.

Joint Commission International. In the US, by far the largest and most respected accreditation agency is The Joint Commission. The agency casts a wide net of evaluation for hospitals, clinics, home healthcare, ambulatory services, and a host of other healthcare facilities and services throughout this country.

Responding to a global demand for accreditation standards, The Joint Commission launched its international affiliate agency in 1994, the Joint Commission International (JCI). To be accredited by JCI, an international healthcare provider must meet a set of rigorous standards similar to those set forth in the US by The Joint Commission.

At this writing, some 600 hospitals and clinical departments in more than 50 countries have been JCI approved, with additional facilities coming onboard each month. This is good news for the medical traveler, who can walk with greater confidence into a JCI-accredited facility knowing that standards are high and that staff, procedures, instrumentation, and administrative infrastructure are monitored regularly.

JCI's website carries far more information than you will likely ever want to explore on accreditation standards and procedures. The agency lists a frequently updated roster of JCI-accredited hospitals abroad, searchable by country.

Please note that many very fine hospitals and clinics throughout the world are not yet JCI accredited, and it's sometimes more difficult for some of these organizations to receive approval for highly specialized or experimental treatments. However, when considering one of these hospitals, you will want to ask some tough questions about accreditation and standards.

Agencies That Accredit Outpatient Specialty Clinics

The cumbersome, decentralized general hospital model is gradually giving way to the vastly more efficient specialty clinic for orthopedics and spine, certain types of cancers, ENT, and a host of other disciplines. Ambulatory care—or outpatient or day visit care—refers to a medical procedure conducted during the course of one day and not requiring an overnight inpatient visit. Dental, cosmetic surgery, fertility, hearing, and vision clinics generally fall into this category. As a result, specialty accreditation agencies now serve ambulatory centers, providing assurance that process and quality standards have been met. Some have established international arms, notably the following three.

The Accreditation Association for Ambulatory Health Care. The Accreditation Association for Ambulatory Health Care (AAAHC) was founded in 1979 "to organize and operate a peer-based assessment, education, and accreditation program for ambulatory health care organizations as a means of helping them provide the highest achievable level of care."

AAAHC surveys and accredits a wide array of ambulatory care organizations, including ambulatory surgery facilities, college and university health services, community health centers, single and multi-specialty group practices, and managed care organizations.

Surveys are conducted by professionals actively involved in outpatient care and who have demonstrated expertise in addressing the specific issues of the facilities they survey. Surveyors vet facilities against prevailing standards and share their knowledge and experience with others to help providers maintain high levels of quality assurance and patient safety.

AAAHC has to date accredited more than 5,000 organizations; in 2010 AAAHC established its international subsidiary (AAAHCI), with a modest beginning in Peru and Costa Rica.

The American Association for Accreditation of Ambulatory Surgery Facilities International. The American Association for Accreditation of Ambulatory Surgery Facilities (AAAASF, or quad SF) also accredits outpatient facilities, focusing upon surgery clinics. AAAASF was founded in 1980 to develop an accreditation program to help establish and oversee quality assurance measures toward creating and improving industry standards that help assure patient safety.

Of particular interest to the medical traveler is AAAASFI, the international branch of AAAASF, established in 2004 to address the growing consumer and industry need for reliable quality standards throughout the world. As of this writing, some 50 international facilities in 15 countries outside the United States have been awarded AAAASFI accreditation, including Brazil, Costa Rica, Mexico, and South Africa.

As with its US counterpart, AAAASFI focuses on three broad quality areas: safe and appropriate facility, safe and appropriate physicians, and appropriate patients. Qualifying facilities are awarded in three-year cycles, subject to random "validation surveys" anytime during the cycle. Among other requirements to achieve accreditation, an outpatient facility must show evidence of active board certification (or the local equivalent) for every doctor engaged by the clinic.

Joint Commission International. JCI accredits outpatient centers, although it mostly accredits same-day departments within hospitals settings.

Other organizations around the world set standards and accredit hospitals, and some may be as careful in their procedures and protocols as JCI—or not.

Other international healthcare accreditation organizations include (to name a few) the Australian Council of Healthcare Standards, the Canadian Council on Health Services Accreditation, the Irish Health Services Accreditation Board, the Malaysian Society for Quality in Health, the Council for Health Services Accreditation of Southern Africa, and the Japan Council for Quality Health Care. If you are considering a hospital accredited by one of these organizations, it pays to investigate the criteria the organization applies and determine to your own satisfaction that the standards are sufficient and appropriate to your needs.

A Word about ISO

When researching hospitals and clinics abroad, you will often come across the phrase *ISO accredited.* Based in Geneva, Switzerland, the International Organization for Standardization (ISO) is a 157-country network of national standards institutes that approves and accredits a wide range of product and service sectors worldwide, including hospitals and clinics. ISO mostly oversees facilities and administration, not healthcare procedures, practices, and methods. That's of limited value in terms of your treatment.

Who Polices the Police?

If you have managed to get this far on the topic of accreditation, you may be wondering which agencies are trustworthy. The International Society for Quality in Healthcare (ISQua), established in 1984, is now the world's leader in accrediting healthcare standards. It is an accreditation agency that blesses the quality of other accreditation agencies around the world through oversight of minimum standards of patient safety. On its website, ISQua publishes a listing of its accredited agencies.

If Healthcare in Other Countries Is So Good, How Can It Be So Cheap?

This question is best answered by another question: Why is US healthcare so expensive? High facilities costs, unpaid hospital bills totaling billions of dollars, high-priced medical education, costly research, and excessive malpractice litigation all add up to exorbitant prices for healthcare in the US.

In addition, US physicians who perform elective and specialty procedures—such as cosmetic surgeries; in vitro fertilization; and certain hip, spine, and cardiac procedures—often command astronomical fees from patients willing and able to pay, leaving those of more modest means in the lurch and seeking alternatives.

Healthcare in other countries is also less costly because standards of living are more modest, doctors and staff command lower wages, government-subsidized healthcare keeps private healthcare costs down, and malpractice attorneys are, if not docile, at least considerably more restrained.

Moreover, the administration of medical care, particularly in Asia, is far more efficient than in legacy nations with burdens of paper-based records, old facilities and instrumentation, and a mind-set not focused on the bottom line. This is evidenced by the fact that the US ranks around 46 among all advanced-economy nations measured by life expectancy. US healthcare spending hovers at nearly 20 percent of our gross national product (GDP). Compare this with nations such as Singapore (rank: #2); South Korea (rank: #8); and the Czech Republic (rank: #34), all of which spend less than 10 percent of GDP on healthcare.

How Much Can I Save?

Your savings will depend on your treatment, your selected destination, and your travel and lifestyle preferences. Patients who travel to India for complex heart bypass surgeries will typically save more than US$50,000 over the price in the US. People traveling to Costa Rica for reconstructive dentistry or extensive breast and abdominal cosmetic surgery can save $10,000 or more.

A good rule of thumb is the $6,000 rule: If your US specialist quotes you a price of $6,000 or more for a treatment, chances are good that one or more foreign countries can offer you the same procedure and quality for less, even including your travel and lodging expenses. If your US quote is less than $6,000, you're probably better off having your treatment at home.

Is It Safe to Travel Overseas?

For many, a medical trip is their first journey abroad. That can be a scary prospect. Relentless news of global social unrest and political instability induces enough fear to make any novice international traveler think twice about packing a suitcase. Yet in the midst of these twenty-first century realities, no medical travel patient has come to harm as a result of terrorism or social unrest.

Further, most leading medical travel destinations enjoy relatively low crime rates. Your own behavior will determine much of your experience abroad. If you follow the common sense rules of travel courtesy and observe cultural norms, you should be safe in any country featured in this book.

Health travelers can be further reassured because from the moment of arrival in another country until departure on a homebound plane, most are under the near-constant supervision of a hospital, health travel broker, tour agency, or other third-party agent. Health travelers are often met at their destination airport arrival gate and whisked to an American-style hospital or hotel. From that point, they are usually under someone's care in a treatment center, getting a bite in a restaurant, or resting in a cozy hotel room.

What Medical Treatments Are Available Abroad?

Although nearly every kind of treatment is possible abroad, most Westerners head overseas for orthopedics (hip replacement, knee replacement, spinal work); cardiovascular surgery (bypass, valve replacement, heart transplant); dental care (usually more extensive cosmetic or restorative surgery); or cosmetic surgery. In addition, patients seek specialty treatments (such as fertility and in vitro fertilization procedures); weight loss procedures (such as bariatric surgeries); and therapies not yet allowed or available in their country (such as certain stem cell treatments). In Part Two of this book, you will discover a range of treatment specialties and super-specialties that run the full medical gamut.

What all those treatments have in common is great expense. The huge savings to be garnered abroad can outweigh the challenges of crossing borders for treatment.

A Note about Prevention and Wellness

In the early days of touring international hospital and clinics as part of my research for *Patients Beyond Borders*, I noticed that patients were generally younger than I had expected them to be, and heavier as well! After witnessing the same phenomenon among Western patients in nearly every facility I visited, I finally questioned a doctor in Taiwan. His reply: "What do you expect? Poor lifestyle causes poor health and premature aging."

We cannot control our genetic programming—and many will require medical care regardless of any precautions we might take. However, most of us can help beat the odds by making good lifestyle choices for us and our loved ones: lose weight, quit or moderate your drinking and smoking, get at least 20 minutes per day exercise. The best way to avoid a trip to the hospital is to reduce your chances of becoming a patient in the first place. If you can help it, why travel crosstown, never mind across the ocean, for medical treatment? ∎

How Do I Know Where to Travel for Treatment?

Many countries are known for a particular category of treatment. Your diagnosis will distill your list of choices down to a handful of destinations. If you are seeking cosmetic surgery, Mexico, Costa Rica, and Thailand rank among the most popular destinations. Dentistry will have you exploring Mexico, Costa Rica, or Hungary. The more expensive, invasive surgeries, such as open-heart surgery or a knee replacement, might make a longer trip to India, Thailand, Singapore, or Malaysia well worth the cost, time, and distance of travel.

To get a preliminary idea of where you are likely to be heading, refer to the "*Patients Beyond Borders* Treatment and Country Finder" at the beginning of Part Two. Use Chapter Two (on planning and budgeting your trip), along with your own travel and lifestyle preferences, to pinpoint your country of choice.

Can Someone Go with Me? I Don't Like Traveling Alone

That's good because we don't recommend your traveling alone. We have found that most health travelers fare better with a companion in tow—a spouse, family member, or friend. Companions do not greatly increase the overall costs of a trip, and they can actually save you time and money in the end because they look out for your interests every step of the way.

Even if you cannot travel with a companion, or prefer not to, you won't be going it alone in-country. If you are staying in a hospital or visiting a specialty clinic, the quality of care and attention received in the better centers is truly remarkable, with low nurse-to-patient ratios and a host of staffers, orderlies, physician's assistants, and dieticians in and out of your room with great frequency. You'll make fast friends during your stay.

If you plan to travel alone, we recommend you consider engaging the services of a health travel agency that offers concierge services. A good agent is with you almost daily, particularly at the more stressful junctures, such as your arrival in-country, medical consultations, and immediately before and after a surgical procedure.

What If They Don't Speak My Language?

Every hospital or clinic catering to international health travelers offers a host of English-speaking physicians, staff, and third-party agents. If English is your native tongue and you are uncomfortable speaking another language, then insist on English. If a hospital or clinic you have contacted cannot furnish doctors and staff who speak your language, don't be embarrassed. Politely thank them and move on. Your continued research will lead you to professionals who can converse in your native tongue.

How Realistic Is the "Vacation" Part of the Trip?

That depends on the type of treatment you are seeking, how much time you have, and how comfortable you feel combining leisure travel with the medical side of your trip. Most patients who take a vacation as part of a healthcare journey are either planning to travel anyway or have allocated a good deal of additional time for recreation as well as recovery. (There's a big difference, which we cover in Chapter Four, "While You're There.")

Throughout this book, we encourage you to focus more on your treatment and recovery than on tourism, even for the less invasive procedures. Websites and health travel brochures peppered with zealous recreational promotion tend to ignore the realities of health travel. Long flights, post-treatment recovery, and just plain being alone in a faraway place can be overwhelming, even for the most optimistic health traveler.

Think of your medical journey more as a business trip than a leisure junket. Consider socking away some of your savings for a separate vacation you and a loved one can take after the primary challenge of managing your immediate health need is behind you. Then, by all means, break out the champagne at a far-flung exotic hideaway to celebrate your health and good fortune.

The exception to this rule is if you are traveling for light, non-surgical medical care, such as a vision or hearing checkup, a teeth whitening, or a second medical opinion. Travelers, particularly those with high-deductible health plans, are increasingly seeing the wisdom of paying for part of their travel with the savings gained from an array of non-invasive procedures or prescription purchases.

Will My Health Insurance Cover My Overseas Medical Expenses?

As of this writing, increasingly so. While the largest employers and healthcare insurers —not to mention our ever-intrusive politicians and corporate interests—struggle with new models of coverage, most plans do not yet cover the costs of obtaining treatment abroad. Yet, with healthcare costs threatening the economic health of many countries, pressures for change are mounting. Recognizing that globalization of healthcare is now a reality, insurers, employers, governments, and hospitals are now more aggressively pursuing models that contemplate international options. By the time you read this book, this list of insurers offering coverage will no doubt have already grown longer. You may want to check with your insurer for the latest on your coverage abroad. Or once you have selected a hospital for your treatment, be sure to check with its insurance representative for a list of insurance carriers for that facility.

Can I Sue? Advice for US Citizens

by Dale Van Demark; Partner, McDermott Will & Emery LLP

In the US, if you believe you have suffered from medical malpractice, you can avail yourself of a robust dispute resolution system with familiar concepts of fault, risk, and fair play.

But what happens if the procedure is performed abroad? Unfortunately, the opportunity to seek redress in court is not clear. Each case is different, national and international regulations vary, and legal standards are evolving. Below are a few guidelines and cautions to clarify both your risks and options.

Can I sue a foreign provider in a US court?

US courts can be the forum for a dispute only if the court can assert jurisdiction over both parties. Generally, US courts have jurisdiction over foreign enterprises only if they have sufficient connections with the US. Most foreign providers attracting foreign patients take steps to avoid creating these types of contacts.

A court can also refuse to hear a case if it determines that a different location is more suitable. Accordingly, foreign providers might argue that because the procedure occurred abroad, witnesses and patient records must be transported to the US, creating an inconvenience to parties and witnesses, and making an overseas venue more appropriate.

Finally, a judgment is only as good as its enforceability, and a US court cannot compel action, such as payment, in a foreign jurisdiction. And enforcing a US judgment in a foreign country means more lawyers and more costs, even if the judgment *can* be enforced abroad.

Can I sue a foreign provider in its country?

Although details of foreign law are beyond the scope of this book, medical travelers should be aware of certain practical considerations:

- Foreign lawyers may not be able to take a contingency fee arrangement (payment only upon success), a customary practice in the US.
- Legal rights may be significantly different than they are in the US.
- Damage amounts may be limited and punitive, and incidental damages may be excluded.
- Standards of practice may result in longer timetables and multiple trips to the foreign location.

Can I sue a US medical travel company?

Most commentators agree that establishing the liability of a medical travel company for the negligent acts of a foreign provider is difficult under current law. Theories of liability require a close connection between the medical travel company and the foreign provider, a connection that generally does not exist with the present business model of most medical travel companies. All of which points to a low likelihood of success in court.

So, what can a medical traveler do? The best course is to take a common sense approach. As medical travel law develops, pathways for lawsuits will either clarify or close. Regardless, it is doubtful that malpractice laws and civil procedures around the world will soon harmonize to the point where a patient's rights and ability to pursue those rights are the same everywhere.

However, the medical traveler need not bear all the risk, and remedies may take non-legal forms. For example, foreign providers may offer a corrective procedure if a problem occurs, or medical travel insurance can offer the promise of remuneration for bad outcomes.

As with all other aspects of medical travel, investigating your options is important. It is also important to understand your own risk tolerance: if low, you may well conclude that medical travel is not for you. However, patients who do their homework and carefully plan travel and treatment can diminish the risk of unfortunate surprises and avoid having to ask—can I sue? ■

Can I Finance My Treatment?

Increasingly, established hospitals abroad and some health travel agents offer financing plans in the form of loans or longer term payment plans (ask your agent or clinic for details). Even though most hospitals, clinics, and health travel brokers accept credit cards, many charge an additional fee to cover their processing costs. Ask beforehand.

Nearly all hotels, restaurants, retailers, and businesses in medical travel destinations happily accept major credit cards. ATMs are now universal; it's fun to watch your cash come out in an unfamiliar currency.

What If Complications Arise after I Return Home?

Depending on your treatment, your physician or surgeon will usually strongly advise you to stay in-country for at least a few days post-treatment. Your doctor will want to make sure that your treatment went well, your medications are working as they should, you are settling into any recommended physical therapies, and required follow-ups are going according to plan. Thus, by the time you board the plane for home, your risk of complications will be greatly reduced.

In the unlikely event that you develop complications after returning home, you will need to decide whether to make a return trip or continue your treatment at home. Some procedures, such as dental work, are guaranteed; so it may well be financially worthwhile, albeit inconvenient, to return. If you choose not to, most overseas dentists and surgeons are happy to talk with your hometown physician to discuss complications and recommend further action. (For more information on complications and other post-treatment considerations, see Chapter Five, "Home Again, Home Again.")

Before traveling abroad for treatment, be sure to let your local doctors know your plans. It's far better to alert them beforehand than to surprise them after the fact.

CHAPTER TWO

Planning and Budgeting Your Health Travel Journey

First Things First: Seek Guidance

As you have probably learned from previous trips, an expert guide can teach you things and take you places you would not have otherwise discovered. Consider Part One of *Patients Beyond Borders* your health travel planning companion, a trusty sidekick to help ease the burdens of your journey. You will progress more safely and easily if you draw upon the collective wisdom of those who have traveled successfully before you.

Although each journey varies according to the traveler's preferences and pocketbook, good planning is essential to the success of any trip. That is doubly true for the medical traveler. In this chapter, you will learn how to become an informed global patient. If you decide that a medical trip is right for you, we'll help you gain confidence about finding the right destination, selecting the best clinic and physician, and working with others to help ensure your success.

Trust Yourself

Most likely, you're considering health travel because you want an elective treatment, such as a cosmetic, dental, or infertility procedure, or because you've been diagnosed with a condition that requires surgical intervention, such as orthopedic or cardiovascular surgery. Whatever the reason, a condition you want or need treated—usually coupled with a desire or need for substantial cost savings (and for some, a sense of adventure or a wish to try something new)—is what brought you to this point.

Other factors may be influencing your decision as well. It is no secret that contemporary economic and medical trends have spawned overworked practitioners, crowded hospitals, and wide variation in the quality of care available to all but the wealthiest citizens. The chatty, all-knowing family doctor has become a medical oddity, supplanted by a bevy of busy assistants, hurried consultations, arms-length testing, ill-informed diagnoses, and increasingly faulty treatment. As a result, the traditional trusting patients of yesteryear, who unquestioningly put their lives in the hands of the medical system, are also a rapidly disappearing breed.

If you're holding this book right now, chances are you have left the old world of blind faith and have adapted to modern medical times, evolving into a curious, assertive, informed patient. Congratulations! Your prognosis for becoming a successful health traveler is vastly improved. Knowledge is power, and the more thought you put into weighing your options, the more confidence you'll gain in reaching the decision best for you and your loved ones.

Even if you only skim the rest of *Patients Beyond Borders*, read this chapter carefully and thoroughly. At the end of it, you will have answered enough questions to know whether, when, and where to travel for your medical care.

Plan Ahead

Long before you pack your bags, you have a lot to do and a logical progression of decisions and events to work through. The first item of business is to plan ahead, as far in advance as you can. Three months before treatment is good. Six months ahead is great. One month is not so good. Here is why.

The best overseas physicians are also the busiest. That is a fact everywhere: doctors, surgeons, and specialists abroad work 24/7, and their schedules are often established a month or more in advance. If you want the most qualified doctors and the best care your global patient money can buy, give the doctors and treatment centers you select plenty of time to work you into their calendars.

The lowest international airfares go to those who book early. As veteran international travelers know, ticket prices rise savagely as the departure date draws closer. Most punishing of all are last-minute fares, reserved for family tragedies, rich jet-setters, and busy corporate executives. Booking at least 60 days before treatment allows you to avoid the unhappy upward spiral of air travel costs.

If you are planning to redeem frequent-flyer miles, try to book at least 90 days in advance, even if not 100 percent certain of your treatment date. At this writing, most airlines don't charge for schedule changes on frequent-flyer fares, and you are better off reserving a date—then changing it later—than being stuck with no reservation at all.

Similarly, for paid fares, it's usually better to reserve your trip as far in advance as you can, giving your best guess at a schedule. Then budget in the US$200 penalty plus change in airfare in case you need to change your flight itinerary.

Peak seasons can snarl the best laid plans. International tourism is again on the rise. If you want or need to travel during the busy tourist season for your chosen region, start planning your global health trip four to six months in advance.

Preparation is a big part of planning. When you paint your living room wall, preparation is usually more than half the effort; by the time you pick up the paintbrush, you're halfway done. The same is true with health travel. Before you can book your flight or reserve your hotel room, you must first confirm your treatment appointment. Before you do that, you'll need to decide which country you want to visit, which physicians will suit your needs, and so on.

Although planning is not rocket science, an organized approach during the preparation stages will save you time and money in the end. In the following pages, we provide a guide to that organized approach.

Set Your Mind to It

As you plan, your attitude is as important as any set of skills. So, cultivate and practice the following:

An open mind. Our twenty-first-century world is increasingly a global village. Contrasts abound: different time zones (they are sleeping while we are working and vice versa); different accents; different clothes (burkas, turbans, exotic neckwear); different cuisine; different greeting etiquette—the list goes on. You need an open mind to accept that other points of view and ways of life are not only valid but also, in some respects, perhaps more refined than yours.

Patience. As you embark on your health journey, you will find that patience is indeed a virtue, particularly in the planning stages. For one thing, the pace abroad may be generally slower—and more cordial—than if your homeland happens to be the US or the UK or Korea. While you might expect your inquiry returned within three hours, you may not hear back from a hospital in Bangkok for three days. Be patient. Call or email a second time. If you don't get an answer in a week, move on. There is now a wide choice of quality international hospitals and clinics willing and able to work with you. Finding the right one is a systematic process, sometimes involving trial and error and false starts.

And what about that receptionist in Mumbai who always wants to know how your family is doing? Well, it is customary in many cultures to talk for a few moments about your personal life, beginning with inquiries about family and loved ones. Take a deep breath and chat it up. You'll be glad you did when working with an in-country doctor willing to spend an hour with you as part of the clinic's normal routine.

Thus, be flexible and persistent in your planning. If Plan A is not working, move to Plan B. You'll sometimes find yourself at Plan D, only to discover that Plan B worked out after all, although not on your expected timetable.

Generally, the early planning stages require the most perseverance. Once in-country, you'll be pleased to see other people sweating the details.

Email and Internet Searching

Although you need not be a computer whiz, you will gain a huge advantage from an internet connection for two important purposes: communication and research.

Communication. Telephones and voice communication have generally given way to more efficient ways of communicating, more so when conducting business from afar with large, decentralized healthcare facilities. Email, on the other hand, knows no time zones, lowers language and culture barriers, and provides an efficient, important written information trail for contacts, recommendations, and myriad other details you would otherwise be obliged to memorize.

Email is vital for making initial inquiries, following up on research, confirming and reconfirming appointments, booking airline and hotel reservations, and keeping records of your transactions with physicians and staff. You need not be a great journalist or business correspondent; if you can email successfully with your kids in Duluth or your Aunt May in Manchester, you'll do fine.

Research. Most of the world's knowledge is now literally at our fingertips. With our laptops, mobiles, or tablets, we can type or tap our way within seconds to find answers to nearly any query. The rise of the web and the refinement of search tools, such as Google and Bing, have enabled anyone with an internet connection to obtain reliable research results.

Primary to successful health travel planning is a basic ability to gather and sort information. The internet offers some big keys to the research kingdom. Indeed, 10 years ago, medical travel as we know it would have been possible only for those with professional knowledge or inside information. Today, the power of that knowledge is available to us all.

For some of us, however, these new internet tools are as bewildering as they are powerful. If you don't like doing the required digging, or if you are not confident in your research skills, perhaps a family member or friend is willing to help. Make your fact-finding a shared project—perhaps working with a younger member of your circle who can show off his or her computer prowess. Although *Patients Beyond Borders* provides sufficient guidelines to get anyone started in finding the right fit for particular treatment needs, the specifics of where to go and which doctor to engage are up to the individual.

Making such decisions requires doing your homework, and the internet is a great and powerful tool, unique to our times. Use it.

Chutzpah!

During the planning stages, make sure you maintain the will to keep moving forward, the courage to do things a little differently, and the confidence that you are making the right choices. Along your health journey you're likely to encounter US physicians unhappy to hear you are heading overseas for treatment, friends and relatives who think you're nuts (even if they didn't previously), and days of genuine self-doubt.

Stick with it. Don't let other people talk you out of your quest because of their ignorance, anxiety, or competitive zeal. If you do your homework and follow the guidelines in this book, you will make the right decisions.

Ten Must-Ask Questions for Your Physician Candidate

Be sure to make the following initial inquiries, either of your health travel agent or the physicians you interview. Note that for some of these questions, there's no right or wrong answer. Your initial round of inquiry will help establish a dialogue. If the doctor is evasive, hurried, or frequently interrupted, or if you cannot understand his or her language, then either dig deeper or move on.

1. *What are your credentials?* Where did you receive your medical degree? Where was your internship? What types of continuing education workshops have you attended recently? The right international physician either has credentials posted on the web or will be happy to email you a complete résumé.

2. *How many patients do you see each month?* Hopefully, more than 50 and fewer than 500. The physician who says "I don't know" should make you suspicious. Doctors should be in touch with their patient load and have such information readily available.

3. *To what associations do you belong?* Any worthwhile physician or surgeon is a member of at least one medical association. Particularly in regions where formal accreditation is weak, your practitioner should be keeping good company with others in the field. For example, if you're seeking cosmetic surgery in Mexico, your surgeon should be a member of the Mexican Association of Plastic, Aesthetic, and Reconstructive Surgery. It's also a plus to see physicians who are members of, or affiliated with, American medical or specialty associations, such as the American Dental Association, the American Academy of Cosmetic Surgery, or the American Academy of Orthopedic Surgeons.

4. *How many patients have you treated who have had my condition?* There's safety in numbers, and you'll want to know them. Find out how many general procedures your hospital has performed. Ask how many of your specific treatment for your specific condition your doctor has conducted. Though numbers vary according to procedure, five cases are not good; 50 or 200 are much better.

5. *What are the fees for your initial consultation?* Answers will vary, and you should compare prices with other physicians you interview. Some consultations are

free; some are deducted from the bill if you choose to be treated by that physician; some are a straight non-refundable fee. In any event, it pays to have this information in advance.

6. *May I call you on your mobile phone before, during, and after treatment?* Most international physicians stay in close, direct contact with their patients, and mobile phones are their tools of choice. When physicians aren't treating patients, you'll find mobile phones glued to their ears.

7. *What medical and personal health records do you need to assess my condition and treatment needs?* Most physicians require at least the basics: recent notes and recommendations from consultations with your local physician or specialist, x-rays directly related to your condition, a patient history, and other health records. Be wary of the physician who requires no personal paperwork.

8. *Do you practice alone or with others in a clinic or hospital?* Safety in numbers is also a good bet on this front. Look for a physician who practices among a group of certified professionals with a broad range of related skills. For example, your initial consultation might reveal that you need a dental implant instead of bridgework, and it just so happens that Dr. Guerrero down the hall is one of the country's leading implantologists. Or, on a return visit, your regular doctor might be on vacation, but Dr. Cho, who is available in the clinic, can access your history and records, check your progress, and help you determine your next steps.

For Surgery

9. *Who holds the knife during my procedure?* Do you do the surgery yourself, or do your assistants do the surgery? This is one area where delegation is not desirable. You want specific assurances that all the trouble you went through to find the right surgeon isn't wasted because the procedure will actually be performed by your practitioner's protégé.

10. *Are you the physician who oversees my entire treatment?* The entire treatment package includes pre-surgery care, surgery prescriptions, physical therapy recommendations, and post-surgery checkups. For more extensive surgical procedures, you want the designated team captain. That's usually the surgeon, but check to make sure. ■

Pack Smart

You have likely heard the cardinal rule of international travel: pack light. Less to carry means less to lose. Don't worry if you leave behind some basic item like toothpaste or deodorant. Once abroad you can always buy essential items you may have forgotten, and picking up socks or toothpaste is a great excuse for you or your companion to hit the local market. The following are items you absolutely, positively should pack:

- passport
- visa (if required)
- travel itinerary
- airline tickets or eticket confirmations
- driver's license or valid picture ID (in addition to passport)
- health insurance card and policy
- enough cash for airport fees and local transportation upon arrival
- credit cards
- ATM card
- immunization record
- hard copies of all appointment schedules and financial agreements
- your prescription medications and copies of written prescriptions
- hard-to-find, over-the-counter drugs you are taking
- hand-sanitizing gel (for cleaning hands while traveling)
- your medical records, current diagnostic images, recent lab reports, and notes
- phone numbers, postal addresses, and email addresses of people you need or want to contact at home or in-country
- travel journal for notes, expense records, and receipts

Budgeting Your Treatment and Trip

As with any other trip, your health travel costs will depend largely upon your tastes, lifestyle preferences, length of stay, side trips, and pocketbook. A patient flying business class and staying at a deluxe hotel can naturally expect less of a savings than one who spends frequent-flyer miles and lodges in a nearby guesthouse.

To set reasonable expectations and avoid surprises, calculate an estimate of your trip's cost. To derive an estimate of your health travel costs and savings, we suggest you use the "*Patients Beyond Borders* Budget Planner" at the end of this chapter. As you get an idea of each separate cost, a realistic estimate will emerge.

Don't feel pressured to fill in every line item in your Budget Planner. Focus on the big expenses first, such as treatment and airfare, and then fill in the remainder as your planning progresses. You probably won't use all the categories. For example, some countries don't require a visa, or you may stay only at a hospital and never visit a hotel.

The Budget Planner simply lists all the common health travel expenses. As you plan, you can fill in the blanks that apply to you and arrive at a rough estimate of your total costs—and your savings!

As you complete the items in your Budget Planner, consider the following cost items.

Passport and visa. If you don't have a passport and are purchasing one for the first time, budget around $200 for fees, photographs, and shipping. If renewing your passport, budget around $150.

Depending on where your travels take you, visa expenses can run from $0 (for those countries that do not require visas) to around $200. To avoid punishing rush charges and needless pre-treatment anxiety, take care of your passport and visa purchases early—passports at least two months in advance of your trip, visas at least 60 days before.

Airfare. Unless you're driving (automobile travel can sometimes have undesirable post-treatment drawbacks), air transportation will likely be your biggest non-treatment cost. It pays to shop hard for bargains. If you're okay flying coach, by all means do so; business-class and first-class international travel are wildly expensive.

Even if uncomfortable using the internet, try to take advantage of one of the many discount online travel agencies, such as Expedia, Travelocity, TripAdvisor, Kayak, or CheapTickets. Or go to individual airlines' websites, where you can often snag special internet-only fares.

Auction and deep-discount services, such as Priceline, take a little more knowledge and patience and come with "gotchas" that often work against the medical traveler. Exercise buyer caution with the lesser-known "cheap-trip" agencies.

If you are flying in-country, discount airlines are now well established all over the world. Southwest and JetBlue lead the pack in the US. Most medical travel destinations now boast low-fare, no-frills airlines, such as AirAsia, which serves all of South, Southeast, and North Asia. Western Europe is served by Ryanair, Norwegian Air, Air Berlin, and a host of others. Cost-conscious Thais love Nok Air. Malaysians use Firefly. Indians find deep discounts with SpiceJet. Beware of non-refundable, non-transferrable fares; strident baggage regulations and fees; and sometimes obscure airports.

International entry and exit fees. They are usually not more than $30 per person, and they may be due at your in-country airport upon arrival, departure, or both. Most countries will not accept credit cards or checks for these fees, only cash. In some countries, your local currency is not accepted, so you'll want to have some extra local cash on hand before leaving for the airport. Many countries do not levy these entry and exit fees.

Rental car. When traveling, some people feel they cannot manage without a car. Yet car rentals are generally expensive, big-city parking is a hassle, and driving on unfamiliar terrain or on the opposite side of the road can land you in the hospital well ahead of your scheduled stay. Even the most adventurous post-op health traveler should think twice about driving a car while full of sutures and medications.

Consider using taxis or limousines. They are comparatively inexpensive and, despite the overworked horror stories, cabs are generally safe and drivers cooperative when you follow the basics found in any travel guide. Seasoned travelers grab taxis from hotel entrances or designated taxi stops.

As a medical traveler, your transportation needs—at least immediately pre- and post-treatment—are likely to be limited to hotels and restaurants. The hospital, hotel, or your health travel agent usually provides local transportation free or at modest cost.

If you're planning to head out of town on a post-treatment vacation, then renting a car is fine. Just be sure that you, your companion, or your agent books the car in advance, as sometimes a conference, festival, or other special event can deplete rental inventories fast.

Other transportation. Transportation to and from the destination airport will probably be handled by the hospital, your health travel agent, or the hotel where you or your companion will reside.

You should budget for the cost of transportation to and from your US airport, as well as in-country transportation costs. Taxis and buses are usually not expensive; $150 should cover nearly any two-week trip.

Companions. Most health travelers we interviewed were glad that a friend or family member accompanied them. In addition to providing love, support, and a shoulder to cry on during difficult moments, companions can attend to myriad details and be a second set of eyes and ears during doctor's visits. Many of those who traveled alone wished a companion or assistant had joined them during those inevitable trying times even the healthiest of tourists experience.

Budget for the additional airfare and meals for your companion and lodging, depending on whether you will be doubling up. Items you can usually share include local taxi rides, mobile phone, and computer and internet services. Items you cannot share include passport and visa costs, airfare, airport fees and taxes, meals, and entertainment.

Treatment costs. Treatment costs vary widely, depending upon the procedure, preferred country, room choice, service options, and post-treatment care. In the Introduction of this book, you'll want to refer to our comparative cost-of-treatment chart, which provides cost estimates for typical treatments. While these figures are not hard and fast, they will give you a good idea of discount ranges to expect. When you are considering a treatment center or physician, request the cost details in writing (email is okay), including the prices for basic treatment plus ancillaries, such as anesthesia, room fees, prescribed medications, nursing services, and more.

Here are some other useful questions to ask regarding costs:

- Are meals included in my hospital stay?
- Do you supply a bed for my companion?
- Is there an Wi-Fi connection in the room or lobby?

If using a health travel agency, make sure your agent gets specific answers in writing to these important questions, along with a firm cost estimate for treatment and ancillary fees. Then, once you've decided to head abroad, check, double-check, confirm, and reconfirm your hospital's and physician's quotes.

The $6,000 Rule Revisited

We have mentioned it elsewhere in this book, but it is worth stating again: a good monetary barometer of whether your medical trip is financially worthwhile is the *Patients Beyond Borders* $6,000 Rule. If your total quote for US treatment (including consultations, procedure, and hospital stay) is US$6,000 or more, you will probably save money traveling abroad for your care. If less than $6,000, you're likely better off having your treatment at home.

The application of this rule varies, of course, depending on your financial position and lifestyle preferences. For some a $500 savings might offset the hassles of travel. Others might be traveling anyway, so savings considerations are fuzzier. ■

Lodging during treatment. These costs are straightforward and largely a function of your tastes and pocketbook. If you're not staying in a hospital or treatment center, search for a hotel near the hospital. Long cross-town treks can be time consuming, hot, frenzied, and costly. Your doctor or your treatment center's international services staff can provide you with a list of preferred hotels nearby.

You may wish to take advantage of the specialty lodging the region offers. Be sure to ask your agent or treatment center about surgical retreats or recovery lodging facilities recommended by, or affiliated with, the hospital.

Post-treatment lodging. Unless you're undergoing nothing more than tests or light dental work, it is a good idea to stick around for at least a week post-treatment instead of jumping on the first plane out. Your physician will want to keep an eye on how your recovery is progressing. We highly recommend taking advantage of this important period to gain strength; guard against complications; and adjust to new medications, physical therapies, and lifestyle changes.

Some hospitals offer nearby recuperation resorts, housing, or other facilities, which include resident nurses and other staff who can assist you with your post-treatment needs. Ask your treatment center or agent about such facilities in your region.

Whether you're recuperating in a recovery resort or hotel, budget $150 to $350 per day to cover lodging, meals, post-treatment services, and tips.

Meals. If staying in a hospital, most of your meals will probably be provided, and the food is often surprisingly good. Many overseas hospitals also offer reasonable meal plans for companions. Ask the facility or your agent about costs. Otherwise, budget your dining out according to taste, both for you and for your companion. Any reputable travel guide can give you a good idea of costs in a given country. Take special care to avoid street food and restaurants of questionable repute before treatment. You do not want to complicate your medical travels with about of "Delhi belly" just before treatment.

Tipping. Tipping protocols vary according to country; check your travel guide on recommended tipping for taxi drivers, baggage handlers, waiters, and maids. A two-week trip should not set you back more than $100 in tips.

We spoke with many patients who were so happy with the quality of service they received that, upon departure, they left an envelope on the bed with $20 to $100 in local currency for nurses, aides, and service personnel. A tip is entirely up to you, and the gesture is generally much appreciated when handled discreetly.

Leisure travel. Many health travelers plan a vacation for either before or after treatment. Although this expense is not strictly a part of your health travel, you may want to add the costs of vacation-related lodging, transportation, meals, and other expenses to your estimated budget.

Patients Beyond Borders Budget Planner

Item	Cost	Comment
IN-COUNTRY		
Passport/Visa		
Rush charges, if any:		
Treatment Estimate		
Procedure:		
Hospital room, if extra:		Often included in treatment package
Lab work, x-rays, etc:		
Additional consultations:		
Tips/gifts for staff:		
Other:		
Other:		
Post-Treatment		
Recuperation lodging:		Hospital room or hotel
Physical therapy:		
Prescriptions:		
Concierge services:		Optional
Other:		
Other:		
Airfare		
You:		
Your companion:		
Other travelers:		
Airport fees:		Baggage and parking
Other:		
Other:		
In-Country Transportation		
Taxis, buses, limos:		
Rental car:		
Other:		
Other:		

Patients Beyond Borders Budget Planner (*continued*)

Item	Cost	Comment
Room and Board		
Hotel:		
Food:		
Entertainment/sightseeing:		
Transportation:		
Other:		
Other:		
"While You're Away" Costs		
Pet sitter/house sitter:		
Other:		
Other:		
IN-COUNTRY SUBTOTAL		
HOME TOWN		
Procedure:		
Lab work, x-rays, etc:		
Hospital room, if extra:		
Additional consultations:		
Physical therapy:		
Prescriptions:		
Other:		
Other:		
HOME TOWN SUBTOTAL		
TOTAL SAVINGS:		Subtract "In-Country" subtotal
		from "Home Town" subtotal

Patients Beyond Borders Sample Budget Planner

Item	Cost	Comment
IN-COUNTRY		
Passport/Visa	$200	For passport and visa, non-expedited
Rush charges, if any:		
Treatment Estimate		
Procedure:	$9,000	
Hospital room, if extra:		Often included in treatment package
Lab work, x-rays, etc:	$45	
Additional consultations:	$200	
Tips/gifts for staff:	$100	
Other:		
Other:		
Post-Treatment		
Recuperation lodging:	$1,100	Hospital room or hotel
Physical therapy:		
Prescriptions:	$65	
Concierge services:	$300	Optional
Other:		
Other:		
Airfare		
You:	$880	
Your companion:	$880	
Other travelers:		
Airport fees:	$25	Baggage and parking
Other:		
Other:		
In-Country Transportation		
Taxis, buses, limos:	$150	
Rental car:		
Other:		
Other:		

Patients Beyond Borders Sample Budget Planner (*continued*)

Item	Cost	Comment
Room and Board		
Hotel:	$1,500	
Food:	$650	
Entertainment/sightseeing:	$500	
Transportation:		
Other:		
Other:		
"While You're Away" Costs		
Pet sitter/house sitter:	$300	
Other:		
Other:		
IN-COUNTRY SUBTOTAL	$15,895	
HOME TOWN		
Procedure:	$55,000	
Lab work, x-rays, etc:	$375	
Hospital room, if extra:	$4,400	
Additional consultations:		
Physical therapy:	$400	
Prescriptions:	$500	
Other:		
Other:		
HOME TOWN SUBTOTAL	$60,675	
TOTAL SAVINGS:	$44,780	Subtract "In-Country" subtotal from "Home Town" subtotal

CHAPTER THREE

The Twelvefold Path to Enlightened Health Travel Planning

———————————————————————————

Diligent research and informed planning are the keys to your successful medical travel journey. The following is drawn from hundreds of interviews with patients and treatment center staff members around the world. Follow the steps and advice outlined here and you'll streamline your planning, organize your trip well, select the best physicians, communicate effectively with staff and agents, save money, and pack your bags with confidence.

Step 1: Confirm Your Treatment Options

Doctors everywhere generally recommend a range of choices for a given condition. They then leave it up to you and your family to settle upon a course of action, based on their recommendations. After all, the buck stops with your body, especially in these days of rushed doctor's consultations and misdiagnosis; no one other than you can or should make those important health-related judgment calls. Most physicians respect that, and that's why they usually stop short of advising you what specific course of treatment to take. That's wise because your body is your own, and you are responsible for owning the final decisions as well.

If you have doubts about your diagnosis or feel dissatisfied in your relationship with your physician or specialist, don't be timid about seeking a second—or even third—opinion. At the very least, a second opinion expands your knowledge base about your condition. The more you and your hometown health team learn about and discuss your condition, diagnosis, and treatment options, the more precisely and confidently you will be able to communicate with your overseas practitioners.

As you sort through your treatment options and consider courses of action, learn as much as you can about your condition. You'll get better care from your overseas practitioners if you are a knowledgeable and responsive patient.

It works both ways. Your experiences and challenges as an informed medical traveler will sharpen your skills on the home front, better equipping you and your loved ones to survive and flourish in the increasingly complex morass of contemporary healthcare.

Step 2: Narrow Your Destinations

Once you've resolved what treatment you're looking for, refer to the "*Patients Beyond Borders* Treatment and Country Finder" at the beginning of Part Two. This handy reference will help you locate the destinations cited throughout the book that offer the care you're seeking. Also consult the web or other trusted sources you may know.

Your searches will likely produce a dozen or so places that offer, for example, excellent dental care. Great! Choice is good. You can then narrow your search based on your circumstance and personal preferences. For example, if you have a choice in travel times, you may prefer the cooler climate of Eastern Europe to the humid heat of Southeast Asia. Or perhaps you speak a little Spanish and are more comfortable conversing with Costa Ricans than with Croatians.

The point is to narrow your options based on your travel preferences, geography, budget, time requirements, and other variables. Part Two, "The Most-Traveled Health Destinations," provides a wealth of information on the world's most widely visited regions and treatment centers. To help narrow your options, ask yourself these questions:

- When do I want—or need—to travel?
- If I am taking a companion, when can he or she travel?
- How much do I mind a 10-hour flight? An 18-hour flight?
- Do I prefer a warmer or cooler climate?
- If I'm planning on leisure activities while abroad, what types most interest me? Hiking? Museum hopping? Shopping? Beaches? Nightlife?
- How much cultural diversity can I tolerate?

For Big Surgeries, Think Big

If you're heading abroad for a liposuction or tooth whitening, you can skip this. However, if you're going under the knife for major surgery—including open-heart surgery, any type of transplant, invasive cancer treatment, orthopedic surgery, or spinal surgery—be certain you are getting the best. Your life is at stake.

For big surgeries, head to the big hospitals that have performed large numbers of exactly your kind of procedure, with the accreditation and success ratios to prove it. A JCI-accredited hospital, such as San José Tec in Monterrey or Bumrungrad in Bangkok, carries the necessary staff, medical talent, administrative infrastructure, state-of-the-art instrumentation, and institutional follow-up to pull off a complex surgery. They make it look easy. They have done thousands of jobs like yours. It's almost routine. You want that.

Be sure to ask about success and morbidity rates for your particular procedure; find out how they compare with those in the US. Also ask your surgeon how many surgeries of exactly your procedure he or she has performed in the past two years. Although there are no set standards, fewer than 10 is not so good. More than 50 is much better. ■

Step 3: Consider Engaging a Health Travel Agent

Good news: if you don't want to do all the planning, research, and booking work yourself, you need not. The medical travel industry has recently given rise to the specialty services of the health travel planner. A qualified agent is usually a specialist in a given region or treatment, with the best doctors, accommodations, and in-country contacts at his or her fingertips.

Once you've settled on your health travel destination, you may elect to seek out the services of that locale's best health travel agent. Agents can pay for themselves in convenience and cost savings. They are usually well worth the relatively modest fees they typically charge.

The better health travel agents do all the work of a traditional travel agent and more, including some or all of the following:

- *Match you with the appropriate clinic and physicians.* By far the most important service a health travel agent provides is that of matchmaker. The best agents have years of experience with treatment centers, physicians, and healthcare staffs, and they are in a position to find the best fit for you among many choices. Because the agency's success depends on references from satisfied customers, top agents work hard to make the physician-patient relationship a good match from the start.

- *Arrange and confirm appointments.* Once you've selected or approved a physician, the agent can handle the details of making appointments for consultations, tests, and treatment. Agents know their way around and can push the right buttons to fast-track your arrangements.

- *Expedite the transfer of your medical information.* Your agent or international patient services center can work with you and your physicians at home and abroad to relay medical data, including history, x-rays, test results, and recommendations. Agents can help you get data into the right format for emailing or help you determine the best way to ship documents.

- *Book air travel.* Agents sometimes have arrangements with airlines for good deals on airfares. Booking international flights is usually a standard part of an agent's service offering.

- *Obtain passports and visas.* For a relatively modest fee, a health travel agent can help you avoid the hassles of purchasing a visa (if required), obtaining or updating your passport, procuring tourist cards, and hounding the appropriate embassy for service.

- *Reserve lodging and other accommodations.* These folks can work with your budget and lifestyle preferences to put you in touch with hotels closest to your treatment center. They often book reservations and arrange amenities, such as private nursing care. Many agents have forged partnerships with hotels for discounted rates.

- *Arrange in-country transportation.* Most agencies either provide transportation from the airport to your hotel or treatment center or work directly with the hotel or hospital to arrange your transport. They also help if transport is required between your hotel and treatment center.

- *Help manage post-treatment procedures.* Agents can be hugely helpful at the point of discharge from your treatment center, ensuring that your exit paperwork and other documentation are in order.

- *Help with recovery and recuperation.* Little publicized and often overlooked are the recovery resorts, surgical retreats, and recuperation hotels that can make a week or two of post-treatment more bearable—sometimes even enjoyable. Agents are likely to know all about accommodations in their service area and work in close partnership with the better ones. The international travel services coordinator at your chosen hospital can also help on this front.

- *Help with leisure activity planning.* If you and your companion are up for a pre- or post-treatment trip, most agents offer assistance with side trips, car rentals, hotels, restaurants, and other travel amenities.

Step 4: Choose a Reliable, Fun Companion

Patients who journey to far-flung places for medical treatment generally fare much better with a companion than if they go solo. Whether a spouse or friend or family member, the right companion can provide essential help and support before, during, and after treatment. Together, you and your companion may also add in some fun and adventure when your health permits.

Most health travelers choose either a good friend or spouse as companion. If you have the luxury of choice, make sure the two of you won't be packing a lot of emotional baggage for the trip. The successful medical journey requires large and prolonged doses of support. In an ideal world, you should get on fabulously with your capable, reliable, organized, and fun companion.

If you've already found a willing and able companion, you are blessed. Be sure to involve him or her in the early planning stages. That's the best way to cement the relationship and to learn at the outset if you'll be compatible. Ask your companion to accompany you to your hometown doctor's appointments, help with second opinions, and make initial international inquiries. You will begin to work as a team. If you don't feel comfortable at the early stages, find a cordial, diplomatic way to part company.

And always remember to be as supportive and complimentary of your companion as you can possibly be. Your companion is a treasure. Cherish the relationship.

How do you choose the right companion? Three words: Capable. Organized. Fun. Above all, travel with an individual you can count on in any number of circumstances. From taking notes in your doctor's office to talking your way past a snarly customs agent to fetching a post-surgery prescription, you'll be immeasurably aided and comforted by having someone beside you who will take the job seriously and stay with the program.

Step 5: Find Dr. Right

For most folks considering a medical trip abroad, this step is the most challenging—and perhaps the most emotionally charged. If you follow a few basic suggestions and caveats, however, you'll find the process far less mysterious and daunting. Remember, the final choice in selecting a physician—like the decision of whether to travel at all—remains always in your hands. Here are some tips to aid you in your search:

- *Insist on your native tongue.* If English is your only language, then insist that the parties you're working with speak English. Your health is too important to risk important information getting lost in translation. Hospitals, clinics, and agents who cater to an international clientele have staff or services that either speak your language or can supply translators to accompany you on your visit.

- *Seek Dr. Right, not Mr. Personality.* Okay, if a practitioner candidate is downright rude to you, then move on; otherwise, give your physician some personality latitude, at least initially. Focus on skill sets, credentials, and accreditations, not charm. Remember that many of the finest medical practitioners are technicians. They may love what they do and be quite good at their chosen specialty, but their personal presentation skills may be lacking. This is doubly true where language and cultural differences create additional social awkwardness. Use your judgment. If credentials and other criteria check out, and if you're otherwise comfortable with your choice, then charm and personality can probably take a backseat.

- *Expect good service.* Although patience is often required when corresponding with international healthcare providers, rudeness should never be excused, and no culture condones it. If anything, you're likely to encounter greater courtesy and graciousness abroad than at home. If parties on the other end appear rude or indifferent, move on.

In corresponding with hospitals and clinics overseas, you may find yourself directly in contact with your physician or surgeon. The good news is that you're engaged in a real dialogue with the professional who will be treating you. The downside is that he or she is probably very busy. Expect delays—sometimes two or three days—for return email or phone calls. If it turns out to be longer, then politely, but firmly, request a response.

Step 6: Get to Know Your Hospital or Clinic

At this point, you've probably chosen a date and destination for your treatment, settled on one or two physicians you like, and perhaps you or your health travel planner have even scheduled a consultation. Excellent! You've made great headway, and most of the heavy lifting is behind you.

Before you start booking air travel and accommodations or planning the more relaxing parts of the trip, do some additional sleuthing, beginning with your treatment center. Although detail driven, this investigation is not as daunting as it sounds, and most of your research involves simple fact-checking. Here's what to do and how:

- *Check hospital accreditation.* If you're looking into a treatment that requires hospital care or an outpatient (day visit) surgery, check to see whether the center is internationally accredited by a reliable healthcare accreditation agency. A handful of international accreditation agencies put their seal of approval on hundreds of hospitals and clinics worldwide. Even though many excellent medical centers have not been awarded international accreditation, it provides an extra layer of assurance and comfort to know your chosen provider is accredited. (For further information and a list of leading accreditation agencies, see "A Briefing on International Accreditation" in Chapter One.)

- *Check for affiliations and partnerships.* Did you know that many of the best overseas hospitals enjoy close partnerships with US universities and medical centers? For example, Johns Hopkins Medicine International has forged relationships with hospitals and clinics in 17 countries. Cleveland Clinic is building a 500+ bed hospital in Abu Dhabi. Hospital San José Tec in Monterrey, Mexico, enjoys a research affiliation with NewYork-Presbyterian Medical Center. While such partnerships do not guarantee succesful clinical outcomes, they are big differentiators for healthcare consumers.

- *Learn about success rates.* Although smaller clinics don't offer such information, the larger and more established hospitals freely publish their success rates and morbidity rates. These are usually calculated as a ratio of successful operations to overall number of operations performed. For larger surgeries (such as cardiovascular and orthopedic), success rates of 98+ percent are on par with those found throughout North America and the EU. For the more common surgeries, you should further investigate any rates under 98 percent.

- *Learn about the number of surgeries.* Although reluctant to do so, most doctors and surgeons, when pressed, furnish information on numbers of surgeries performed. Generally, the more the better; there's safety in numbers on this front.

Step 7: Follow-Up on Credentials

Once you've located one or two suitable physicians, be sure to obtain their résumés. Many physicians post such data on the web. If your candidates don't, then request that they or your health travel agent send you full background information, including education, degrees, areas of specialty, number of years in practice, number of patients served, and association memberships.

Get references, recommendations, and referrals. If possible, speak with some of the doctors' former patients to get their feedback. Understandably, many former patients wish their privacy respected, and international law protects us all in that regard. Thus, it's often difficult for a physician to put you in direct contact with a former patient.

If you're unable to talk with former patients, ask the physician to provide you with testimonials, newspaper or magazine articles, and letters of recommendation—in short, anything credible that will help you assess this individual's expertise. If you're using the services of a health travel agency, ask your representative to check credentials and backgrounds of physicians to help you narrow your search. Specifically, here is what to look for:

- *Education.* What degrees has the doctor received and when were they awarded? Where did he or she attend medical school? Has he or she completed a fellowship? If yes, where and in what specialty?
- *Certification.* Exactly what is this physician licensed to practice? If you're having implants done, then you want a certified implantologist's fingers in your mouth.
- *Professional history.* How long has he or she been practicing, and where? If a surgeon, how many surgeries has the surgeon performed, and what types of procedures? Information on presentations, publications, honors, and awards gained along the career path will help you evaluate a doctor's talent, performance, and commitment to his or her trade.
- *Affiliations.* With what medical and related associations is the physician affiliated? Information about community involvement is useful as well.
- *Continuing education.* Mandatory in many countries, continuing education helps

a physician stay abreast of new trends in his or her field. Most good physicians travel at least once a year to accredited conferences and workshops. Find out where your doctor goes and how often.

- *Patient references and letters of recommendation.* Nearly as useful as professional histories are reference letters or letters of recommendation from patients, colleagues, or other credible sources.

Ask your physician candidate or medical staff to email you a copy of the doctor's résumé. If you want to take your search a step further, contact the universities, associations, and references listed in the résumé to verify its authenticity. (For more information, see "Ten Must-Ask Questions for Your Physician Candidate" in Chapter Two.)

Step 8: Gather Your Medical Records

Once you've established a relationship or scheduled a consultation with one or more overseas physicians, they will probably ask to see supporting information about your medical needs. Such data usually include the following:

- reports or written recommendations from your local specialist related to your condition
- x-rays or imaging reports from your specialist's office or your radiology lab
- test results from your specialist's office or third-party laboratories
- general medical history, health record, or pathology reports from previous treatments, depending on your treatment

Some patients are timid about requesting health information from their doctors. If you're one of those people, it's important for you to know that as of 2003, any physician, surgeon, specialist, hospital, or laboratory you visit is required by law to provide you with copies of all medical information they have compiled about you.

These data include consent forms, consultation records, lab reports, test results, x-rays, immunization history, and any other information compiled as a result of your visits. Although most don't require payment for making copies, your doctor or laboratory has the right to charge you a nominal fee for this service.

Most medical information has gone digital, particularly all-important x-rays and other imaging data. When you request your medical records, ask the staff to email you the data in digital form and to provide you with a hard copy. If you can obtain only hard-copy documents, then have them scanned and converted to either .pdf or .jpg format.

If you're uncomfortable with technology and computers, perhaps your companion or friend or family member can tweak the paperwork into the form of an electronic file (scanning is not expensive or time consuming for those who know how). A full-service copy shop or office supply center can convert hard-copy paperwork to digital files for a nominal fee. And you'll save real money on international courier rates if you transmit via email instead. Overseas physicians generally prefer digital records, particularly x-rays, which are easier to study and manipulate than old-fashioned film.

Step 9: Plan Your Recuperation and Recovery

For patients abroad, the days or weeks spent post-treatment can be particularly challenging. Perhaps you were on the road vacationing before treatment, and now you are eager to head home. Or urgent tasks are piling up back at the office. Or you are just feeling far away and becoming homesick.

Any surgeon, dentist, or other medical specialist can tell you that if complications are going to develop, they're most likely to occur in the first few days following treatment. That's the time when your body is doing everything it can to compensate for the stress and trauma of your treatment. Rest and a healthful lifestyle are essential during recovery. But in these busy, overworked times, many people don't take recuperation as seriously as they should.

Do yourself and your loved ones a big favor: follow your doctor's post-treatment orders, allowing your body and spirit time to return to health. It's not that much more time out of your life. For extensive dental work, recovery is usually a matter of a few days. Even the more invasive surgeries have you back to something approaching normalcy within a couple of weeks.

You might be surprised—and encouraged—to learn that many international health travelers enjoy recovery and recuperation accommodations not available in the US. Recovery resorts, surgical retreats, hospital residences, and a host of other options are available at many of the destinations featured in this book. Services offered include:

- on-site medical staff to assist with bathing, getting in and out of bed, physical therapy, medication, and more

- gyms and other accommodations for physical therapy and daily exercise
- room service for meals and laundry
- internet access
- liaison with hospitals

Another big plus for recovery accommodations is the company you keep. The guests are people like you who have recently undergone treatment. There is comfort in sharing experiences, and dinner-table conversations with fellow patients can yield a wealth of medical tips and travel advice. If recovery retreats are not offered in your region of choice, ask your health travel planner or hospital for recommendations on hotels or apartments near your treatment facility.

Step 10: Create Your Health Travel Vacation

For most health travelers, a vacation takes a backseat to treatment and recovery. Many simply do not have the time or the motivation to add a vacation to an already time-consuming health travel trip. Some patients require more invasive procedures with longer recovery, and the planning alone (not to mention the usual discomforts of recuperation) knocks a relaxing Riviera jaunt clean out of the picture.

If you're planning for less demanding treatments, such as light cosmetic surgery or nonsurgical dentistry, take a brief inventory of your treatment schedule and time requirements. Ask the following questions:

- How many appointments does my treatment require?
- How long should I remain near my treatment center during my stay?
- How long is my expected recuperation period?

Unexpected tests, appointment reshuffles, and travel delays can eat up leisure time. As a rule, the treatment part of your trip will probably be three or four days longer than your appointment schedule indicates.

Whether you can squeeze in a vacation or not, the most important consideration is your health. Focus on your treatment, and try not to bite off too much. Remember that you can always take a vacation later, happily spending the money you saved by being treated abroad. And if you find yourself feeling up to a little sightseeing post-procedure, you can usually schedule tours while in-country, with a day or two notice.

Step 11: Book Air Travel and Accommodations

Why is this not the first step? Although it may seem counterintuitive to book your travel and accommodations last, remember that you must first determine where you want to go, select a treatment center and physician, and schedule your consultations or procedure. Only at that point does it make sense to begin contacting airlines and hotels; otherwise, you're likely to spend needless effort and expense changing itineraries.

You can see now why planning ahead is so important to successful medical travel. Some airlines and most hotels levy stiff penalties for changes and cancellations. That's another reason why it pays to begin your initial planning 60 to 90 days before your expected departure date and to book your flight after you've scheduled your treatment.

The same holds true for airfares. First-class and business-class fares are usually quite punishing; they are best paid by jet-setters, corporate executives, and frequent flyers. If you do not mind traveling coach or economy class, you'll save a bundle.

If you're making your travel plans on your own, ask your in-country contact to recommend some hotels nearby. Snarled traffic is the norm in most medical travel destinations, so the closer your accommodations, the better. Some of the larger hospitals have partnerships with hotels at discounted rates. Such information is usually posted on their websites.

Step 12: Triple-Check Details and Documents

In addition to ensuring that the kids, dog, and other loved ones are looked after in your absence, it is crucial on a medical trip to remember to take everything that you and your companion will need. Unlike forgetting your favorite tie or blouse, leaving important documents behind can create unnecessary hassles on the other side of the world.

Make sure you have all your paperwork in order, including travel itinerary, airline tickets or etickets, passports, visas, immunization records, and cash on hand for airport taxes and other unexpected expenses. Be sure to pack all medical records, consultation notes, agreements, and hard copies of email correspondence. Also remember to take the telephone numbers and email addresses of all your contacts, at home as well as in-country.

CHAPTER FOUR

While You're There

First Things First: Arm Yourself with Information

Now that you have settled on a destination, made appointments with one or more physicians, booked your airfare and hotel, and arranged transportation, the hard part is behind you—except, of course, for your treatment! You'll find that once you arrive in-country, you will be greeted graciously, with help and support from hotel and hospital staff, your health travel agent, and sometimes even a friendly bystander.

But before you embark on an airplane journey overseas, read, ask questions, and learn as much as you can about your destination. *Patients Beyond Borders* cannot begin to provide all the important information you need about international travel, much less the specifics of your chosen destination. Yet we do want to point you to a few important basics to get you started. Everything else you need is readily available through any number of travel guides and online resources now available at the touch of your keyboard.

If you've not done much international travel before booking your health journey, keep in mind that you need not be a seasoned travel veteran to have a successful trip. In fact, most international tourists board their outbound flight uninformed of their destination's culture, customs, and language, and they do just fine. Armed with multiple credit cards, they rent a car or hire a limousine at the airport and head for a ubiquitous beach resort, without giving a thought to the country they are visiting. Many scarcely speak to a local resident, except perhaps to mumble a few words during shopping sprees or dining out.

Health travel is different. Unlike that dimly recollected junket to Belize last summer, you're now far more concerned about practical matters. Getting things done cooperatively and efficiently will help you and your companion preserve your physical and mental health. And most health travelers are interested in saving money when it is prudent to do so.

You will be interacting closely with local physicians, staff, health planners, and others who live and work in-country. Thus, knowing a little something about the culture, history, geography, and language of your host country will buy you boatloads of goodwill and appreciation. A small investment of time and effort in learning something about your destination will help you make the right choices and become more confident and proficient when you arrive in-country.

General Guidelines and Cautions

Safety and security. The overriding concern of most patients new to global health travel is safety. That's understandable. In the past five years, this old world has seen several terrorist plots at UK airports (a frequent medical tourist stopover), an airport siege in Bangkok (one of the most-traveled medical tourist destinations), social and political unrest in Mexico and Turkey, rioting in Budapest (a popular dental and cosmetic surgery destination), and never-ending strife in Israel (an important destination for reproductive and high-acuity procedures), to mention only a few.

Obviously, we live in a troubled world. Yet this fact remains: of the tens of millions who have visited international hospitals for medical treatment in the last five years, not one patient has come to harm as a result of political or social unrest. As you read this chapter, you'll learn that most health travelers are quite sheltered. They're chauffeured from the airport to the hospital or hotel, personally driven to consultations, given their meals in their rooms, then driven back to the airport when it's time to go home, all with good reason. It has always been in a healthcare facility's interests to protect an unwell patient. Perhaps more important, as a medical traveler, you'll be too busy achieving your health goals to be booking boisterous nights out on the town, hazardous wilderness tours, or adventurous side trips of uncertain outcome.

Currency, credit cards, and banking. Much has changed in our new era of electronic banking, and currency is no exception. Check your local travel guide for specifics. Also, check with your health travel broker and hospital beforehand to determine accepted forms of payment.

Cash. Good old reliable local currency is usually the best way to get the most for your money without all the surcharges and hassles that come with traveler's checks and credit cards. If you want to bring cold hard cash to cover your entire trip and treatment, be sure that you are confident about carrying large sums. Check with your hotel staff or hospital administration beforehand to determine whether they offer room or lobby safes.

Traveler's checks. These outdated instruments are still accepted by most hotels, hospitals, and restaurants—but usually only for a fee. Be sure to check first with your treatment center on the types of traveler's checks accepted.

Credit cards. As convenient as they are, credit cards may not always be your best method of payment, particularly for large transactions (such as settling your hospital bills). Some establishments add service charges as high as 10 percent, negating the value of any frequent-flyer miles you might want to earn. Then, adding insult to injury, upon your return, your bank statement may reflect an additional 2–5 percent fee on each transaction. If possible, avoid using your credit card for cash advances because banks charge big commissions on those. Before you leave home, check with your bank or credit card company about its policies concerning international transactions.

ATMs. Miraculous, magical cash-dispensing machines are everywhere now. ATMs usually offer exchange rates equal or close to the day's official rate. Before departing, check with your bank on its ATM surcharges, if any.

International wire transfers. Avoid them, particularly for smaller amounts where the surcharges are not worth it. They are prone to frustrating, bungled transactions at one end or the other. Also avoid black markets and money changers.

Hotel safes. Most hotels and hospitals offer personal safes where you can stash your cash, passport, airline tickets, and other important belongings. Just remember to clean out your safe as you pack for departure. One dental patient reported getting to the airport still woozy on painkillers, fumbling for tickets and money, and becoming hysterical when he realized he had forgotten to empty his safe. He made the plane, a little poorer and more gray haired, after a hectic taxi ride back to the hotel.

Change. When traveling on your own—as you might when shopping for gifts—be sure to leave the hotel or medical center with lots of small bills or coins. You do not want to be seen on the street sorting through a pile of large bills, and most vendors cannot or will not break them, leaving you standing there while they trot next door for change. Yet large bills are what you usually get from ATMs, banks, and money exchange offices. Ask your hotel desk or hospital cashier for smaller denominations.

Water. The last thing you need as a patient, pre- or post-treatment, is a case of "green apple quickstep." Check to ensure that the cap's seal on bottled water is unbroken. Plastic bottles are sometimes "recycled" by enterprising vendors, then filled with local tap water.

Food and dining. One of the most frequently heard comments from on-the-road patients is about the food. Surprisingly, the complaint is not about the quality of the hospital meals. Indeed, the heart of the problem is that institutional meals abroad tend to be too robust, particularly post-treatment. Patients just out of surgery who are taking antibiotics, painkillers, and other pharmaceuticals should not be sampling exotic new taste delights. Until you are well on your way to recovery, ask your hospital dietician for the blandest food possible, and pass on the tray of spicy tandoori chicken!

Dress. If you're staying in a hospital, comfort is your first priority, and your gown will be about as elegant a fashion statement as you'll make. Once on the outside, respect local customs for dress. As a nearly universal rule, shorts are frowned upon except at the beach. And shirtless men are almost never seen in town, even in the hottest climates. When walking the city, check out what the folks on the streets are wearing; if you're comparably dressed, you'll be fine.

Women should make sure to bring a scarf to Middle Eastern countries, India, and Malaysia, as well as some Mediterranean countries like Greece and Turkey. There may be times when you are expected to cover your head. Also, sleeveless garments, tank tops, and camisoles are often frowned on; unless you're heading to the beach, leave them home.

Getting Around Town

Ground transportation varies, depending upon your destination—from rickshaws and bicycles to motorcycles, buses, and stretch limousines. Generally, your best bet is a good old-fashioned motorized sedan taxi. They come in different shapes and sizes and are usually reliable. Be sure you use only authorized, licensed, or certified taxis. Your local travel guide or hotel concierge can give you specific information on finding the right services at the right price.

Taxi drivers and honesty do not always coincide. Agree on the price—or insist on using the meter—before getting into the car. Also, make sure your driver understands your destination; if not, find a driver who does. Carry the address and phone number of your hotel, hospital, or recovery resort with you at all times so you can show your driver where you need to go or phone your hotel if necessary.

Remember to tip. Although in many countries it's not expected, a tip is seldom refused.

Operator, Information: Staying in Touch While on the Road

When in-country, most folks want to communicate with friends, family, and coworkers back home, and good communications with your caregivers and medical staff is essential during your stay. Gone are the days of postcards, faxes, and landlines, now largely replaced by email, handheld devices, instant messaging, texting, chat, and other helpful tools.

If you're already using email and mobile phones at home, you'll no doubt be comfortable with them in-country once you learn a few new ways of doing things.

Email and chat. The most hassle-free and least expensive way to keep current with loved ones and coworkers is via email. Most countries featured in this book offer excellent internet access, either free or inexpensive. If you cannot access your email using a web browser (such as Chrome, Explorer, or Firefox), consider setting up a temporary email account with one of the many free web-based services, such as Gmail or Yahoo. You can easily cancel the account after you return home. You'll have no trouble finding internet access abroad.

All hotels now offer high-speed Wi-Fi, which you can access via your laptop, tablet, or smartphone, either in your room or in the lobby. If you choose not to take a laptop or tablet, you'll find that many hotels have terminals in their lobbies with internet connectivity, but the price is often high and the wait may be long. It is usually cheaper and easier to find an internet café on the street, if you're healthy enough to venture out.

Internet cafés and coffee shops. They abound abroad and are usually inexpensive, with reliable, fast connections. Internet cafés and small eateries can be a welcome change of scene from your hotel or treatment center, and they sometimes afford you an opportunity to meet and chat with a fellow traveler. Your hotel or treatment center staff can tell you where the nearest internet café or Starbucks equivalent is located. Or you can do a Google or Yelp search by entering the search terms <internet café> <city> <country>. Expect to pay US$2–6 an hour in an internet café.

Mobile phones. If you want to hear your loved ones' voices from afar, do a little research into the country you'll be visiting before you leave home. International telecommunications standards vary, as do costs, international service plans, and quality of service. Your phone carrier likely supports most of the medical travel destinations listed in *Patients Beyond Borders,* and you can usually sign up on a monthly basis. Don't forget to discontinue your international plan when you return home!

Even if you cannot or do not want to use your normal mobile phone abroad, pack it anyway. Many folks find that upon returning, a cell phone is useful in communicating from the airport or on the way home. Make sure to switch it off before packing so the battery doesn't lose its charge.

If you want to place international calls directly from your hotel room, inquire about the rates before you connect. There is usually a high premium for room phone services.

Communicating with Your In-Country Caregivers

Voice. Most folks who travel abroad for treatment are stunned to find that physicians and surgeons are generally accessible. When you're in-country, your doctor's preferred method of communication may well be his or her mobile or tablet for voice, voice messaging, and text messaging. As part of your early planning and screening for the right doctor, be sure to ask for his or her mobile phone number, and ask if it's okay to call with questions or concerns. If not okay, then ask how the doctor prefers to stay in touch. Ask also for the names and contact information of key staff members. Email is great during the early planning stages, but once in-country you'll want to be assured of immediate direct contact and prompt responses to your queries.

Because doctors are among the busiest and most harried professionals in the world, remember to keep phone conversations concise and have a good idea what you want to say before you call.

Text messaging. Knowing how to use text messaging on your mobile phone is a real plus when communicating with your caregivers. Texting is more widely used abroad than traditional email is. Keep your text messages concise, for example, "Doctor Alvarez, please call me back soon. I have a problem."

Going under the Knife? Pre- and Post-Surgery Tips and Cautions

Be informed about general and specific pre-treatment precautions. If your physician has not already briefed you (usually in writing), be sure to ask about food, alcohol, pharmaceuticals, and physical activities that may be prohibited before surgery. Ask also about the aftercare regimen you will need to follow. Even though all surgeries come with similar general precautions, take the time to learn the instructions specific to your treatment. ∎

Ask Questions

Too often, patients are timid about asking questions or raising concerns. Or, smitten by a nostalgic notion of yesterday's paternal, omniscient physician, patients trust their doctors to provide them with all necessary information. Remember, times have changed, doctors are busy, and being chronically overbooked is now a routine part of their work.

Thus, especially as medical travelers, you and your companion have a right—and an obligation—to ask questions. If things don't feel right, voice concerns politely and firmly. Don't allow a procedure to move ahead until you feel good about the answers you receive. If your surgeon fails to provide adequate information, ask questions like these:

- How long will my recovery period be?
- How much pain will I experience?
- What kinds of physical therapy will I require?
- How will I know when it's safe to take a long flight home?
- When I return home, how will I know when it's safe to return to my normal routine?

Your doctor should welcome such questions. If you don't understand the answers, or if you don't clearly understand your doctor, ask that the explanation be repeated, or request a translator. It's okay to be something of an annoyance. Your health is at stake, and getting this information right is essential to your well-being.

Be Germ Obsessed

Food-borne and water-borne pathogens are a significant concern. The Centers for Disease Control and Prevention estimates that nearly 100,000 patients die each year in the US from hospital-acquired infection. That does not count the millions of cases of food poisoning acquired at home and while eating out. At least one-third of such cases are preventable by simple measures and precautions.

The good news is that of all the patients, staff, and visitors who walk a given clinic's floors each year, fewer than 5 percent become infected, and far fewer die. Although standards of cleanliness vary among countries, infection rates in nearly all internationally accredited hospitals abroad generally rank on par with, or a little lower than, rates in North America or in the EU.

Thus, whether here or there, risk does exist, however slight, and it pays to be vigilant and to follow a few simple precautions when in the hospital and before and after treatment:

- Make sure you wash your hands thoroughly, particularly after using the toilet. If necessary, remind your companion, physician, nurse, and other hospital staff to do likewise before and after attending to you. They should be wearing gloves; if not, insist that they do.
- Inform your nurse if the site around the needle of an IV drip is not clean and dry.
- Ask that hair around the site of a surgical incision be clipped, not shaven. Razors cause tiny lacerations where infections can invade.
- Tell your nurse if bandages or other dressings are not clean and dry or if they are sticking to incisions. Ask that discolored, wet, or foul-smelling dressings be changed.

- Ask staff members to check on tubes or catheters that feel displaced or may be malfunctioning.
- Do deep-breathing exercises to help prevent chest infections.
- Ask relatives or friends who have colds or are unwell not to visit. If your companion contracts a cold or flu, postpone visits or keep them as brief as possible.
- Watch out for unclean clothing, floors, or instruments, and bring such breaches of hygiene to the attention of physicians or staff.
- Eat only cooked foods, even in the hospital. Drink only bottled water, and say no to ice.

Manage Post-Treatment Discomfort and Complications

You have been out of surgery for two days, you hurt all over, your digestive system is acting up, and you're running a fever. Was the dinner you just ate simmered in sewer water? Have you somehow contracted an antibiotic-resistant staph infection? Will you die here, alone and unloved, a stranger in a strange land?

Coping with post-surgery discomfort is difficult enough when you're close to Mom's chicken soup. Lying for long hours in a hospital bed, far away from home, family, and *Monday Night Football*—that's often the darkest time for a health traveler.

Knowledge is the best antidote to needless worry. As with pre-surgery preparation, ask lots of questions about post-surgery conditions before heading into the operating room. Be sure to ask doctors and nurses about what kinds of discomforts to expect following your specific procedure.

If your discomfort or pain becomes acute, bleeding is persistent, or you suspect a growing infection, you may be experiencing a complication more serious than mere discomfort and that requires immediate attention. Contact your physician without delay!

Get There Good to Go

Did you know that patients planning to undergo LASIK eye treatment must not wear contact lenses for two weeks before the operation? Imagine disembarking from a 23-hour trip to Bangkok, walking into your doctor's office for your initial consultation wearing contacts, and hearing that for the first time!

The point is this: take the time to learn about the dos and don'ts for your specific procedure. Do not assume that your physician has already told you everything you need to know—or that you heard, understood, and remembered all of the instructions your healthcare provider gave you. Ask about pre-treatment precautions specific to your procedure. And ask well in advance. As with passports and visas, the earlier the better.

The healthier you are before your treatment, the better your chance of a positive outcome. Before your procedure, follow these steps:

- Stop smoking. Smoking impedes the healing process. Smoking also damages your air passages, which makes lung infections more likely. If you're planning major surgery, and particularly cosmetic surgery, your physician will insist that you stop smoking before the procedure.
- Maintain a healthy weight. Overweight patients are more prone to infection.
- Inform your doctor of any current or recent illness. A cold or the flu can lead to a chest infection and other complications. Let your physician or health travel agent know if you don't feel well.
- If diabetic or pre-diabetic, make sure that your blood sugar levels are under control. ■

Before Leaving the Hospital: Get All the Paperwork

Wonderful! Your treatment was a success! You have rested a little, and you're now more than eager to leave the hospital for the comforts of home or of that five-star recovery retreat you booked on the Bay of Bengal. Not so fast. Impatient to be gone, and often suffering the woozy side effects of surgery and post-operative pharmaceuticals, patients too often find themselves back at home missing important documents that could have more easily been obtained on site. So before you hightail it out of your hospital or clinic, be sure that you have all of your important documents.

Generally, larger hospitals provide complete medical documentation as part of the standard exit procedure. However, some smaller clinics may rely more on verbal instructions, and they are less likely to build and maintain a dossier on your case.

Regardless, be sure that you have the following in your possession before you walk out of the hospital (ideally, before making final payment):

- Any x-rays your surgeon and staff may have taken. Try to get all x-rays and images in digital form (.jpg or .tif files), as well as hard copy.
- Any pre- or post-operative photographs. If your doctor does not take them, you might ask your companion to snap a few close-ups. Even though not entirely complimentary, photographs provide additional visual information for your specialists back home, as well as backup should complications arise.
- Any test results from exams, blood work, or scans.
- Post-operative instructions, for example, diet and physical activity precautions, bed rest, bandaging, bathing. If your doctor doesn't furnish you with such instructions, ask for them. If you cannot obtain written instructions, arrange a time to talk with your doctor, and take careful notes.
- Prescribed medications and the written prescriptions, including instructions on dosage and duration. If the pharmaceutical is a brand name manufactured in a country outside your home country, be sure to ask your doctor what the comparable prescription would be when you return home in need of a refill. Your doctors at home may not know, and they will feel more confident prescribing for you if you can provide them with documentation from your overseas practitioners.
- Physical therapy recommendations or prescriptions, including full schedules and instructions.
- Exit papers that indicate your discharge with a clean bill of health.
- Insurance claims forms, if you've determined that your treatment is covered by your health plan.
- Receipts for payment, particularly if you paid in cash.

Alert your doctor before treatment that you'll be requesting copies of all images, instructions, and notes. Then a medical staffer can arrange to have duplicates made for you. Alerting your doctor serves notice that you're serious about wanting documentation, and the staff will be more likely to assemble and duplicate all materials as treatment proceeds.

Speaking of paperwork, it's a good idea to keep a journal near your bed so that you or your companion can easily jot notes and keep them in a central place. Keep lists of questions so you don't forget to ask them. Record all verbal instructions and important observations for future reference.

The Straight Dope on Pharmaceuticals

If you travel from a country where prescription drugs are expensive, chances are you will want to visit a reputable in-country pharmacy for significant savings on pharmaceuticals that may require prescriptions in your home country.

The overwhelming number of tourists who carry pharmaceuticals purchased abroad cross the border with no trouble, their medications usually unnoticed. The best advice is to use common sense. You're far less likely to be hassled for carrying US$100 worth of amoxicillin than if your suitcase is seen bursting with enough tramadol to supply the streets of Los Angeles for a year. And, as always, if you're carrying drugs that are illegal in your home country—prescription or otherwise—you may be subject to arrest, as well as seizure of the prohibited items. Singapore and other medical destinations post threats of capital punishment for those bringing in heavy narcotics. Enough said. ∎

Leisure Time: Before or After Treatment?

Since the recent dawn of contemporary medical travel, the media have had a field day promoting the image of sophisticated, devil-may-care patients jetting overseas for treatment and then heading to exotic resorts for two-week romps. Truth is, few health travelers match that description. The overwhelming majority of health travelers we interviewed had focused on researching, locating, and receiving quality healthcare at significant cost savings. Vacation and leisure time played second fiddle.

The decision of when or whether to include a vacation as a part of a medical journey depends upon a number of important variables. Thus, before booking a week at that yummy-looking mountain rain forest spa retreat, consider the following points.

Intensity of treatment and length of recovery period. Even though promoters of health travel may imply otherwise, there is a big difference between tooth whitening and a hip replacement. Or, in the words of one physician, "Minor surgery is what other people experience." When it's you, it's major, and even a simple tooth extraction or brow lift involves pain, swelling, post-treatment care, pharmaceuticals, and possible complications.

If you're undergoing surgery, focus on your recuperation. If your surgeon or health travel agent recommends a specialized recovery accommodation nearby, take that advice seriously. Recovery lodges often offer 24-hour nursing services and rapid on-call physician care should you develop complications. Even if you're planning only minor surgery (such as simple oral treatment or light cosmetic surgery), build in at least three days of recovery immediately following your treatment before heading out on a vacation.

Also remember that for many surgeries—and for all cosmetic treatment—you are required to avoid exposure to the sun for at least two weeks (so much for the fun-'n-sun part of the trip). Remember also that air travel too soon after surgery increases the risk of deep vein thrombosis (DVT), which is the formation of a thrombus (clot) in one of the deep veins, usually in the lower leg. The immobility of long flights increases DVT risk, as does recent surgery. You can take preventive measures, including wearing compression stockings and moving about while on planes and trains. Ask your doctor about how soon after surgery you can undertake a long sedentary trip (see "Caution: Blood Clots in the Veins" in Chapter Five).

Your availability. Most health travel journeys take at least 10 days: three or so for consultation and treatment and at least seven for recovery. Thus, if you or your companion works for a living, an extended stay may be out of the question. On the other hand, if you are retired or you have vacation days accrued, building leisure activities into the trip could be good medicine. If you do not have at least three weeks to travel, reconsider combining treatment with pleasure and focus on what's most important—your health!

Your pocketbook. The idea of saving a lot on airfare because you're already there is attractive. An added vacation may feel like a bonus. But vacation expenses add up, and you're still spending real cash for every vacation day you take. Are you sure you want to spend the money you saved by getting healthcare overseas on a vacation you might never have taken otherwise? If money is tight, perhaps you're wiser to plan shorter, simpler, cheaper vacations at some other time, when you are feeling your best.

Maybe the money you save on treatment can be put to better use if saved for later. Patients who opt out of long, potentially stressful vacation trips tacked on to their health travel tend to return home in a better frame of mind—and with fewer complications.

Your personal preferences. Some health travelers we interviewed had no problem taking a week's vacation in-country before heading into the hospital for treatment. Others worried the entire time. "All I did was fret about the procedure and all the unknowns before me," said one patient, who underwent a successful knee replacement in Malaysia. "I would have been better off postponing the fun part for another time."

Your companion. When planning your medical journey, consider your companion's interests as well as your own. One patient found that her companion—although a great friend and ally and a huge contributor to her successful heart surgery—was not the ideal fun mate. While in Austria, they had different notions about how to spend their leisure time. Carol liked playing the blackjack tables at Casino Wien; Jennifer preferred chamber music at the Conservatory.

Your first priority. We have found the most successful health travel vacationers were either veteran medical travelers who knew the ropes or patients who had lots of time on their hands—at least a month—to add a vacation to their treatment and full recovery period.

If you fall into neither of those categories, consider earmarking some of your medical savings for some delayed gratification in the form of an unfettered, fully relaxing vacation once you have successfully recovered. Why rush it, when in truth, a successful medical treatment and a fun vacation usually make for strange bedfellows. For the moment, know that most successful health travelers focus their efforts on taking care of their bodies, recovering successfully, and returning home happy and well.

CHAPTER FIVE

Home Again, Home Again

Beating Those Home-Again Blues

It's something of a paradox: arriving home from a long trip is at once joyful—and challenging. After all, you've just been to a new and perhaps exciting place. If you're not a frequent traveler, the richness of the culture, the cordiality of the people, or the quality of the healthcare you received may have surprised you. You might have delighted in learning a thing or two about a new land. Maybe you even picked up a bit of wanderlust on the road.

On the downside, you're probably experiencing the expected discomforts of surgery, the side effects of pharmaceuticals, and the annoyances of jet lag. You'll likely return home exhausted, only to face backlogged bills, clogged email, endless voice mail messages, demanding kids, and a house in need of a cleaning. Take a deep breath and try to relax. It's important to pace yourself, particularly your first few days back home, allowing yourself time to settle back into a routine. It's even more important if you're not completely healed and you need additional recovery time.

Communicate Your Needs to Family Members

Yay! Dad's home! He went all the way to India for a knee replacement and came back alive to tell about it. In all the hubbub, family members also need to know that the returned health traveler still needs prescriptions filled, physical therapy, follow-up consultations with physicians, additional tests, x-rays, and lab work. You may be unable to get back to your full pre-treatment load of tasks and responsibilities—at least not right away. Let family members know how they can help. Support—as simple as a son who does his own laundry for a while or a mother-in-law who brings over a casserole—can make a world of difference.

At home, some patients feel timid about asking for help, particularly if they managed to work a vacation or extended recovery period into the medical trip. Yet the fact remains that the healing body needs a great deal of rest and attention. Do not be afraid to voice a gentle reminder that you're still recuperating.

Touch Base with Your Local Doctor

If you have followed our advice in previous chapters, you've informed your local doctor or specialist about your health trip before departure. When you sent your medical records abroad, you established the basis for a continuing communication between your local healthcare provider and your overseas physician (see "Continuity of Care" in Chapter Seven).

Shortly after your return, pay a brief visit (or send an email) to your healthcare provider's office to let your contacts there know that you're back. Chances are you'll have specific needs based on your overseas physician's instructions or recommendations. You might need an antibiotic prescription refilled or six weeks of physical therapy approved. Thus, it is best to touch base as soon as you reasonably can, both as a courtesy and for practical reasons.

Most physicians are understanding and cooperative, particularly if you've brought home complete, accurate paperwork. If for some reason you find your physician uncooperative or uncommunicative, then consider seeking an alternative healthcare provider sooner rather than later.

Anticipate Longer Recovery Periods

Whether treated at home or abroad, most patients can expect recovery periods of three months—sometimes even more—for large, invasive surgeries. For less intensive treatments, recovery periods range from a few days to several weeks. Regardless of the intensity of your treatment, don't be surprised if you find that you need what seems like a long time to feel fully yourself again, particularly after a long trip.

It's easy, for example, to underestimate the effects of jet lag. In fact, seasoned travelers know that for every one hour of time zone difference, travelers should allow one day to fully recover from jet lag. For a trip to Asia, that's nearly two weeks! Typical jet lag discomforts include feelings of disorientation, fatigue, inability to sleep, loss of concentration, loss of drive, headaches, upset stomach, and a general feeling of unwellness.

Add symptoms of jet lag to the list of unavoidable post-treatment discomforts, and your body's inner voices will be pleading with you to take things easy, at least during the first week after your return.

Hold On to Your Paperwork

Remember all those documents, files, and assorted gobbledygook the hospital gave you before your departure? Forms, instructions, prescriptions, notes, and recommendations ad nauseam—keep it all! Your hometown health providers and caregivers will need that information as a road map to your recovery.

Take it all with you when you visit your local doctor, who is likely to find those documents more informative and reliable than your personal account of the trip. If your physician wants to keep any of the documents, ask for a copy for your files.

Stay with the Program

We have said it elsewhere in the book: pre- and post-procedure is all about compliance, compliance, compliance. If you've just had dental surgery, for example, you might be instructed to use a special antiseptic rinse twice a day. Do so. Or after an orthopedic procedure, patients are usually required to undergo a rigorous physical therapy program. Do it. Nearly all procedures come with a regimen of antibiotics and other prescriptions, sometimes lasting weeks. Follow doctor's orders. That means you!

Granted, it's no fun to take those big horse capsules or drag yourself to that physical therapy appointment when you really need to clear those 400 emails sitting in your inbox. But consider the alternative: after all that work and investment and travel, do you really want to develop complications that could cost you extra time and money—if not your life?

Fully inform your family members and close friends about your post-treatment procedures and regimens. Loved ones should encourage you to do everything you can to get better, and they should help you follow your program in every way possible. Pepper your calendar and to-do list with reminders of your medications, appointments, therapy sessions, and other health-promoting activities.

Get Help or Farm Out the Work

If you've come this far in your health travel experience, chances are you're one of those people who does it all. You're good at planning and problem solving, juggling many balls at once, keeping myriad tasks and projects in the air, and managing to walk the tightrope of a complex contemporary life. That's why an otherwise challenging, difficult journey turned out so well. You managed it!

Now that you're home, cut yourself some slack. Don't try to return immediately to your pre-treatment pace. If housecleaning was one of your daily chores, and your doctor admonishes you not to overdo it, then use some of your treatment savings to hire temporary help for house chores, yard work, or any other tasks that might have you overstressing too soon. If you need to repair a lawn mower so you can cut the grass, send it to the shop. You get the idea. For the first month or so after your trip, demand less of yourself, and work back gradually into your normal routine.

Stay Mentally and Socially Active

During long recovery periods, it's easy to become bored, isolated, and listless, falling into a rut of watching endless TV or updating your Facebook page for hours on end. If your recovery keeps you from being as physically active as you would like or returning to work immediately, try to stay as emotionally fit as possible. Get a friend to bring you a stack of your favorite reading and viewing materials from the local library. Invite friends and family members to watch a good movie with you. Take up chess again or whatever activity keeps you stimulated. Studies have shown that patients who stay mentally and socially active post-treatment recover better and faster than those who become couch potatoes.

If Complications Develop . . .

If your overseas doctors played your treatment by the rules, they probably insisted that you remain in-country for at least a few days following your procedure. The main reason was to observe your progress and monitor your condition for any signs of complications, which are more serious than the usual discomforts experienced post-surgery. Most complications arise within a week after surgery. Even though 95 percent of all surgical patients experience no post-treatment complications, every patient should be able to recognize the warning signs and promptly seek medical help.

> ## Caution: Blood Clots in the Veins
>
> **A**ir travel after surgery may put you at risk of deep vein thrombosis (DVT), a term that describes the formation of a thrombus (clot) in one of the deep veins, usually in the lower leg. The immobility of long flights increases the risk, as does recent surgery—a potential double whammy for some medical travelers. The symptoms of DVT include pain and redness of the skin over a vein or swelling and tenderness in the ankle, foot, or thigh. More serious symptoms include chest pain and shortness of breath.
>
> You can take preventive measures to reduce your risk of DVT. Wear compression stockings, and move about frequently while on planes and trains. Ask your doctor about how soon after surgery you can undertake a long, sedentary trip. ■

Post-Treatment:
Normal Discomfort or Something More Complicated?

Before your surgery, your doctor should have thoroughly explained the procedure and informed you about any discomforts post-op. Discomforts differ from complications. Discomforts are predictable and unthreatening. Complications, though rarely life threatening, are more serious and may require medical attention. These are some common discomforts you can expect following your surgery:

- minor local pain and general achiness
- swelling (after dentistry)
- puffiness (after cosmetic surgery)
- bruising, swelling, or minor bleeding around an incision
- urinary retention or difficulty urinating (side effect of anesthesia and catheters)
- nausea and vomiting, headache, dry mouth, temporary loss of memory, lingering tiredness (all common side effects of anesthesia)
- hunger and under-nutrition

Most surgically induced discomforts recede or disappear altogether during the first few days after treatment as the body and spirit return to normal. Be sure to report discomforts that persist or become more pronounced; they might be early warning signs of more serious complications.

Complications vary according to each type of surgery, and you should be aware of the more common ones. Complications are scary, and many doctors would rather not go into morbid detail about them unless pressed. Complications are rare; most arise in fewer than 5 percent of total cases—and generally among patients who are aged or infirm in the first place. So though it's wise to be informed and vigilant, there is no need to worry yourself sick anticipating the worst. Common symptoms of complications include:

- infection, increased pain, or swelling around an incision
- abnormal bleeding around an incision
- sudden or unexplained high fever
- extreme chest pain or shortness of breath
- extreme headache
- extreme difficulty urinating

If you experience any of the symptoms listed above, call your hometown physician immediately!

The Trip Home

Now that you are finally going home, remember to take care of yourself on the way. Before you travel:

- Book a seat (exit row or bulkhead) that provides sufficient leg room.
- Wear loose clothing.
- Reserve an aisle seat on the airplane so you can get up and move around easily.
- Ask your surgeon about using a pneumatic compression device during and after surgery.
- Before your return flight home, ask your surgeon if you need an anticoagulant.
- Walk briskly for at least half an hour before takeoff.

And, once you are on the plane:

- Don't stow your carry-on luggage under your seat if it restricts your movement.
- Flex your calves and rotate your ankles every 20 to 30 minutes.
- Walk up and down the aisle every two hours, more often if you can. If airline staff hassle you back into your seat, let them know you are DVT prone; they usually back off.
- Sleep only for short periods.

- Do not take sleeping pills.
- Drink lots of water to avoid dehydration.
- Avoid alcohol, caffeine, and diet soda.
- Wear elastic flight socks or support stockings.
- Don't let your socks, stockings, or clothing roll up, pinch up, or constrict your legs.
- Take deep breaths frequently throughout your flight.

CHAPTER SIX

Dos and Don'ts
for the Smart Health Traveler

Much of the advice in this chapter is covered in greater detail elsewhere in this book. Consider this a capsule summary of essential information, sprinkled with practical advice that will help reduce the number of inevitable "gotchas" that health travelers encounter. You may want your travel companion and family members to read this chapter, along with the Introduction, so they better understand medical travel. They can use this information as a gateway to the more in-depth sections of this book.

Do Plan Ahead

Particularly if you'll be traveling at peak tourist season, the further in advance you plan, the more likely you're to get the best doctors, the lowest airfares, and the best availability and rates on lodging. Remember, you'll be competing for treatment with other health travelers. You'll also be competing with other tourists for hotels and amenities. If possible, begin planning at least three months before your expected departure date. If you're concerned about having to change plans, *do* be sure to confirm cancellation policies with airlines, hotels, and travel agents. (For more information, see Chapter Two, "Planning and Budgeting Your Health Travel Journey.")

Do Be Sure about Your Diagnosis and Treatment Preference

The more you know about the treatment you're seeking, the easier your search for a physician will be. For example, if you're seeking dental work, you should know specifically whether you want implants or a bridge. If the former, then you'll be narrowing your search to accredited implantologists. *Do* work closely with your hometown doctor or medical specialist, and make sure you obtain exact recommendations—in writing, if possible. If you're unsure of your needs or not confident of your doctor's diagnosis, seek a second opinion. Then, when you know your specific course of action, learn as much as you can about your procedure, using textbooks, medical references, and reliable sites on the internet. (For more information on recommended health research sites, see Part Three, "Resources and References," in the back of the book.)

Do Research Your In-Country Doctor Thoroughly

This is the most important step of all. By following a few basics, you'll see the process is not so daunting. When you have narrowed your search to two or three physicians, invest time and money in personal telephone interviews, either directly with your doctor or through your health travel planning agency. Don't be afraid to ask questions—lots of them—until you arrive at a comfort level with a competent physician. (For more information, see Chapter Two.)

Don't Rely Completely on the Internet for Your Research

Even though the online world has matured over the last few years, searching for information is not yet on automatic pilot. Deeper digging and more effort on your part are usually required. It's okay to use the web for your initial research, but don't assume that websites offer complete and accurate information. Cross-check your online findings with referrals, sources of accreditation and certification, articles in leading newspapers and magazines, word of mouth, and your health travel agent. You'll begin to find the same names of clinics and physicians popping up. Narrow your search from there.

Do Get It in Writing

Cost estimates, appointments, recommendations, opinions, second opinions, air and hotel accommodations—get as much as you can in writing, and *do* be sure to take all documentation with you on the plane. Email is fine, as long as you have retained a written record of your key transactions. If you prefer to use the telephone, confirm your conversations with a follow-up email: "As we discussed, it is my understanding that the cost for my treatment, including an extraction and two implants, will be US$1,250. Is that correct? Could you please confirm that in a letter or email?"

The more you get in writing, the less the chance of a misunderstanding, particularly when confronting language and cultural barriers.

Do Insist on Your Native Tongue

As much as many of us would like to have a better command of another language, the time to brush up on your Spanish is most definitely not when negotiating that new set of porcelain-on-titanium crowns in Costa Rica.

As you begin your research into a medical trip, consider the language barrier as an early warning sign in your screening process. If a clinic, physician, or health travel service that claims to serve international patients does not have a good grasp of a language in which you're conversant, then politely apologize for your lack of language skills and move on. There are now plenty of options in the global healthcare arena, and establishing a comfortable, reliable rapport with your key contacts is paramount to your success as a health traveler.

Don't Schedule Your Trip Too Tightly

Most veteran health travelers admit that one of their biggest surprises was the efficiency of medical services they received abroad. Staff-to-patient ratios are generally lower than in US treatment centers, and the level of personal commitment is often better.

Yet it is best not to plan your trip with military precision. A missed consultation or an unanticipated extra two days of recovery overseas can mean rescheduling that non-refundable $1,300 airfare, with penalties. More important, scheduling a little leeway lets everyone breathe more easily and gives you the flexibility of adapting seamlessly when things don't go precisely as planned.

A good rule of thumb is to add one additional day for every five days you have already scheduled for consultation, treatment, and recovery. If you're planning a face-lift and tummy tuck, consultation and surgery might require three days, with a recommended recovery of 10 days (totaling 13 days). Thus, you should add two or three more days to your travel schedule to allow for weather-related delays, missed appointments, additional tests, and other unexpected events.

Don't Forget to Alert Your Bank and Credit Card Company

The consumer fraud units of banks and credit card institutions now deploy hair-trigger monitoring for unusual spending activity. Thus, overseas travelers often find their accounts canceled immediately after using them in-country, just when they need their credit cards and ATM access the most. Then the fun begins as you try to connect with your bank's voice-activated customer service line, using your mobile phone's expensive international voice plan.

The easy fix is to contact your bank and credit card company (or companies) before your trip. Inform them of your travel dates, and tell them where you'll be. If you plan to use your credit card for large amounts, alert the company in advance. Also, if you plan to use your credit card to pay for expensive treatments, this might be a good time to reconfirm your credit limits.

Do Learn a Little about Your Destination

Once you've settled on your health travel destination, spend a little time getting to know something about the country you're visiting. You'll find a little knowledge goes a long way: the locals will differentiate you from less caring travelers and express sincere appreciation for your interest. *Do* buy or borrow a couple of travel guides, learn a little history, and practice a few basic phrases (such as *hello, goodbye, please, thank you,* and *excuse me*). When in-country, pick up an English-language newspaper, which will get you up to speed on current events, happenings around town, and local gossip.

Do Inform Your Local Doctors Before You leave

Telling your doctor you're planning to travel overseas for treatment is a little like calling your auto mechanic just to announce you're taking your business to a competitor down the road. However, although you may never again see your former car mechanic, you do want to preserve a good working relationship with your family physician and local specialists.

Although they may not particularly like your decision, most doctors will respect your desire to travel overseas for medical care. Even if they privately question your judgment, they will appreciate learning about your plans before your trip. If your physician attempts to dissuade you, do be attentive and polite, but stay firm in your resolve if you've done your homework and made your choice. The pre-trip notification will pay off for you, too. When you return, you'll not have to make an awkward call to your doctor just when you most need a follow-up consult or a prescription refilled.

Don't Scrimp on Lodging

Unless your finances absolutely demand it, avoid hotels and other accommodations in the "budget" category. In foreign lands, particularly Asia and Central and South America, there is often a world of difference between "moderate" and "no frills." The latter can land you in unsavory parts of town, with cold-water showers and shared bathrooms of questionable cleanliness. On the other hand, hospitals and travel agents sometimes recommend deluxe hotels that charge astronomical rates, even by US standards.

Press your health travel contacts to recommend a good, moderately priced hotel in the US$125-per-night range, or search online using hotels.com or tripadvisor.com (both now offer a robust inventory of international lodging; many brands will be familiar to you). Even though such affordability may not be possible or desirable in certain cities—some in India, for example—there is often a huge price difference at the four-star or three-star levels just below deluxe, where a range of perfectly comfortable, service-rich accommodations can be found.

Don't Stay Too Far from Your Treatment Center

When booking hotel accommodations for you and your companion, make sure the hospital or doctor's office is nearby. This is doubly true in large cities. Although in-town transportation costs are usually low, traffic and noise levels can be horrendous, and long stop-and-start cross-town trips can be as stressful as a 24-hour flight. Check with your doctor, hospital, treatment center, or health travel planner for conveniently located lodging.

Do Befriend Staff

Nurses, nurse's aides, paramedics, receptionists, clerks, and even maintenance people—consider each of them a vital member of your health team. Often overlooked and always overworked, these professionals are omnipresent in the day-to-day operation of a hospital or clinic, and they wield a good deal of quiet power. You and your companion might find you need one of these folks most in the wee hours when no one else is around. Invariably, it will be the second-floor lobby clerk who knows how to get in touch with your doctor or the night-shift nurse assistant who fetches a clean bedsheet.

You and your companion should take the time to chat with medical staff members, learn their names, inquire about their families, and proffer any small gifts you might have brought. Above all, treat staff with deference and respect. When you're ready to leave the hospital, a heartfelt thank-you note and a modest cash tip make a memorable farewell.

Do Comply with Doctor's Orders

One of the best ways to assure a successful medical travel journey—and to avoid unnecessary complications—is to follow the pre- and post-procedure program set forth by your in-country and local MD. It's easy to return home and go lax on your physical therapy program or fail to refill your prescription or less than diligently manage your surgical wounds. To ensure a successful recovery, redouble your efforts to rigorously follow all of your doctor's orders.

Don't Return Home Too Soon

After a long flight to a foreign land, multiple consultations with physicians and staff, and a painful and disorienting medical procedure, most folks feel ready to jump on the first flight home. That is understandable but not advisable. Your body needs time to recuperate, and your physician needs to track your recovery progress. As you plan your trip, ask your physician how much recovery time is advised for your particular treatment. Then add a few extra days, just to be on the safe side.

Don't Be Too Adventurous with Local Cuisine

Chicken vindaloo in Bangalore! Spicy prawn soup in Bangkok! Grilled snapper picante in Puerto Vallarta! Yes, it's true that most health travel destinations also have robust, tasty cuisine, with a variety of local culinary fare to tempt nearly any palate. But one sure way to get your treatment off to a bad start is to enter your clinic with a case of traveler's diarrhea or even a mild stomach upset caused by local water or food intolerance.

So when hunger calls, go easy with your food choices. Before treatment, avoid rich, spicy foods and exotic drinks. And eat only cooked foods. If you cannot survive without fresh fruits and vegetables, follow the international travel rule: Boil it, cook it, peel it (yourself), or forget it! And use bottled water when you can always making sure the seal is intact.

If staying in the hospital as an inpatient, don't be afraid to ask the dietician for a menu that is easy on your digestion.

Finally, find out about food interactions for any pharmaceuticals you're taking before or after your procedure. Some drugs don't work—or become downright risky—if certain foods are consumed. In short, play it safe on your medical trip; your digestive tract will thank you.

Do Set Aside Some of Your Medical Travel Savings for a Vacation

You and your companion deserve it! If you're not able to take leisure time during your trip abroad, then set aside the extra money for some time off after you return home, even if only for a weekend getaway. You've demonstrated great courage and perseverance in making a difficult trip abroad, and you have earned some downtime with your cost savings.

Don't Ever Settle for Second Best in Treatment Options

Even though you can cut corners on airfare, lodging, and transportation, always, *always* insist upon the very best healthcare your money can buy. Go the extra mile to find that best physician or surgeon. Although everyone likes a bargain, the best treatment does not always come from the lowest bidder. Focus on quality, not just price.

Do Get All Your Paperwork Before Leaving the Country

Understandably, after you have undergone a treatment—whether a simple root canal or complex hip replacement—you're eager to get home or go on vacation or just get your life back. Too often and in too much of a hurry to leave, patients exit their treatment center lacking instructions, prescriptions, and other essential paperwork. Get copies of everything. (For more information, see Chapter Four.)

Do Trust Your Intuition

Your courage and good judgment have brought you this far. Continue to rely on your sixth sense throughout your trip. If, for example, you feel uncomfortable with your in-country consultation, switch doctors. If you get a queasy feeling about extra or uncharted costs, don't be afraid to question them. Thousands of health travelers before you have beaten a successful path abroad, using good information and common sense. If you have come this far, chances are good you'll join their ranks.

CHAPTER SEVEN

Checklists for a Successful Health Journey

The five checklists that follow will remind you of some important issues you need to consider in planning your health travel.

Checklist 1: *Should I Consult a Health Travel Planner?*

Health travel planners answer to many names: brokers, facilitators, agents, expeditors. Throughout this book, we use the phrase *health travel planner* or *health travel agent* to mean any agency or representative who specializes in helping patients obtain medical treatment abroad. Before engaging the services of a health travel agent, ask yourself these questions:

Should I consult a health travel planner?	Yes	No	Not Sure
Will a health travel planner save me time?			
Am I willing to pay for the convenience of a health travel planner's services?			
Will I feel more confident about health travel if I use the services of an agency?			
Does the agent I'm considering have the knowledge and experience I need?			
Does this planner have a track record of successful service to the health traveler?			
Does this agent speak my language well enough for us to converse comfortably?			
Can I get at least two recommendations or letters of reference from former clients of this agency? Have I checked these references?			
Can I get at least two recommendations or letters of reference from treatment centers that work with this agency? Have I checked these references?			
Can this agency give me complete information about possible destinations and options for my procedure?			
Will this agent put me in touch with one or more treatment centers and physicians?			
Will this agent work collaboratively to help me choose the best treatment option?			
Is this agent responsive to my questions and concerns?			
Does the service package this agent is offering meet my needs?			
Does this agent have long-standing affiliations with in-country treatment centers and practitioners?			
Has this planner negotiated better-than-retail rates with hospitals, clinics, physicians, hotels, and (perhaps) airlines?			
Can this agent save me money on other in-country costs, such as airport pickup and dropoff or transportation to my clinic?			
Can this agent provide personal assistance and support in my destination country?			

Should I consult a health travel planner?	Yes	No	Not Sure
Is this planner willing to work within the constraints of my budget?			
Do I know (and have in writing) the exact costs for this agency's services?			
Do I have a suitable contract or letter of agreement with this agency?			
Do I feel comfortable with this agency? Have we built a sense of trust?			

Of all the services a health travel planner offers, the most important are related to your treatment. Start your dialogue by asking the fundamental questions:

- Do you know the best doctors?
- Have you met personally with your preferred physicians and visited their clinics?
- Can you give me their credentials and background information?
- What about accommodations?
- Do you provide transportation to and from the airport?
- Do you provide transportation to and from the treatment center?

If an agent is knowledgeable and capable with these details, the rest of the planning usually takes care of itself.

Just Ask

When it comes to asking for special assistance from the airlines, many travelers believe they must be severely handicapped to request a wheelchair or some other service. And some folks are just shy about asking for help or embarrassed to be wheeled around airport corridors and jetways.

Get over it! If you're heading to India for hip surgery and you've been in chronic pain for three years, there is no shame in requesting a wheelchair. Every airline we contacted happily supports medical travelers. In the same vein, if you still feel the effects of surgery on your homebound trip, it's perfectly reasonable to request wheelchair assistance.

Airlines ask that you or your companion request a wheelchair 48 hours before your flight. Then, when you arrive at the airport, check in with the skycap at curbside, where a wheelchair is usually nearby. Remember to tip folks a few dollars for assisting you; they will appreciate the gesture and remember you the next time your paths cross. ■

Checklist 2: *What Do I Need to Do Ahead of Time?*

This checklist covers some of the planning you'll need to do to become a fully pre-pared and informed global patient.

Have I completed these planning steps?	Yes	No
Engaged the services of a health travel planner (if desired—see Checklist 1)		
Obtained a second opinion—or a third if necessary—on diagnosis and treatment options		
Considered a range of treatment options and discussed each option with potential providers		
Reviewed the various hospitals, clinics, specialties, and treatments to select an appropriate destination (see Part Two)		
Chosen a reliable, fun travel companion		
Obtained and reviewed the professional credentials of two or more physicians or surgeons (see "Ten Must-Ask Questions for Your Physician Candidate" in Chapter Two)		
Selected the best physician or surgeon for the treatment I need		
Researched the history and accreditation of the hospital or clinic (see Chapter One)		
Checked for the affiliations and partnerships of the hospital or clinic		
Learned about the number of surgeries performed in the hospital or clinic (generally, the more the better)		
Learned about success rates (these are usually calculated as a ratio of successful operations to the overall number of operations performed)		
Gathered and sent all medical records and diagnostic information that my physician or surgeon needs to plan my treatment		
Pre-arranged travel, accommodations, recovery, and leisure activities (if desired)		
Pre-arranged amenities, such as concierge services in-country or wheelchair services on the return trip		
Packed the essentials (see Checklist 3)		
Double-checked everything—then checked again		

Checklist 3: *What Should I Pack?*

You have likely heard the cardinal rule of international travel: pack light. Less to carry means less to lose. Don't worry if you leave behind some basic item, such as shampoo or a comb; you can always pick it up at your destination. That said, this checklist covers the items you absolutely, positively need to take with you. And make sure you pack these things in your carry-on bag. A prescription or passport lost in checked luggage creates unnecessary discomforts.

Is this item packed in my carry-on bag?	Yes	No
Passport		
Visa (if required)		
Travel itinerary		
Airline tickets or eticket confirmations		
Driver's license or valid picture ID (in addition to passport)		
Health insurance card(s) or policy		
ATM card		
Credit card(s)		
Enough cash for airport fees and local transportation upon arrival		
Immunization record		
Prescription medications		
Hard-to-find over-the-counter drugs		
Medical records, current x-rays/scans, consultations, and treatment notes		
All financial agreements and hard copies of email correspondence		
Phone and fax numbers, mailing addresses, and email addresses of people I need or want to contact in-country		
Phone numbers, mailing addresses, and email addresses of people I need or want to contact back home		
Travel journal for notes, expense records, and receipts		

Continuity of Care

Continuity of care can be a challenge for patients who travel for medical proce-dures. Excellent communication—with both your hometown doctor and your international healthcare team—is critical to the success of your treatment. Many hospitals offer an international patient services center with medically knowledge-able staff fluent in English and other languages.

Make sure you take full advantage of this resource, and work with them to coordinate your appointments and healthcare plan before you schedule your travel. Make sure, also, that you work with them to establish communication between your primary (local) doctor and your in-country medical team. Early communication with all parties can ensure better follow-up care after you return home.

Current Medical Records

Once you have established contact with your selected facility's international patient center, work with staff there to make sure your in-country physician has access to your most current medical records, including up-to-date laboratory tests, x-rays, and scans.

Medical records are most often transmitted digitally. Ask your hometown physi-cian to email copies of your complete record to you. If you can obtain only hard-copy documents, then have them scanned and converted to either .pdf or .jpg format.

Collaboration among Doctors

Transferring your medical records may get your local doctor communicating directly with your in-country physician for the first time. The next collaboration should occur after your treatment or surgery. Work with the international patient center to make sure your local physician is notified of the details of the surgery and the aftercare protocol.

Once you return home and are again under the care of your local physician, this collaboration and consultation should continue until you're released from care with a clean bill of health.

Complete Documentation

Too often patients return home lacking the complete documentation their local physician needs to oversee ongoing care. The absence of information compromises the physician's effectiveness and threatens the patient's health. Make sure you get complete records before you return home. ∎

Checklist 4: *What Do I Do after My Procedure?*

Coping with post-surgery discomfort is difficult enough when you're close to home. Lying for long hours in a hospital bed, far away from family—that is often the darkest time for a health traveler. Knowledge is the best antidote to needless worry. As with pre-surgery preparation, ask lots of questions about post-surgery discomforts before heading into the operating room. Be sure to ask doctors and nurses about what kinds of discomforts to expect following your specific procedure.

If your discomfort or pain becomes acute, bleeding is persistent, or you suspect a growing infection, you may be experiencing a complication that is more serious than mere discomfort and requires immediate attention. Contact your physician immediately!

This checklist will help you make the most of your post-treatment period and know when it is appropriate to seek medical assistance.

What do I do after my procedure?	Yes	No	Not Sure
Have I received all of my doctor's instructions for my post-treatment care and recovery? Do I understand them all?			
Am I following all of my physician's instructions *to the letter*?			
Do I know what post-treatment signs and symptoms are normal?			
Do I know what post-treatment signs and symptoms indicate a need for prompt medical attention?			
Do I have copies of all my medical and treatment records, including x-rays/scans, blood test results, prescriptions, and others?			
Do I have itemized receipts for all the bills I have paid?			
Do I have itemized bills for all the costs I have not yet paid?			
Do I have completed insurance claim forms (if applicable)?			
Have I allotted ample time for recovery?			
Do I know how to prevent blood clots in my legs after surgery and on the airplane?			
Do I know what follow-up treatment I will need when I return home, including physical therapy?			
Have I let my family know what help I will need when I return home?			
Have I checked in with my local doctor to share information about the procedure I had and my post-treatment care needs?			
Am I staying mentally, physically, and socially active following my procedure?			

Checklist 5: *What Does My Travel Companion Need to Do?*

A person who accompanies a health traveler gives a great gift. Here are some questions for potential companions to answer before they commit themselves to accompanying a health traveler abroad.

Considerations for travel companions	Yes	No	Not Sure
Am I sure I want to go? Am I sure I'm up to the task? (If you hesitate in answering either question, you may want to reconsider.)			
Am I willing and able to take responsibility for handling details, such as obtaining visas and passports?			
Do I feel comfortable acting as an advocate for the health traveler at times when he or she may need assistance?			
Have we agreed on the costs of the trip and on who is responsible for paying what?			
Do I feel sufficiently confident about handling experiences and challenges in a foreign country, such as getting through airports, arranging for taxis, or finding addresses?			
Do the health traveler and I communicate well enough to identify problems and solve them together amicably?			
Am I prepared to listen to and record doctor's instructions and provide reminders for the health traveler when needed?			
Can I help the health traveler stay in touch with family, friends, and healthcare providers back home?			
Have I allowed for "downtime" and time for myself during the medical travel?			
Do I have the patience to help the health traveler through what might be a long and difficult recovery period, both abroad and back home?			

The Most-Traveled
Healthcare Destinations

The Most-Traveled
Healthcare Destinations

━━━ ━━ ━━━ ━━━ ━━━━ ━━━ ━━ ━━━ ━━━ ━━ ━━━━

Introduction

Having read Part One, you now have a fair idea of what it takes to be an informed health traveler. If you're reading this section of the book, chances are you have already reached a decision about your course of treatment, and you may even have narrowed your search to several countries or a particular region.

Part Two, "The Most-Traveled Healthcare Destinations," gives an overview of hundreds of destinations in 20 countries. It includes important information about accreditation, leading medical centers and their top specialties, approximate cost savings, and cultural considerations.

To help you navigate this section, we have provided a quick-reference Treatment and Country Finder, following. Consult that chart to locate the specialty you're seeking, and you'll quickly discover which countries specialize in your area of interest. Then hunker down and explore the destinations on the following pages. As you read, consider the following points.

Things change. Although *Patients Beyond Borders* is the cumulative result of thousands of hours of research, keep in mind that contemporary medical travel is undergoing rapid changes. New hospitals gain (and lose) accreditation by the month, and entire countries are on the verge of emerging as leading medical travel destinations. Moreover, travel and treatment prices fluctuate, countries become more or less stable, and monetary exchange rates move buying power in and out of favor. Depending upon current events, attitudes vary toward health travel—and travel in general.

Despite the oft-shifting global landscape, if you stay informed, shop wisely, and always keep high-quality, reliable treatment at the top of your priority list, you'll be on a firm path to success as a global health traveler. If you've decided to travel abroad for treatment, we hope you'll continue to look to *Patients Beyond Borders* for guidance. For updates and additional services, visit our website at patientsbeyondborders.com.

Prices and savings. In previous editions of *Patients Beyond Borders*, we listed typical treatment costs for featured destinations. As this sector grows, so does competitive pricing, coupled with innovation around minimally invasive procedures, telemedicine, and other advances. In addition, following in the footsteps of retail, many respected hospitals are offering special discounts and package pricing on selected procedures. Thus, in lieu of price listings, we have furnished estimated cost savings for each destination, based on our work with hospitals, hospital networks, governments, and research groups, to bring you a more realistic expectation of general savings ranges for each destination.

Why such a wide range? During the long and winding course of our research, we have received sometimes significantly varying cost estimates from hospitals in the same country, sometimes in the same city. Perhaps those savings differentials are significant, so it pays to shop around because there are bargains to be had. However, some of the cost variations result from the addition or subtraction of included services. For example, you may find that a lower estimate might not include your hospital stay, anesthetist's charges, operating room expenses, or even doctors' fees. A higher estimate, on the other hand, might include most, if not all, of a procedure's costs.

Thus, we advise you to use our "typical cost savings" only to arrive at a general idea of what to expect. When doing your research, make sure your quote contains specifics, in writing, about all the included fees as well as any extra costs. In health travel, the old Latin adage applies doubly: "Caveat emptor": Let the buyer beware!

Customer service. Hospitals and clinics are busy places. As much as these organizations would like to cater to medical travelers, truth is they are in the healthcare business, not the travel business. So don't be surprised if some hospitals are slow to respond. And, despite their excellent reputation, accreditation, and references, some may not respond at all.

If you experience poor customer service in your initial contacts with a hospital or clinic, try working through a reputable health travel agent. You may have learned about an agency or planner from a friend or a web search. Many agents have partnerships with hospitals, clinics, hotels, and airlines. All of the better agents have strong contacts with the best physicians in a given treatment area. Unlike hospitals and other treatment centers, a health travel planner's job is to do exactly that—plan health travel.

Accreditation. You may notice that for some countries we did not provide information on all internationally accredited hospitals. There are good reasons. For example, although Brazil boasts a high number of Joint Commission International (JCI)-accredited hospitals, the country generally does not cater to North American health travelers. Websites of leading Brazilian hospitals are generally not in English, and we found the customer service to be poor to non-existent. Similarly, if a hospital in a given country did not respond within a reasonable amount of time to our inquiries and requests for information, we excluded it from our list.

Even though international accreditation is a benchmark of quality and an indicator that patients should seriously consider when making their healthcare choices, it is not the only measure of quality. All the countries featured in this section impose internal accreditation standards on their hospitals and clinics. Requirements and oversight vary with each country: Mexico's standards and enforcement, for example, are far lower than Thailand's or Malaysia's. At this writing, no international organization rates accreditation standards by country or region.

If you're considering a hospital or clinic that's not internationally accredited, double and redouble your research efforts for that facility. Has your hospital met its country's accreditation requirements? How many patients does your hospital see annually? How many surgeries of your specific procedure have been performed there? What are the hospital's morbidity and success rates?

Medical jargon. *Patients Beyond Borders* was written as a consumer reference for you, the layperson, not as a formal medical resource. Even though we have taken great pains to ensure medical accuracy throughout these pages, we often use lay terminology interchangeably with medical terminology, particularly when treatment names themselves tend to be used interchangeably by physicians. For example, you might see "tummy tuck" instead of the tongue-twisting "abdominoplasty" and "gum disease treatment" in place of "periodontics." If you need clarification on a medical term, please consult the Glossary in the back of this book. There we have listed and defined the medical terms most frequently used in *Patients Beyond Borders*. For more information on terms not covered in the Glossary, consult a good medical dictionary or your physician.

Safety in numbers. As you read this section, you'll see numerous references to specific numbers of procedures, surgeries, specialties, and super-specialties. As any medical professional will tell you, one of the best ways to gauge the success of a hospital or clinic is by learning the number of procedures performed there. This statistic, combined with the success rate of a specific procedure, tells as much or more about a hospital's practices as any other number. Thus, a hospital that claims 2,700 angioplasties with a success rate of 98.4 percent should give you more confidence than one that has performed 65 and cannot furnish a success rate. You'll get an even better picture if you can find out the number of procedures performed by your specific physician or surgeon.

Old school, new school. The date a hospital was established is often a good clue to its appearance. But looks are not the health traveler's most important consideration. Although some hospitals have been operating for decades in what has become an old building, they may well offer excellent physicians and state-of-the-art equipment. Other newly opened facilities may boast shiny Italian marble lobbies and five-star accommodations yet lack a track record you can use to assess the quality of care. For new hospitals, you may need to dig deep into your research to make sure your physicians and surgeons have gained ample experience at other institutions.

Data. The information in the following pages was gleaned from a long and exhaustive research process, including hospital surveys, hundreds of hospital site visits, interviews with hospital administrators and patients, and research on the web. Despite the thoroughness of our research, please know that it's impossible for us to audit hospitals' records or authenticate their statements. We believe that our information is correct. But it is up to you, the patient, whether seeking treatment across the water or across the street, to validate information about accreditation, physicians' credentials, numbers of surgeries, success rates, and other information. Once you've zeroed in on your hospital of choice, take the extra step of revalidating and cross-checking the information found in these pages.

Completeness. With all the changes occurring in the medical travel sector, this edition of *Patients Beyond Borders* cannot possibly include every excellent dental clinic, cosmetic surgery center, or specialty hospital out there. But we add new entries with every edition, and we are constantly updating our website. Did you have a successful treatment at a place we have not yet mentioned? If so, we hope you'll visit our website (patientsbeyondborders.com) and let us know about it so that we may further research your findings and broaden the base of information for our readership. You can remain anonymous, and any information you provide will remain completely confidential.

■ TREATMENT AND COUNTRY FINDER

TREATMENT	Brazil	Costa Rica	Czech Republic	Hungary	India	Israel	Malaysia
Cardiology and Heart Surgery	■				■	■	■
Cosmetic and Reconstructive Surgery	■	■	■	■			■
Dentistry	■	■			■		■
Fertility and Reproductive Health					■	■	
Health Screening		■			■		■
Neurology and Spine Surgery	■				■		■
Oncology	■		■		■		■
Ophthalmology					■		■
Orthopedics	■	■			■	■	■
Stem Cell and Regenerative Therapy						■	
Transplant					■		■
Weight Loss Surgery	■	■			■		■
Wellness and Prevention		■			■		■

Primary destination for health travelers

Secondary destination for health travelers

Mexico	Singapore	South Africa	South Korea	Taiwan	Thailand	Turkey	UAE	US

DESTINATION: **BRAZIL**

■ AT A GLANCE

Rio de Janeiro, São Paulo

Languages	Portuguese, Spanish, limited English
Time Zones	GMT −4, GMT −3, GMT −2
Country Dialing Code	+55
Electricity	127V and 220V (Brazil's electricity is notoriously nonstandard; check your specific destination for plug type.)
Currency	Brazilian real (BRL)
Leading Specialties	Cardiology and heart surgery, cosmetic and reconstructive surgery, dentistry, neurology and spine surgery, oncology, orthopedics, weight loss surgery
Typical Savings (over USD retail)	20%–30%
Standards and Affiliations	Brazilian Society of Plastic Surgery; International Society of Aesthetic Plastic Surgery; Brazilian Society of Aesthetic Dentistry; National Epidemiology Center; National Health Foundation
International Accreditation	Joint Commission International; American Association for Accreditation of Ambulatory Surgery Facilities International

■ TREATMENT BRIEF

Brazilians take beauty seriously, perhaps to a fault. If, for example, you'd like perkier ears on the family schnauzer, Dr. Edgado Brito, a São Paulo veterinarian of 25 years, has performed thousands of cosmetic alterations on pets worldwide—undoubtedly an extreme spillover from one of the world's most body-conscious countries.

Brazil boasts more than 4,500 licensed cosmetic surgeons, with the highest per capita number of practicing cosmetic physicians in the world. Most international patients head to São Paulo and Rio de Janeiro, Brazil's two largest cities. Smaller destinations—such as Recife, Porto Alegre, and Santos— are also popular. Only in the US and China are more plastic surgeries performed than in Brazil.

■ BRAZIL AND MEDICAL TRAVEL

Prices vary widely. Although the celebrity "surgeons to the stars" command fees comparable to the highest found in the US, dozens of excellent, lesser-known clinics serve patients from all regions and income brackets. Even though cosmetic surgery is Brazil's biggest international health travel draw, some 40 JCI-accredited hospitals throughout the country offer nearly every specialty to the medical traveler. São Paulo, the country's largest city, boasts several world-class hospitals, including Hospital Israelita Albert Einstein, the world's first hospital to receive JCI accreditation.

Brazil welcomes most of its 50,000+ medical travelers from neighboring countries seeking access to Brazil's more robust healthcare system. Patients also arrive from relatively nearby Angola, where Portuguese is the predominant language.

Brazil is home to the internationally revered Ivo Pitanguy, the world's most renowned plastic surgeon. The clinic and institute bearing his name were established in 1963. More than 4,000 surgeons have visited there for training, workshops, and continuing education. The 87-year-old Pitanguy and his staff of 70 have set high international standards for cosmetic and aesthetic surgery, although recently challenged by competing clinics and doctors in Korea, Thailand, and Costa Rica.

Yet, for all its notoriety, Brazil lacks the medical travel infrastructure found in nearby Costa Rica or Colombia. The Brazilian government is at long last awakening to international medical travel, with corresponding investment in partnerships, conferences, and infrastructure building.

The language barrier (principally Portuguese) looms large, and most of Brazil's 40 JCI-accredited providers have little to offer the English-speaking patient. Nonetheless, health travel services are gradually gaining ground, with growing numbers of conscientious, reliable agents; recovery accommodations; and travel support services. Health travelers intent on visiting Brazil should redouble their efforts to work from a base of reliable information or through a trustworthy third-party agent.

SOME CAUTIONS

For North Americans and Asians, travel times are long and often involve multiple hops. Brazil's two principal medical travel destinations—Rio and São Paulo—are sprawling urban giants with legendary traffic snarls. Crime is a concern: 25 percent of São Paulo's luxury cars are customized to be bulletproof. Patients traveling to these areas should insist upon door-to-door hospitality from their selected facility.

Prices vary widely, and travelers will find medical treatment in Brazil to be generally more expensive than in Mexico, Costa Rica, or Southeast Asia. The best known medical centers cater to high-profile clients, often driving prices to nearly US levels.

For those planning to attend the 2016 Summer Olympics, hosted by Brazil, emergency services are available at most JCI-accredited hospitals, with English-speaking personnel or access to translators.

SELECTED HOSPITALS AND CLINICS

Hospital do Coração
Street Judge Elisha William, 147–Paradise
São Paulo-SP, BRAZIL
Tel: +55 11 3053.6611
Email: hcor@hcor.com.br
Web: hcor.com.br

Hospital do Coração translates as "Hospital for the Heart," and that is exactly what this treatment center is. Since its founding in the 1980s, it has operated as a philanthropic institution providing cardiac care to needy infants and children. Its future plans call for expansion to become a major center for the treatment of cardiovascular illnesses in Latin America.

Cardiology is not the only specialty on offer at Hospital do Coração. Located in the Paraiso neighborhood of São Paulo, the hospital offers treatment in 37 medical specialties, including orthopedics, oncology, neurology, urology, gastroenterology, and general surgery. More than 700 physicians practice there. Hospital do Coração was a pioneer in the performance of cardiac transplants and, in 1985, was the first in Brazil to perform a cardio-pulmonary transplant.

This facility initially received JCI accreditation in 2006 and was most recently re-accredited in 2013.

Accreditation: Joint Commission International

Leading Specialties: Cardiology and heart surgery, oncology, orthopedics

Hospital Israelita Albert Einstein
Avenida Albert Einstein, 627/701
Morumbi, São Paulo 05651-901, BRAZIL
Tel: +55 11 2151.1301
Email: international@einstein.br
Web: apps.einstein.br/english

Hospital Israelita Albert Einstein opened its doors in 1971 as a non-profit diagnostic and treatment center. Today it boasts more than 5,000 employees, including 500 full-time physicians. Einstein is the world's first hospital to have been awarded JCI accreditation.

Einstein's specialties include integrated cardiology, neurology, oncology diagnosis and treatment, organ transplantation, orthopedics, dermatology, gastroenterology, hematology, ophthalmology, plastic surgery, and urology. Einstein's Diagnostic and Preventive Medicine Center offers numerous options for medical assessment. Einstein's Bariatric Surgery Excellence Center opened in 2007.

Einstein prides itself on personalized care for its patients, employing state-of-the-art protocols, procedures, and technologies. Recent equipment acquisitions include a 64-row CT scanner, image-guided radiation therapy (IGRT), three-dimensional transthoracic echocardiograph, high-resolution electrocardiogram (HRECG), cardiac event monitoring, a da Vinci surgical system, and OSCAR (one-stop clinic for assessment of risk), one of the most advanced prenatal screening tools available.

Einstein is Latin America's largest liver transplant center, performing some 200 transplants annually. In 2006 the Einstein Transplant System passed the 1,000-transplant mark. The hospital boasts a consistent liver transplant success rate of 90 percent, on par with the best US and European hospitals.

The bilingual staff of the hospital's Commercial Service Center works with international patients on price checking and negotiation with insurance companies. The hospitality and concierge departments can assist with travel plans, local accommodations, and other amenities.

A multi-million dollar renovation and facility addition was unveiled in 2012.

Einstein was first accredited by JCI in 1999 and then re-accredited in 2002, 2006, 2009, and 2012.

Accreditation: Joint Commission International

Leading Specialties: Cardiology and heart surgery, oncology, weight-loss surgery, transplant

Hospital Samaritano
Rua Conselheiro Brotero, 1486
Higienópolis, São Paulo 01232-010, BRAZIL
Tel: +55 11 3821.5300
Email: international@samaritano.org.br
Web: www.samaritano.org.br

In business for more than a century, Hospital Samaritano has been JCI accredited since 2004. More than 1,300 credentialed physicians practice there. The 19-story building boasts a heliport, a 200-seat auditorium, gastronomy and nutrition services, 10 surgical suites for high-complexity procedures, an intensive care unit, and other modern amenities.

Specialties include orthopedics, cardiology, oncology, neurology, nephrology, diagnostic and therapeutic medicine, and emergency care. Samaritano is recognized as a reference center for bariatric surgery, epileptic surgery, cosmetic and reconstructive plastic surgery, and cochlear implants.

If you research this hospital, don't be surprised if some webpages pop up in Portuguese.

Leading Specialties: Cardiology and heart surgery, nephrology, neurology, oncology, weight loss surgery

Ivo Pitanguy Clinic
Rua Dona Mariana, 65 Botafogo
Rio de Janeiro 22280-020, BRAZIL
Tel: +55 21 2266.9500
Email: ivopitanguy@pitanguy.com.br
Web: pitanguy.com.br/pitanguy/en

Dr. Ivo Pitanguy, considered a founding father of plastic surgery, established his world-famous clinic in 1963 after first studying in the US and England. The clinic also houses the Pitanguy Institute, where plastic surgeons from 40 countries learn Pitanguy's techniques during a three-year master apprentice study program.

In Brazil 80 percent of all plastic surgery is cosmetic. In a country with a surplus of plastic surgeons, Pitanguy stands out. The clinic specializes in cosmetic surgeries, including those of the face, nose, and ears, in addition to body contouring and hair transplants. Reconstructive surgeries include scar revision, skin grafts, skin expansion, and breast reconstruction.

The Pitanguy Clinic is the only known center where two patients receive surgery (even different procedures) simultaneously in the same operating room. Despite this, infection rates are low. Only local and regional anesthetics are used, and it is not uncommon for patients to converse during their surgeries.

It is a paradox that the most prominent treatment center in Latin America, serving celebrity patients, is situated in one of the largest and poorest shantytowns in Brazil. The crime rate is high in Rio de Janeiro, and the Pitanguy Clinic is located in a dangerous neighborhood.

Leading Specialties: Cosmetic and reconstructive surgery

DESTINATION: **THE CARIBBEAN**

■ AT A GLANCE

Christ Church, Nassau, St. Johns

Language	English
Time Zones	GMT −5, GMT −4
Country Dialing Code	+1
Electricity	230V and 115V, plug types A and B
Currency	East Caribbean dollar (XCD), US dollar (USD)
Leading Specialties	Addiction and recovery, cardiology and heart surgery, fertility and reproductive medicine, health screening, oncology, orthopedics
Typical Savings (over USD retail)	25%–40%
Standards and Affiliations	National Association of Addiction Treatment Providers; Association for Addiction Professionals; European Association for the Treatment of Addiction; American Society of Addiction Medicine; Human Fertilisation and Embryology Authority; American Society for Reproductive Medicine
International Accreditation	Joint Commission International

■ TREATMENT BRIEF

Although a convenient destination for North American health travelers, the Caribbean region offers only a few high-quality healthcare options: one JCI-accredited hospital (Doctors Hospital in the Bahamas) and two renowned specialty facilities, the Barbados Fertility Centre (for assisted reproductive technologies) and the Crossroads Centre in Antigua (for substance abuse and addiction treatment). Still, the region's white sand beaches, laid-back lifestyle, and welcoming hospitality attract health travelers who appreciate short travel times and a chance to mix healthcare with a vacation in a culturally familiar environment.

■ THE CARIBBEAN AND MEDICAL TRAVEL

Those who typically experience digestive upset when traveling face a lower risk in the Caribbean than in Asia or the Middle East. Sanitation standards are high in urban areas, and food choices are similar to those at home. There are cost savings to be had there too, with in vitro fertilization fees in Barbados, for example, running around half the price quoted in most US fertility centers.

No discussion of the Caribbean as a healthcare destination would be complete without mention of the newly opened Health City Cayman Islands, a 140-bed, tertiary-care hospital founded by famed Indian heart surgeon Dr. Devi Shetty and catering to the nearby North American patient. Current specialties are cardiac surgery, cardiology, and orthopedics. Over the next decade, the hospital plans to expand to a 2,000-bed facility, providing care in all major specialties, including neurology and oncology. The complex is also slated to include a medical university and an assisted-care living community. Its leaders plan to apply for JCI accreditation soon. The hospital is located near High Rock in the East End District of Grand Cayman.

Although not yet included as a *Patients Beyond Borders* medical travel destination, nearby Colombia is a frequently traveled health venue for Caribbean patients who take advantage of prices some 40 percent lower than in the US. Excellent facilities, such as Fundación Cardioinfantil (a JCI-accredited heart specialty hospital), Calle Doce Clínica Odontológica (dentistry), the San Diego Ophthalmologic Clinic in El Poblado (eye care), and Hospital San Vicente (Colombia's largest hospital network) serve thousands of affluent Caribbean patients annually.

■ SELECTED HOSPITALS AND CLINICS

Barbados Fertility Centre

Christ Church
Hastings, Barbados BB15154, WEST INDIES
Tel: +1 246 435.7467; 866 246.8616 (US toll free)
Email: contact@barbadosfertility.com
Web: barbadosfertility.com

Barbados Fertility Centre (BFC) is a JCI-accredited center of excellence, specializing in all aspects of infertility management. BFC opened its doors in 2002. Exactly nine months later, its first in vitro fertilization (IVF) baby was born. And in 2008, the center celebrated its thousandth egg collection.

BFC treats couples ages 26 to 46 who have been unable to conceive a child for a year or more. Infertility has many different causes, and BFC tailors its treatments to meet individual needs. The center's unique approach combines rest, relaxation, and holistic therapy with medical intervention. BFC's cutting-edge technology and stress-reducing environment give couples the best possible chances of conception.

BFC's high success rates and relatively low treatment costs attract regional and international

patients in growing numbers annually. Couples travel from Europe, the UK, the US, and Canada to seek treatment. However, the center has not forgotten its closer-to-home clientele. BFC's main facility is located in Christ Church, Barbados, and partnerships with gynecologists on other islands have made assisted reproduction accessible to couples throughout the Caribbean. Satellite offices also operate in Antigua, St. Maarten, and Trinidad.

BFC's international couples usually find that their infertility treatment costs less in Barbados than it would at home. Patients from the UK report that their public health system funds only 25 percent of the cost of IVF treatments. Patients' out-of-pocket costs may run as high as £5,000 (about us$8,3600) for a single cycle. Patients from the US often report cost estimates as high as $30,000.

Dr. Juliet Skinner, BFC's medical director, is Barbadian by birth. She trained as an obstetrician/gynecologist at Trinity College in Dublin, Ireland. "I returned to Barbados [after my training]," she says, "and it was obvious that choices for couples with infertility were very limited." Using her connections in Ireland, Skinner seized an opportunity to develop an IVF unit on the island in conjunction with the largest unit in Ireland.

From 2005 onward, BFC has achieved success rates comparable to, if not better than, those in the US—and twice those achieved in the UK. The reasons for BFC's success? "Our philosophy, our team, our approach, anything that can make a difference," Skinner says. "The most important message we can get out there is that infertility is common. It affects one in six couples. There is a host of reasons why it may occur—and the vast majority of them have a solution. Treatment options are effective, especially if we are treating a couple early on."

Accreditation: Joint Commission International

Leading Specialties: Fertility and reproductive medicine

Crossroads Centre Antigua

Willoughby Bay
St. Philip Parish
PO Box 3592
St. John's, Antigua, WEST INDIES
Tel: +1 268 562.0035; 888 452.0091 (US and Canada toll free)
Email: info@crossroadsantigua.org
Web: crossroadsantigua.org

Founded by Eric Clapton in 1998, the 32-bed Crossroads Centre Antigua is a non-profit international center of excellence for the treatment of alcohol or drug addiction and other addictive disorders. The center's mission is to help people and their families make the changes necessary to find health, a sense of well-being, and a new life of recovery.

The center deploys the "whole-person approach" to healing and recovery by assisting each client in improving the quality of his or her relationships; career; and social, emotional, physical, and spiritual well-being. The program offers 29-day and six-week residential chemical dependency programs that include medical detoxification services, 12-step meetings and groups, individual and group therapy, individual assignments, nutritional and spiritual counseling, and recovery lectures.

Additional program services provided as part of the package to enhance recovery include yoga, auricular (ear) acupuncture, fitness training, and therapeutic massage. Included in the total cost is a four-day family outpatient program. Medical and clinical health professionals help families understand the disease of addiction, improve family relationships, and support the recovery process.

Free ground transportation is provided to and from the airport, and patients are met at the airport by a staff member. Family members attending the family outpatient program may opt to stay on campus in a separate residence or at a nearby hotel.

Continuing care is a vital aspect of the recovery process, so all clients are provided with ongoing referrals before they are discharged from the facility. An alumni services department follows up with clients for at least two years post-treatment to support the ongoing recovery process. Alumni chapter groups are located in various US states and parts of Europe. Crossroads Centre offers five-day renewal programs for people in recovery or those struggling to maintain sobriety. Participants need not have completed treatment at Crossroads to attend.

Crossroads is affiliated with the Sanctuary in Delray Beach, Florida, a transitional living home for men in recovery.

Accreditation: Joint Commission International

Leading Specialties: Addiction and recovery

Doctors Hospital Bahamas

#1 Collins Avenue
Nassau, THE BAHAMAS
Tel: +1 242 302.4600
Email: info@doctorshosp.com
Web: doctorshosp.com

With 1,300 outpatient surgeries and 4,250 annual admissions, the Caribbean's only JCI-accredited hospital is best known for general internal medicine, pulmonology, orthopedics, cardiac surgery, general surgery, and bariatrics. Frequently performed procedures include balloon angioplasty with stent, coronary artery bypass graft (CABG), valve replacement, total hip and knee replacements, and the full range of bariatric and cosmetic procedures and surgeries. The first open-heart surgery in the Bahamas was performed at Doctors Hospital in 1994.

Doctors Hospital boasts a three-room operating suite, an eight-bed intensive care unit, a rehabilitation department, and a maternity wing equipped with a newborn nursery. Diagnostic equipment includes a 16-slice CT scanner and an MRI. The hospital's half-day Executive Health and Wellness program includes a complete medical history and physical, lab tests, electrocardiogram (ECG), chest x-ray, nutrition assessment and counseling, and vision and hearing exams.

Doctors Hospital owns Bahamas Medical Center, which opened in 2012, offering specialty services in dentistry, cosmetic surgery, bariatrics, gynecology, and high-intensity focused ultrasound (HIFU), often used for the treatment of prostate cancer. The HIFU program attracts about 200 patients per year, mostly from North America.

The International Patient program for both facilities is staffed by two certified nurses. In total, the hospital and the center treat about 1,000 tourists from the US and Canada annually. The facility offers concierge and travel planning services, along with transportation from the nearest airport and translators for French, Spanish, Italian, and German.

Accreditation: Joint Commission International

Leading Specialties: Cardiology and heart surgery, orthopedics, oncology (prostate), weight loss surgery

DESTINATION: **COSTA RICA**

■ AT A GLANCE

San José, Escazú

Languages	Spanish, English widely spoken
Time Zone	GMT –6
Country Dialing Code	+506
Electricity	120V, plug type A
Currency	Costa Rica colon (CRC)
Leading Specialties	Cosmetic and reconstructive surgery, dentistry, health screening, orthopedics, weight loss surgery, wellness and prevention
Typical Savings (over USD retail)	45%–65%
Standards and Affiliations	Costa Rican Department of Social Insurance; Council for the International Promotion of Costa Rica Medicine; Ministry of Health, Costa Rica
International Accreditation	Accreditation Association for Ambulatory Health Care; American Association for Accreditation of Ambulatory Surgery Facilities International; Joint Commission International

■ TREATMENT BRIEF

No longer a sleepy destination for cost-conscious American expats seeking dental care, Costa Rica's two JCI-accredited hospitals and numerous smaller private AAAASF- and AAAHC-accredited clinics offer a wide range of medical services, including orthopedics, cardiology, cancer treatments, cosmetic surgery, and bariatrics. Idyllic scenery and unique recovery lodges make Costa Rica a prime destination for the medical traveler.

With its comparative wealth as a Central American nation, emphasis on ecotourism, and long history of relative political tranquility, Costa Rica, Spanish for "rich coast," can hardly be labeled a third-world country. Few tourist destinations offer such easy access to leisure activities.

Breathtaking national parks of volcanoes and cloud forests are less than an hour's drive from the capital, San José. Both the Pacific and Caribbean coasts are easily accessible, with plenty of local and westernized accommodations. With so many Americans vacationing in, traveling to, or buying real estate in Costa Rica, many "Ticans" wonder if their country won't soon become the US's fifty-first state.

■ COSTA RICA HEALTHCARE AND MEDICAL TRAVEL

The World Health Organization has ranked Costa Rica as one of the top three healthcare systems in Latin America. The nation consistently ranks higher in healthcare than many of its industrialized counterparts, including Canada and the United States. Similarly, life expectancy is among the world's highest: 78.7 years, one year higher than in the US.

Health travel is huge as well. In 2011 the country welcomed some 48,000 medical and health travelers, mostly from the US, Canada, and the EU.

Neighboring countries—such as Nicaragua, Guatemala, and Honduras—also seek out Costa Rica for access to higher-quality medical services. Some 5 percent of Costa Rica's international tourists visit this small, lush country to take advantage of its medical services, mostly cosmetic surgery and dental care.

For those planning minimally invasive procedures, Costa Rica's proximity to the US and reputation as a tourist destination offer the best of both worlds. In fact, Costa Rica is one of the top five countries most visited by Americans seeking medical treatment.

Costa Rica boasts hundreds of board-certified physicians, surgeons, and dentists, mostly practicing in or near San José. Capitalizing on Costa Rica's success in cosmetic surgery and dentistry, the country's international medical offerings have expanded in recent years to include eye surgery and other elective procedures, such as bariatric surgery (for weight loss) and orthopedics. In addition, Costa Rica has launched research and clinical initiatives for Parkinson's, multiple sclerosis, pain management, and diabetes.

Three hospitals—CIMA San José, Clínica Hospital la Católica, and Clínica Bíblica—have recently undergone extensive expansion and modernization to attract a broader mix of international patients. Clínica Bíblica was the first in the country to achieve JCI accreditation. American-owned Hospital CIMA in San José achieved JCI status in 2008. Both are full-service hospitals offering patients a wide array of specialties and procedures previously unavailable to medical travelers in Costa Rica.

Although Costa Rica enjoys a reputation for cosmetic surgery, many of the country's noted surgeons do not have their own facilities, but rather practice in one of the respected private hospitals, such as Católica, Bíblica, or CIMA. For patients who prefer the comparative intimacies of a clinic, the less cozy hospital setting may be off-putting.

■ RECOVERY RESORTS: A UNIQUE FEATURE

One of Costa Rica's health travel specialties is the recovery retreat, a hotel or ranch-style accommodation that serves recovering patients exclusively. Situated close to clinics, these retreats have all the amenities of a typical hotel, but they are staffed with nurses and interns who attend to the special needs of recovering patients.

Transportation to and from the airport is usually included with the cost, as is transport to clinics for consultation and treatment. Guests in these retreats chat at breakfast and dinner about their latest treatment. A snapshot of the clientele at any time is usually a portrait of recovery's progress—from the bruises of yesterday's facelift procedure to the confident smile and gait of the patient heading home.

International patients will be pleased to learn that Costa Rica's hospital and clinic websites are increasingly in English, and patient services are improving. Do not expect large-scale grandeur. Costa Rica's hospitals are generally small compared to the top international hospitals in India, Korea, Malaysia, or Thailand. However, health travelers to Costa Rica can find excellent services in some of the smaller, private facilities located in San José and its Americanized suburb, Escazú.

■ SELECTED HOSPITALS AND CLINICS

Advance Dental
Hospital CIMA, Torre 2, Suite 618
Escazú, COSTA RICA
Tel: +506 2208.8618
Email: info@advancedentalcostarica.com
Web: advancedentalcostarica.com

Established in 2007, Advance Dental Costa Rica moved its offices in 2010 to the JCI-accredited Hospital CIMA campus (for further details on CIMA, see listing). Two specialists, Dr. Eugenio Brenes and Dr. Luciano Retana, received their training at Loma Linda University School of Dentistry and New York University Advanced Program in Implant Dentistry, respectively. Specialties include dental aesthetics, prosthodontics, dental implantation, periodontics, and general dentistry.

Advance Dental is accredited by the American Association for Accreditation of Ambulatory Surgery Facilities International. Its affiliations include American College of Prosthodontists (all ACP members must be in or have completed an American Dental Association-accredited advanced education program in prosthodontics).

All dentists and staff are fluent in English, and translators are available for Chinese- and Japanese-speaking patients. Private drivers and tour facilitators can be arranged for additional fees. Accommodations in various price ranges are available at nearby Marriott Courtyard, Holiday Inn, and Intercontinental Real, in addition to Costa Rica's unique recovery resorts, all listed on the Advance Dental website.

Accreditation: American Association for Accreditation of Ambulatory Surgery Facilities International

Leading Specialties: Dentistry

CIMA San José
Los Laureles San Rafael de Escazú
Escazú, COSTA RICA
Tel: 855 782.6253 (US toll free)
Email: intlpatientservices@cimamedicalvaluetravel.com
Web: cimamedicalvaluetravel.com/sjos

The 62-bed CIMA San José was the first Costa Rican hospital to be accredited by the Costa Rica Ministry of Health and is the only hospital in Central America accredited by the US Department of Veterans Affairs. CIMA San José is also the first hospital in Latin America to receive accreditation under JCI's new patient safety standards, scoring a 99.5 percent, one of the highest scores in Latin America.

Located in the elegant San José suburb of Escazú, CIMA boasts more than 170 physicians representing more than 60 specialties. The hospital offers a complete imaging department, including open MRI, CT scanner, x-ray, ultrasound, and endoscopy as well as a full-service laboratory and a 24-hour pharmacy.

CIMA's specialties include cardiology, orthopedic surgery, cosmetic and reconstructive surgery, laparoscopic surgery, neurology, urology, ophthalmology, and otolaryngology (ear, nose, and throat). More than 400 breast augmentations and 500 arthroscopic procedures are performed annually at CIMA.

International patients contribute to more than 25 percent of CIMA's occupancy. Health travelers most often visit CIMA for cosmetic, eye, hip, and knee surgery, for which it reports some of the lowest prices in the country.

The hospital received JCI accreditation in 2008 and was re-accredited in 2011. This American-owned hospital network also operates facilities throughout Mexico and Brazil.

Accreditation: Joint Commission International

Leading Specialties: Cardiology and heart surgery, cosmetic and reconstructive surgery, dentistry, ophthalmology, orthopedics, weight loss surgery

Dentavac Dental Clinic
Highway 121
PO Box 906–1250
Escazú, COSTA RICA
Tel: +506 2288.5959; 877 317.3048 (US toll free)
Email: info@dentavac.com
Web: dentavac.com

Founded in 1988 and in its present offices since 2006, four dental surgeons, two oral surgeons, two periodontists, one endodontist, one orthodontist, and one pediatric dentist treat more than 6,000 patients annually. More than half of these patients travel from outside Costa Rica, largely from the US. Specialties include cosmetic and restorative dentistry, implants placement and rehabilitation, general dentistry, endodontics, periodontics, and pediatric dentistry.

Dentavac is accredited by the American Association for Accreditation of Ambulatory Surgery Facilities International and is a member of the American Academy of Cosmetic Dentistry. Dentavac is in the ritzy San José suburb of Escazú, where Western-style accommodations, restaurants, and shopping abound. Many of Costa Rica's renowned recovery resorts are nestled in the surrounding hills, within

20 minutes of Dentavac's offices. Most dentists and staff speak English.

Accreditation: American Association for Accreditation of Ambulatory Surgery Facilities International

Leading Specialties: Dentistry

Hospital la Católica

San Antonio de Guadalupe
Goicoechea, COSTA RICA
Tel: + 506 2246.3000
Email: servicioalcliente@hospitallacatolica.com
Web: hospitallacatolica.com/en/homepage

Hospital la Católica was founded in 1963 by Franciscan nuns and physicians. Since then, the hospital has grown and changed. In 2002 its new, expanded facilities opened, housing emergency and observational services.

The hospital provides all the usual departments for services and surgical procedures and employs a variety of technologies for diagnosis and treatment, including a hyperbaric oxygen chamber and a state-of-the-art Philips Allur Xper FD apparatus for shadowless angiography. There is a handy chat function on the website, and patients can subscribe to an email newsletter.

Leading Specialties: Cardiology and heart surgery, dentistry, ophthalmology, urology

Hospital Clínica Bíblica

1st & 2nd Streets, 14th & 16th Avenues
PO Box 1307–1000
San José, COSTA RICA
Tel: +506 2522.1000; 800 503.5358 (US toll free)
Email: international@clinicabiblica.com
Web: clinicabiblica.com

In 2008 Hospital Clínica Bíblica became the first hospital in Costa Rica and the second in all of Latin America to receive JCI accreditation. Even though it has been around since 1929, don't expect anything old-fashioned about its facilities or services. Clínica Bíblica boasts a us$50 million infrastructure (including a new $35 million hospital building) for 200 physicians who specialize in cardiology, cosmetic and reconstructive surgery, ophthalmology, orthopedics, and preventive medicine.

Doctors there also perform a large number of minimally invasive laparoscopic procedures, such as bariatric surgery, arthroscopy, hernia repair, prostatectomy, gallbladder removal, and colonoscopy. Many of the physicians are bilingual and US or European trained. More than 20 percent of Clínica Bíblica's patients are international travelers.

Clínica Bíblica's International Department assists patients with all aspects of treatment planning. Each patient is assigned a personal healthcare assistant to coordinate physician contact; pre-procedure consultations; price quotes; airport pickup and drop-off; recovery retreat and hotel bookings; VIP concierge services (superior-class lodging, transfers, and sightseeing tours); hospital admittance; bedside follow-up; contacts with family via phone or email post-surgery; regular post-surgery visits by a qualified medical staff; and patient follow-up back home.

Patients at Clínica Bíblica can expect to save as much as 70 percent compared to prices in the US or Canada. For example, a knee replacement at a US hospital costs approximately $40,000; at Clínica Bíblica, the procedure (using the same equipment and techniques) costs $10,700.

Clínica Bíblica was most recently awarded JCI accreditation in 2011.

Accreditation: Joint Commission International

Leading Specialties: Cardiology and heart surgery, orthopedics, weight loss surgery

Integral Plastic Surgery and Maxillofacial Clinic

Hospital la Católica, Guadalupe
San José, COSTA RICA
Tel: +506 2246.3100
Email: info@plasticarivera.com
Web: plasticarivera.com

Integral Plastic Surgery and Maxillofacial Clinic was founded in 2005 by two brothers. Dr. Erik Rivera specializes in oral and maxillofacial surgery; Dr. Christian Rivera is a plastic and reconstructive surgeon. They operate a full-service clinic within the walls of Hospital la Católica, one of Costa Rica's leading private hospitals.

Cosmetic surgery procedures include breast augmentation and post-cancer breast reconstruction, vibroliposuction surgery, abdominoplasty (tummy tucks), rhinoplasty (nose reconstruction), and facelift. Dental procedures include dental implants, orthognathics (corrective jaw surgery), surgical management of temporomandibular (jaw joint) conditions, extraction, and general cosmetic dental procedures.

The clinic utilizes some of the latest instrumentation, including the Cynosure Icon fractional laser (skin resurfacing and scar removal); Syneron VelaShape II (body contouring, cellulite reduction); Viora Reaction; Biomet GPSIII (used in gravitational platelet separation); BIOPHYMED U225 Mesotherapy injector gun; and Ethicon Harmonic scalpel.

The clinic performs more than 360 procedures annually, around 20 percent with international patients, mostly from North America. English and Spanish are both spoken. Consultations and second opinions are offered by both surgeons via Skype for us$50.

Note: Many of the procedures and much of the instrumentation deployed by Integral and other cosmetic surgery clinics are not FDA approved and are sometimes subject to differing clinical opinion. Patients should check into the efficacy of such treatments.

Leading Specialties: Cosmetic and reconstructive surgery, dentistry

Meza Dental Care Clinic

Condominium Torres del Campo
Barrio Tournon
San José, COSTA RICA
Tel: +506 2258.6392; 877 337.6392 (US toll free)
Email: mezadentalcare@mezadentalcare.com
Web: mezadentalcare.com

Alberto Meza founded the clinic more than 15 years ago, specifically to cater to North Americans. He and Dr. Marianella Marin both received their postgraduate training at UCLA. They are well known for providing best-in-class cosmetic dental services, including implants, porcelain veneers, full porcelain crowns, dental implants, root canal therapies, and gum surgeries.

Although Meza is somewhat pricier than neighboring facilities, the clinic is known for its high standards of quality, particularly with cosmetic and restorative dentistry.

Meza Dental is a longtime member of the American Academy of Cosmetic Dentistry. The clinic employs a Johns Hopkins graduate who works in-house to oversee standards and to assist patients. Meza Dental works with an agency to help patients with travel arrangements and lodging.

Leading Specialties: Dentistry

Nova Dental

Plaza Itskatzu, Suite 212
Escazú, San José, COSTA RICA
Tel: +506 2228.0997; +1 760 666.8227 (US)
Email: info@novadentalcr.com
Web: novadentalcr.com

Founded in 2005 by Costa Rican dental luminary Dr. Luis Obando, Nova Dental is located in the wealthy Americanized suburb of Escazú, just outside San José. Specialties emphasize cosmetic and restorative work, including implant dentistry and oral surgery (implants, bone grafts, sinus lifts); full mouth reconstruction (zirconium crowns, e.max crowns, hybrid bridge, dentures over implants); cosmetic work (veneers, smile makeover); and endodontics (root canals).

Three highly credentialed specialists work with a staff of six to treat more than 400 new patients annually with 90 percent arriving from Canada or the US. Nova Dental is one of the few dental clinics accredited by the Accreditation Association for Ambulatory Health Care. Nova is also a member of the American Academy of Implant Dentistry and the International Congress of Oral Implantologists and is affiliated with New York University College for Dentistry. The affiliation is for training.

In addition to state-of-the-art offices, Nova has a digital x-ray system designed to reduce radiation exposure; microscope-enhanced dentistry; and digital panoramic equipment that aids patient and doctor alike, particularly with complex root canal, bone graft, and reconstructive work.

All dentists at Nova Dental are fluent in English as well as Spanish. International patient services include help with travel plans, airport and local transportation as needed, booking of nearby hotels and recovery resorts, and recommendations for side trips for patients and companions.

Accreditation: Accreditation Association for Ambulatory Health Care

Leading Specialties: Dentistry

Rosenstock-Lieberman Center for Cosmetic Surgery

28th Street & 2nd Avenue
San José, COSTA RICA
Tel: +506 2223.9933
Email: info@cosmetic-cr.com
Web: cosmetic-cr.com

Founded in 1982 by Drs. Noe Rosenstock and Clara Lieberman (both still practicing), the Rosenstock-Lieberman Center focuses on cosmetic procedures.

Rosenstock-Lieberman offers a variety of procedures, including hair transplant, facelift, blepharoplasty (eyelid surgery), otoplasty (ear surgery), rhinoplasty (nose surgery), fat transfer, lip enhancement, neck lift, brachioplasty (arm lift), breast augmentation, breast reduction/lift, liposuction, thigh lift, lower body lift, and tummy tuck.

Head surgeon Dr. Rashi Rosenstock is a member of the American Society for Aesthetic Plastic Surgeons. Head surgeon Dr. Joseph Cohen is a member of the American Academy of Cosmetic Surgery.

Because most procedures at Rosenstock-Lieberman are done on an ambulatory basis, patients should plan to stay in one of the nearby recovery retreats or hotels.

Since 1997, the Rosenstock-Lieberman Center has been offering courses on cosmetic surgery to selected physicians worldwide under the sponsorship of the American Academy of Cosmetic Surgery.

Leading Specialties: Cosmetic and reconstructive surgery

DESTINATION: **CZECH REPUBLIC**

■ AT A GLANCE

Prague

Languages	Czech, German, some English
Time Zone	GMT +1
Country Dialing Code	+420
Electricity	230V, plug type E
Currency	Czech koruna (CZK)
Leading Specialties	Cosmetic and reconstructive surgery, dentistry, oncology
Typical Savings (over USD retail)	40%–65%
Standards and Affiliations	Czech Medical Chamber; Czech Dental Chamber; Czech Society of Aesthetic Plastic Surgery; Czech Plastic Surgery Association; Czech Society of Burn Plastic Surgery; European Societies of Plastic, Reconstructive and Aesthetic Surgery; International Societies of Plastic, Reconstructive, and Aesthetic Surgery; Ministry of Health of the Czech Republic
International Accreditation	Joint Commission International

■ TREATMENT BRIEF

One of the most popular tourist destinations in Eastern Europe is the Czech Republic's fairy tale capital city, Prague, where health travelers find most of the country's best clinics. Although the Czech Republic offers an array of surgeries and other general treatment, health travelers generally head to Prague for either cosmetic surgery or dental care.

Since the early 2000s, several privately funded clinics have opened that cater mostly to international patients from Western Europe and the UK. Staff and physicians speak English and provide medical care based on Western-style models. Prague has also recently seen a great increase in Western-trained doctors opening private practices.

That said, the Czech Republic's healthcare system is in transition. The Czech Republic enjoys long-standing healthcare oversight and stringent requirements for physicians and surgeons. Cosmetic surgery is strictly regulated by the government and by the Czech Medical Chamber.

For example, standards to become a plastic surgeon in the Czech Republic are rigorous, requiring a minimum of six years at an accredited university, followed by a minimum of two years of post-graduate work under the supervision of a senior doctor, two years in general surgery, and four years of plastic surgery theoretical and practical practice in a state-certified clinic for plastic surgery. Yet, in a country where many physicians in the public sector earn less money than office workers, health travelers must double their research to ensure quality of care.

■ THE CZECH REPUBLIC AND MEDICAL TRAVEL

Patients who travel for medical care cite Prague as a favorite sightseeing destination. Many factor extra travel time into their trips, taking advantage of less-invasive procedures and shorter recovery times to enjoy a vacation or weekend getaway.

Fees for medical services vary widely. Quoted prices usually include all pre-operative tests, examinations, surgery, medications, overnight stays, and post-operative treatments.

Health tourism packages often include bike tours through the wine country, mountain exploration, hiking, horseback tours, and art and heritage festivals

For those concerned about antibiotic-resistant infections, the Czech Republic is reputed to have one of the lowest methicillin-resistant *Staphylococcus aureus* (MRSA) rates in Europe (meaning that unlike in the US, most staph infections in the Czech Republic can still be treated effectively with certain antibiotics).

JCI accreditation is relatively new to the Czech Republic. Since 2010, JCI accreditation has been awarded to four hospitals and clinics.

■ SELECTED HOSPITALS AND CLINICS

Elite Dental
Vodickova 5/12, Praha 2
Prague, CZECH REPUBLIC
Tel: +420 222 510.888
Email: reception@elitedental.cz
Web: elitedental.cz

Elite Dental's offices are somewhat removed from Prague's tourist crush, but within walking distance of Prague's most renowned sites. A team of nine dentists are certified through the Czech Republic's strident quality standards and licensing program and have received training in Germany, Switzerland, France, and Israel. English is fluently spoken.

Specialties include restorative dentistry, pediatric dentistry, oral surgery, orthodontics, treatment of periodontitis and root canals, cosmetic dentistry, and implantology. Elite Dental offers a lifetime warranty on all American implant procedures performed at the clinic. Elite is one of the only dental clinics in Prague to deploy a Zeiss dental microscope, used for endodontics (root canals) and other procedures requiring greater magnification and accuracy.

Elite has also pioneered the use of CEREC technologies, which combine the latest CAD/CAM software to design crowns and manufacture them with 3-D milling. Creation of the crown usually takes 4 to 20 minutes, allowing busy or fidgety patients to receive crowns at one sitting.

Elite offers special transportation and accommodations packages to its international patients.

Leading Specialties: Dentistry

Esthé Clinic
Esthé Clinic; Na Príkope 17
110 00 Prague, CZECH REPUBLIC
Tel: +420 222 868.811; +420 731 188.478
Email: esthe@esthe-plastika.cz
Web: www.esthe-plastika.cz/en/

Founded in 1996, Esthé Clinic has two centers, one devoted to cosmetic surgery and the other to laser resurfacing. Esthé's six plastic surgeons and four laser and dermatology specialists form one of Eastern Europe's largest cosmetic surgery centers.

Esthé's Plastic Surgery Center performs breast, eyelid, facial, nose, and outer-ear surgeries; lip enlargement; liposuction; and tummy tucks, often using endoscopic procedures.

Esthé's Laser Center has amassed an impressive arsenal of the latest laser machines and instrumentation, including many of Candela Laser Corporation's high-end devices.

Acne scars, facial wrinkles, and other irregularities can be corrected using cosmetic injections. The volume of the injections and subsequent water retention smooth the skin's uneven surface and diminish wrinkles. The injections are most frequently used to fill nose-mouth lines and fine lip lines or to correct deeper forehead, cheek, and chin wrinkles.

Esthé uses a high-performance V-beam laser to treat spider veins on the face, thighs, and lower legs.

The vascular laser is also helpful in removing warts and other skin outgrowths.

Tired of that "Robert Still Loves Me" tattoo? The Alexandrite laser focuses a powerful beam to pulverize unsightly pigment into small segments, which are then washed away by the cellular system. Pigmentations resulting from age or sun, birthmarks, freckles, permanent makeup, scars, and other hyper-pigmentations are treated using this technique.

Permanent removal of unwanted hair from face, thighs, underarms, and other parts of the body is carried out with the Candela GentleLase laser.

Esthé uses Candela's Smoothbeam laser to inter-rupt the cycle of acne scarring caused by hardening of the upper layer of skin. This non-invasive pro-cedure is used to treat ongoing acne as well as old acne scars. Up to three sessions are usually required, combined with chemical peeling.

Leading Specialties: Cosmetic and reconstructive surgery

Na Homolce Hospital

Roentgenova 2 150 30
Prague 5, CZECH REPUBLIC
Tel: +420 257 273.036
Fax: +420 257 273.097
Email: vladimir.dbaly@homolka.cz
Web: homolka.cz/en-cz/

The first building of what is now Na Homolce Hos-pital was constructed between 1984 and 1989 as a medical facility for top communist functionaries. At that time it was known as the State Institute of National Health and more commonly as Sanopz. It opened in 1989 as a private "luxury facility" with an outpatient unit, rehabilitation unit, and wards in internal medicine, cardiology, and neurology. Within months, it reopened to the general public under the new name of Na Homolce Hospital (from Homelike Hill on which it stands).

Today the full range of services is available, and the hospital's specialties are grouped into three pri-ority clinical programs in which all the individual departments participate: the cardiovascular pro-gram, neuro program, and general medical care

program. Na Homolce has 357 beds. Annually, Na Homolce's physicians and surgeons treat nearly 18,000 inpatients, perform more than 14,000 surger-ies, and examine more than one million outpatients.

JCI accreditation came in June 2005; the facility was re-accredited in 2013.

Accreditation: Joint Commission International

Leading Specialties: Cardiology and heart surgery, neurology

Laderma Klinik

22 Rumunska Street (4th Floor) 120 00
Prague 2, CZECH REPUBLIC
Tel: +420 775 118.005
Email: laderma@laderma.com
Web: laderma.com

Laderma Klinik offers the full range of cosmetic, aesthetic, and reconstructive procedures, including eyelid surgery, ear surgery, nose surgery, chin aug-mentation, facelift, breast enlargement, breastlift/reduction, tummy tuck, liposuction, and Botox. Laderma's cosmetic surgeons boast training in the US and Europe. The chief surgeon, Dr. Zuzana Černá, is certified to perform operations in the Czech Republic, Austria, and the UK. Potential patients can submit photos online and receive an opinion from a Laderma surgeon.

Leading Specialties: Cosmetic and reconstructive surgery

Prague Proton Therapy Center

Budínova 2437/1a
Prague 8, 180 00, CZECH REPUBLIC
Tel: +420 222 999.000
Email: info@ptc.cz
Web: proton-cancer-treatment.com

The Prague Proton Therapy Center opened its doors in 2012. It is one of the few medical facilities in Eastern Europe offering proton therapy.

A relatively new (and expensive) option for treat-ing certain types of tumors, proton therapy uses en-ergy from positively charged particles called protons to irradiate diseased tissue. More precise than other forms of external beam radiation, proton therapy is less harmful to surrounding healthy tissue. As of this writing, the technology is available in fewer than 20 countries.

Prague Proton treats some 2,500 patients annually. The center offers a full range of diagnostic imaging equipment such as CT, MRI, and a PET/CT scanner. Proton beam specialties at the center include prostate, lung, pediatric, as well as other complex cancers. The center is capable of treating a wide range of conditions, including base-of-skull, brain, head, and neck tumors; breast, prostate, and gastrointestinal tumors; and tumors near the spine.

Services offered international patients include airport and hotel transportation, a personal interpreter, translation of medical documents into the patient's language, a children's playroom, and tourist/sightseeing arrangements. Staff members are fluent in English and Russian. Patients from EU countries can ask for reimbursement of the treatment under the S2 Route or the EU Directive on Cross-Border Healthcare.

With new treatment applications and falling prices for equipment, proton therapy has only recently begun to gain mass medical appeal. The non-profit Particle Therapy Co-Operative Group (PTCOG) publishes a roster of proton therapy centers around the world.

Leading Specialties: Oncology

Schill Dental Clinic

Lumírova 21, 128 00
Prague 2, CZECH REPUBLIC
Tel: + 420 224 936.389
Email: info@schilldental.cz
Web: schilldental.cz/en

Schill's seven dentists—whose biographies are posted online—handle the usual range of dental services, including bridges, cosmetic dentistry, crowns, dentures, fillings, implants, pediatric dentistry, periodontics, root canals, and tooth whitening. Most frequently performed surgeries at Schill include dental implant placement, tooth extraction, apicoectomy (root end), hemisection, amputation, replantation, pre-prosthetic surgery, surgical periodontal therapy, incision, and excision.

Leading Specialties: Dentistry

DESTINATION: **HUNGARY**

■ AT A GLANCE

Szombathely, Budapest, Héviz, Mosonmagyaróvár, Győr

Languages	Hungarian, German, some English
Time Zone	GMT +1
Country Dialing Code	+36
Electricity	220V, plug type B
Currency	Hungarian forint (HUF)
Leading Specialties	Cosmetic and reconstructive surgery, dentistry
Typical Savings (over USD retail)	40%–60%
Standards and Affiliations	Association of Hungarian Medical Societies; Hungarian Accreditation Council; Hungarian Dental Association; Hungarian Medical Chamber

■ TREATMENT BRIEF

Hungary is no stranger to health tourism; for centuries the well heeled have been flocking to its restorative mineral springs, lakes, baths, and spas. German and Swiss patients head to Budapest and Hungary's border towns—literally by the busload—for inexpensive, high-quality dental work. Patients from the US and Canada are beginning to catch on as well.

Hungary boasts more dentists per capita than any other country, and post–Cold War Hungarian dentists pride themselves on their state-of-the-art equipment. Since the country's admission to the European Union in 2004, travel and communications have grown easier, and Hungary has begun to upgrade accreditation and care standards to match those of Western Europe.

Hungary's cosmopolitan capital, Budapest, boasts the country's largest number of dental clinics—although they tend to be the region's most expensive. Dental travel agents also offer trips to smaller, sleepier (and more economical) towns, such as Mosonmagyaróvár, Héviz, Sopron, and Győr, all near the Austrian border. Although populated by only 32,000 inhabitants, Mosonmagyaróvár is home to an incredible 160 dental offices!

It is economical for Europeans, western Russians, and Middle Easterners to travel to Hungary for a dental checkup or a cleaning. However, most North American patients traveling to Hungary are seeking more extensive care, including full-mouth restorations and implants. Such work can be had at less than half the US price, including travel.

■ HUNGARY'S HIGH HEALTHCARE STANDARDS

Hungarian dentists must complete five years of dental training. To practice, a dentist must be registered with the Hungarian Medical Chamber. Accreditation and standards are set by the State National Health Commission and Medical Service, Hungarian Medical Chamber, and International Society of Aesthetic Plastic Surgery. All that said, compliance to standards varies widely in Hungary, and health travelers should rely on trusted sources, such as referrals or a reputable health travel agent.

■ HUNGARY AND MEDICAL TRAVEL

Dental clinics literally line the streets in northwestern Hungarian towns—such as Hévíz, Mosonmagyaróvár, Sopron, and Győr—with wide variations in service and expertise. Even the top clinics can vary in the amount of English spoken and the level of customer service provided. Travelers to Hungary should make an extra effort to attain the highest comfort level with their clinic and doctor beforehand. The services of a good health travel agent are recommended.

■ SELECTED HOSPITALS AND CLINICS

Eurodent Aquadental Dentistry
Győri Kapu Utca 7
Mosonmagyaróvár H-9200, HUNGARY
Tel: +36 96 578.250
Email: eurodent@eurodent.hu
Web: eurodent.hu

Established in 1993, Eurodent Aquadental Dentistry's six dentists and staff of 20 serve mostly Europeans seeking to combine Viennese vacations with dental checkups and cleanings. Vienna is less than 90 minutes away, and border crossings have become much easier for tourists. Treatments at Eurodent include closed sinus elevations; cosmetic and preservative fillings; inlays and veneers; laser therapies; oral surgery (extractions, root canals); prosthetics (crown and bridge removal and a variety of metal and non-metal crowns, including zirconium); and restorations.

Leading Specialties: Dentistry

Gelenscér Dental Clinic
Vörösmarty u. 75
8380 Hévíz, HUNGARY
Tel: +36 83 340.183
Email: info@gelencserdental.hu
Web: zahnarzt-ungarn-heviz.de

Gelenscér provides a full range of dental treatments, including orthodontics and periodontal treatments, oral surgery, and dental laboratory services. More than 1,000 dental implants are performed annually. The center also offers general dentistry to hotel guests via its clinics at NaturMed Hotel Carbona and Danubius Health Spa Resort Hotel Aqua. The clinic's nine doctors—one oral surgeon/implantologist, five dental surgeons, one orthodontist, one chief anesthetist, and one anesthetist—are multilingual, and most widely used languages can be accommodated.

Gelenscér boasts the latest technology and imaging solutions, such as digital dental x-ray; intraoral camera; dental laser; and BriteSmile, a tooth-whitening system with plasma lamp. All crowns, bridges, and dentures are made in Gelenscér's own lab, which reduces treatment time. The clinic runs a dental taxi service from selected hotels in Hévíz. Telephone consultations are free online, and all work carries an international guarantee.

Leading Specialties: Dentistry

Isis Dental Clinic
Thököly Utca 16
Szombathely H-9700, HUNGARY
Tel: +36 94 339.155
Email: isisdental@isisdental.hu
Web: isisdental.hu/en/

Located at the foot of the Alps in Szombathely (one of Hungary's oldest towns, established in 43 AD by the Roman emperor Claudius), Isis Dental Clinic offers the full range of diagnoses, treatments, and surgeries. An on-site laboratory helps shorten wait periods for crowns, dentures, and implants.

Implantologists at Isis boast the use of products from Oraltronics and Nobel Biocare, two well-known European dental manufacturers. Other aesthetic services include permanent bleaching with the BriteSmile system and a wide range of tooth jewelry.

Isis offers three-, six-, and nine-day "Dental Week" packages that include consultations, various treatments, and free pickup and drop-off to and from Vienna (50 minutes) or Graz (40 minutes).

For patients planning annual visits, the clinic offers a five-year guarantee on all prosthetic work with annual checkups.

Leading Specialties: Dentistry

Kreativ Dental Clinic

1141 Vezér Utca 100
Budapest, HUNGARY
Tel: +36 12 220.199; 888 573.2848 (US toll free)
Email: office@kreativdentalclinic.eu
Web: kreativdentalclinic.eu

Established in 1996 in suburban Budapest, Kreativ Dental employs 12 full-time dentists working from 10 examination rooms with a staff of some 50 assistants, hygienists, interpreters, receptionists, and drivers.

Specialties run the gamut: implants, artificial bone replacement, sinus lifting, periodontal surgery, inlays, porcelain crowns, bridgework, and full restorative and cosmetic dentistry. An in-house CT scanner allows convenient and accurate diagnosis without painful investigative procedures. Kreativ's in-house laboratory employs 17 technicians who work with clinic dentists to efficiently deliver crowns, dentures, bridges, and other work under one roof.

Kreativ carries a three-year guarantee for veneers; five-year guarantee on crowns, inlays, and bridgework; and a lifetime guarantee for implants (device only). An unusual offer allows for one-night hotel accommodation and partial airfare reimbursement if received treatment resulting from a free consultation is valued at more than US$3,000.

Services to international patients include free airport transportation, hotel shuttle, and local transportation travel pass; interpreters (Danish, Norwegian, Italian, Swedish, French, German, Russian); and access for patients and companions to Kreativ's rooftop Sky Café.

Accreditation: Accreditation Association for Ambulatory Health Care

Leading Specialties: Dentistry

Smile Zentrum Dental Clinic and Implantation Center

Bálint Mihály Utca 121
Győr H-9025, HUNGARY
Tel: +36 96 528.910
Email: info@smilezentrum.hu
Web: smilezentrum.hu

Győr offers elegant old architecture and charming shopping streets, but at the same time, it is a fast-developing industrial town, where you find factories for Audi, Leier, Wolf, Philips, and other major companies. So if you are traveling on business, you may opt to have some dental work done while there.

Smile Zentrum offers the full range of dental services, including radiography (panoramic or small size), ultrasound scaling of tooth film, mycoderm treatment, groove closing, bleaching, fillings, prostheses, inlays/onlays of gold and ceramics, ceramic caps, crowns, dentures, oral surgery, implants (Titan), root canals, and extractions.

Leading Specialties: Dentistry

TriDent Budapest Cosmetic & Family Dentistry

17 Nádasdy Kálmán St.
Budapest H-1046, HUNGARY
Tel: +36 20 945.8797
Email: dentist@drtooth.hu
Web: drtooth.hu

Established in 1995 as a family enterprise, TriDent has now welcomed patients from more than 20 countries. Dr. George Toth serves English-speaking patients. His drtooth.hu website was named in response to affectionate ribbings from his patients. TriDent specializes in cosmetic and advanced restorative work, but its dental team is equipped to handle implants, crowns, veneers, inlays, implants, dentures, and fillings.

The clinic emphasizes minimally invasive dentistry, promoting the least possible tissue loss, combined with preventive strategies for maintaining healthy teeth and gums. Yet it is also committed to the latest technology, including radiosurgery, in-house panoramic x-ray, intraoral cameras, and conscious sedation (nitrous oxide) for those averse to topical anesthesia.

Free patient amenities include airport transfer, consultation, intraoral x-ray, use of a local mobile phone, and corporate rates on partnered hotel accommodation. TriDent offers two- to five-year guarantees on most of its work, with the usual caveats. With the completion of the new M0 highway, TriDent is only 30 minutes from Budapest's Ferihegy Airport.

Leading Specialties: Dentistry

Patient Experience

Brenda B., Minnesota

Brenda B. received the antibiotic tetracycline as a child, so her teeth were tinted yellow. She dreamed of an attractive smile, but the costs of having her teeth capped in the US were too high for her budget. So she started investigating the dental tourism industry.

"Hungary was my country of choice," said Brenda, "because of the large number of highly qualified dentists offering services at competitive prices. I also liked the fact that it is in Europe and I could visit capitals in surrounding countries.

"I chose the city of Mosonmagyaróvár for several reasons. I liked the idea of relaxing in the thermal spa pool after a long session in the dental chair. Mosonmagyaróvár turned out to be a charming little town with an old-European feel to it. There were quaint bakeries and coffee shops to enjoy along its cobblestone streets and avenues. The people were friendly, and I felt extremely safe walking the streets alone (even at night). From Mosonmagyaróvár, I took day trips to Bratislava (capital of Slovakia), Budapest, and Vienna."

Brenda was happy with the dental services she received. Her dentist took care to avoid the pain Brenda had previously experienced from her sensitive teeth. After doing tests that confirmed Brenda's allergy to the metals cobalt and nickel, her dentist removed amalgam from her mouth and used gold to make her new crowns.

"Now I have a pretty smile, and my teeth aren't overly sensitive," Brenda said. "Much appreciation and gratitude goes to my heath travel agent and my dental team for enabling me to fulfill this dream." ■

DESTINATION: **INDIA**

■ AT A GLANCE

Mumbai, Delhi, Bangalore, Chennai, Hyderabad

Languages	Hindi, English widely spoken
Time Zone	GMT +5
Country Dialing Code	+91
Electricity	220V, plug types B and E
Currency	Indian rupee (INR)
Leading Specialties	Cardiology and heart surgery, dentistry, fertility and reproductive medicine, health screening, neurology and spine surgery, oncology, ophthalmology, orthopedics, transplant, weight loss surgery, wellness and prevention
Typical Savings (over USD retail)	65%–90%
Standards and Affiliations	British Medical Association; General Medical Council; Ministry of Health and Family Welfare; Indian Healthcare Federation; Indian Medical Association; National Accreditation Board for Hospitals and Healthcare Providers; Quality Council of India
International Accreditation	Joint Commission International

■ TREATMENT BRIEF

Who could have guessed at the start of the twenty-first century that India would grow into one of the world's most important destinations for health travelers? Driven by a surging economy, a surplus of well-trained healthcare practitioners, low infrastructure costs, and a proven national penchant for international outsourcing of customer service, India is now the world's value leader for the cost-conscious international health traveler.

Patients willing embrace some of India's cultural challenges will realize savings of up to 85 percent on high-acuity procedures such as heart and joint surgery. Serving more than 250,000 international patients annually, the vast subcontinent welcomes international medical travelers in several large metro areas: Bangalore, Chennai, Hyderabad, Mumbai, and New Delhi.

Unlike its Asian counterparts, which have traditionally encouraged medical travel by aggressively recruiting top-of-the-line physicians from other countries, India produces some of the world's finest physicians and surgeons internally, with excellent teaching hospitals and research centers. (Tens of thousands of Indian physicians have joined hospitals outside their homeland. At last count some 35,000 Indian specialists practice in the US and more than one in six US surgeons is of Indian descent.)

India clearly has a two-tier health delivery system. Because of the country's widespread poverty, the Indian public healthcare system offers medical care to the poor at little or no cost. Few in India can afford the large, complex surgeries and elective treatments that attract foreign patients. The good news is that many large private hospitals are comitting a portion of profits from international business to improved healthcare services for the indigent.

■ INDIA AND MEDICAL TRAVEL

Despite—or because of—the global economic downturn, India's medical travel industry is clipping along at a 20 percent growth rate annually. India welcomes most of its cross-border travelers from the immediate region (Bangladesh, the Turkic States, the Middle East, East Africa). However, some of those gains have arisen from increasing numbers of Americans, Canadians, and Europeans seeking treatment, particularly the more expensive cardiac and orthopedic surgeries, for which health travelers can save tens of thousands of dollars compared to the cost of treatment at home.

India's official national health policy encourages medical travel as part of its economy's "export" activities, although the services are performed within India. The government uses revenues generated from medical travel to increase its holdings in foreign currency. With government and corporate investment solidly behind its healthcare system, more international hospitals and super-specialty centers are opening every year.

Cardiology and cardiac surgery have become a specialty in India, with centers such as Fortis (Mumbai), Apollo (New Delhi and Chennai), and the Institute of Cardiovascular Diseases (Bangalore) leading the way. Success and morbidity rates are on par with those found in the US and Europe, with major surgeries at 15–60 percent of the cost.

In 2014 India's JCI-accredited hospitals numbered 21, up from only two in 2005.

■ SELECTED HOSPITALS AND CLINICS

Apollo Hospitals Group
Apollo Hospitals–Bangalore
154/11, Opp. IIM B
Bannerghatta Road
Bangalore, 560076 INDIA

Apollo Hospitals–Chennai
No. 21, Greams Lane, Off. Greams Road
Chennai, 600006 INDIA

Indraprastha Apollo Hospitals–New Delhi
Sarita Vihar, Delhi Mathura Road
New Delhi, 110076 INDIA

Apollo Hospitals–Hyderabad
Jubilee Hills
Hyderabad 500033, INDIA
Tel: +91 404 344.1066
Email: enquiry@apollohospitals.com
Web: apollohospitals.com

Now one of Asia's largest private healthcare groups, Apollo began in 1983 as a 150-bed hospital. Apollo Hospitals Group includes 54 hospitals in India and overseas, has a total bed capacity of 8,700, offers 55 medical specialties, and annually treats more than 255,000 inpatients and two million outpatients.

Apollo has five JCI-accredited hospitals, four of which welcome a high volume of international patients. Apollo's hospitals in Chennai, Delhi, Bangalore, and Hyderabad collectively treat more than 50,000 international patients from 55 countries every year.

The Institutes of Cardiology and Cardio-Thoracic Surgery at Apollo Hospitals form one of the largest cardiovascular groups in the world. With locations in Delhi, Chennai, Hyderabad, Ahmedabad, Kolkata, and Bangalore, the institutes have collectively performed more than 100,000 heart surgeries, including coronary artery bypass, heart valve surgery, heart transplants, and minimally invasive cardiac surgery. Cardiologists at the institutes have performed more than 85,000 angiographies and 50,000 coronary angioplasties. Only 10 other hospital programs in the world claim such a high volume of procedures. The institutes have a 99.6 percent success rate for cardiac bypass surgeries, the vast majority of which were beating-heart surgeries.

Apollo's Cancer Institutes in Chennai, Delhi, Kolkata, and Hyderabad offer comprehensive medical, surgical, and radiation oncology services. The institutes emphasize a multi-disciplinary approach combined with the latest treatment technologies. Cancer Institutes in Delhi and Hyderabad use the Novalis Tx radiotherapy and radiosurgery system to eradicate tumors without incision. The institute in Chennai uses the CyberKnife robotic-assisted radio surgery system to treat tumors anywhere in the body with a high level of accuracy. Additional treatment options include linear accelerator for radiotherapy (LINAC), brachytherapy, and stereotactic radiosurgery.

The Bone Marrow Transplant Unit performs both autologous and allogenic bone marrow transplants. The units treat acute myeloid leukemia, lymphatic leukemia, and Hodgkin's disease. Although still experimental, bone marrow transplants have yielded hopeful results for genetic disorders, such as thalassemia and sickle cell anemia. Apollo's Cancer Institutes have performed more than 150 bone marrow transplants with a high success rate.

Surgeons at Apollo's Institutes of Orthopedics in Delhi, Chennai, Hyderabad, Ahmedabad, Kolkata, and Bangalore perform a wide range of procedures, including major joint replacement, arthroscopy, delicate hand surgery, spine surgery, limb lengthening, and treatment of bone tumors. Institute surgeons use computer navigation and imaging equipment with robotics-assisted technology to improve outcomes. The Institute of Orthopedics in Chennai has performed thousands of hip resurfacing surgeries, with a success rate well ahead of facilities in other countries.

Apollo's Transplant Institutes in Delhi, Chennai, Hyderabad, Ahmedabad, Kolkata, and Bangalore have collectively completed more than 6,700 kidney transplants and 775 liver transplants. In 2010 the institutes performed more than 746 transplants, making the group one of the world's largest transplant programs and the busiest outside the US. The institutes have a 90 percent success rate and are known for several firsts in India, including the first pediatric liver transplant, the first adult liver transplant, the first cadaver liver transplant, the first transplant in acute liver failure, and the first liver-kidney transplant.

Apollo offers several additional centers of excellence and specialty centers. Some of the most recognized include the Institute of Neurosciences, the Center of Cosmetic Surgery, the Center for Assisted Reproduction, the Institute of Preventive Medicine, the Institute of Gastrosciences, and the Center for Gastroenterology and Hepatology, which performs weight loss surgery.

Apollo offers comprehensive international patient services, including appointment scheduling, direct admission, language translation, and support for travel arrangements. Upon arrival international patients are received at the airport and taken directly to a hotel or hospital. Inpatient rooms are designed to feel more like a hotel than a patient ward and offer satellite TV, internet access, room service, and laundry service.

For patients interested in alternative therapies, Apollo Chennai offers a comprehensive, hospital-based wellness center. Holistic healing therapies—such as Ayurveda medicine, aromatherapy, pranic healing, yoga, meditation, and music therapy—are offered to international patients as part of the hospital's complimentary recovery package.

Accreditation: Joint Commission International

Leading Specialties: Cardiology and heart surgery, cosmetic and reconstructive surgery, fertility and reproductive medicine, oncology, ophthalmology, orthopedics, spine surgery, transplant, weight loss surgery

Apollo White Dental Centre
21, Greams Road Opp. M.R.F
Chennai 600–006, INDIA
Tel: +91 90 0311.5000, +91 90 0311.3000 (international patients)
Web: apollodentalcentre.com

Apollo White Dental, the dental branch of Apollo Hospitals, is the largest dental chain in India, with more than 50 centers in nine cities. Apollo is aiming to reach 100 centers in 2015. The corporate headquarters is located in Chennai, and 14 Apollo White clinics serve that city. (A full list of addresses and phone numbers is available on the website.) The Greams Road site is adjacent to the main Apollo Hospital in Chennai. It offers a full range of dental services, including crowns and bridges, fillings, dentures, dental implants, root canals, restorative dentistry, cosmetic dentistry, and pediatric dentistry.

All Apollo dental clinics are equipped with high-tech dental chairs, CACTI and Instant CAD-CAM crown machines from Germany, implants from Switzerland, and crowns and aligners from the US.

Leading Specialties: Dentistry

Asian Heart Institute and Research Centre
G/N Block, Bandra Kurla Complex, Bandra (E)
Mumbai 400 051, Maharashtra, INDIA
Tel: +91 99 2015.5000
Email: internationalassist@ahirc.com
Web: asianheartinstitute.org

JCI accredited since 2006, the 250-bed Asian Heart Institute and Research Centre (AHIRC) was established by Contemporary Healthcare, Pvt. Ltd., and six of India's top cardiac specialists. A 15-minute drive from Mumbai's domestic and international airports, the hospital forms part of the new Bandra Kurla Complex , a US$250 million business-shopping-healthcare-living development in northern Mumbai. The institute follows treatment and facilities guidelines established by the Cleveland Clinic in the US.

In 2013 surgeons at the hospital performed 1,430 coronary artery bypass grafts, with a mortality rate of 0.5 percent. Virtually all of them were performed using the off-pump (beating-heart) technique, which reduces post-operative complications and the length of hospital stays. In addition to coronary artery surgery, AHIRC specializes in the Maze procedure for atrial fibrillation, valve repair and replacement, and aneurysm surgery of the aorta and other blood vessels. A special pediatric team operates on all types of cardiac conditions in children.

Asian Heart Institute's international patients department offers airport pickup and drop-off, hotel accommodations and local travel arrangements for companions, consultations with physicians and surgeons, prayer rooms, and internet access.

Accreditation: Joint Commission International

Leading Specialties: Cardiology and heart surgery

Columbia Asia India
Corporate Office: The Icon, #8, 80 Feet Road
HAL III Stage, Indiranagar
Bangalore 560075, INDIA
Tel: +91 80 4021.1000
Email: international.patients@columbiaasia.in
Web: india.columbiaasia.com/international-patients/

Columbia Asia is India's new kid on the block, competing with giants Fortis and Apollo with smaller, nimbler specialty facilities (usually around 60 beds) in rural areas or suburban neighborhoods of larger cities. Although most of this healthcare network's international patients are regional, patients from the West are drawn to facilities in Gurgaon (just outside Delhi and near the international airport) and Bangalore.

Because Columbia Asia focuses on efficiency, its no-frills approach to quality care makes prices jaw-droppingly low, even by India's standards. Most of Columbia Asia's facilities are accredited by the National Accreditation Board for Hospitals and Healthcare Providers, India's government-supported and most prestigious healthcare accreditation agency.

Specialties include bariatric surgery; oncology (breast cancer, bone marrow transplant); neurology (minimally invasive spine surgery); orthopedics (joint replacement); urology; and transplants (kidney and liver).

The centralized International Patient Services Center helps patients match conditions with the appropriate facility and doctor; provides airport transportation; and offers teleconsultation directly with the treating doctor, treatment estimates, language interpretation services, and assistance with insurance. The group has formed arrangements with leading health plan carriers, including Bupa International, Vanbreda, Blue Cross Blue Shield, Aetna, AXA Assistance, and Cigna.

Columbia Asia claims that in the future all hospitals will look like Columbia Asia facilities. Evidence lies in its regional, specialized focus; streamlined services; a 24-hour help line; and online publication of package pricing, where patients can view all-inclusive deals on a wide range of procedures.

Columbia Asia also operates facilities in Malaysia, Indonesia, and Vietnam, with aggressive growth plans throughout Asia.

Leading Specialties: Cardiology and heart surgery, oncology, orthopedics, spine surgery, weight loss surgery

Dr. L H Hiranandani Hospital
Hill Side Avenue, Hiranandani Gardens
Powai, Mumbai, INDIA
Tel: +91 22 2576.3333; +91 22 2576.3300
Email: wecare@hiranandanihospital.org
Web: hiranandanihospital.org/index.html

This tertiary- and quaternary-care medical center was established in 2004 in honor of its namesake, Dr. L. H. Hiranandani, one of India's most innovative surgeons, and the first Indian appointed as a member of the American Society of Head and Neck Surgery. In the heart of Mumbai along the water, this 240-bed facility is among the most respected hospitals in western India.

Centers of excellence include the advanced Cancer Care Center (specializing in bone marrow transplant); Center for Advanced Dental Surgery (mostly restorative, aesthetic, and corrective procedures); Physical Rehabilitation and Sports Medicine Center; Ophthalmology Center; and a new Executive Health Check Center.

Other specialties include cardiology, joint replacement, hip resurfacing and hip arthroscopy, and bariatrics/weight loss.

In 2007 Hiranandani became the first hospital in western India to receive the prestigious National Accreditation Board for Hospitals and Healthcare Providers accreditation.

Accreditation: Joint Commission International

Leading Specialties: Cardiology and heart surgery, fertility and reproductive medicine, oncology, ophthalmology, orthopedics, weight loss surgery

Fortis Escorts Heart Institute
Okhla Road
New Delhi 110 025, INDIA
Tel: +91 99 1099.0342
Email: international.escorts@fortishealthcare.com
Web: fortisescorts.in

Headquartered in New Delhi, with 20 centers and associated hospitals throughout India, Fortis Escorts Heart Institute now manages nearly 900 beds and carries out 5,000 open-heart surgeries, 5,000 angioplasties, and 15,000 angiographies annually. The 285-bed New Delhi facility has nine operating rooms, with 200 doctors managing around 14,000 admissions annually.

Known primarily for cardiology and cardiac surgery, the institute also specializes in orthopedics, respiratory, kidney (transplant and dialysis), neurology (brain, spine, and peripheral nerves), and dental surgery. In 2013 The Week/Nielson ranked the institute the top private heart hospital in Delhi and fifth best in cardiology in India.

Cardiac specialties include standard and specialty coronary bypass surgery, transmyocardial laser revascularization (TMLR), heart port surgery, robotic-assisted surgery for aortic aneurysms and dissections, carotid endarterectomy, valve surgery, and treatment of peripheral vascular disease.

Escorts also emphasizes preventive cardiology with a fully developed program of monitored exercise, yoga, meditation, and lifestyle management.

The institute's latest addition is its Cardiac Scan Center, where state-of-the-art MRI and CT scanners are used to diagnose coronary artery disease at its earliest stages.

Fortis Escorts' network-wide International Services Department offers airport pickup and drop-off, assistance with travel arrangements, a local interpreter, currency exchange, customized in-hospital cuisine, and sightseeing.

Accreditation: Joint Commission International

Leading Specialties: Cardiology and heart surgery, health screening, orthopedics, spine surgery

Fortis Hospital Bangalore
154/9, Bannerghatta Road, Opp. IIM-B
Bangalore 560 076, INDIA
Tel: +91 80 6621.4444; +91 80 7101.2300
Email: enquiries@fortishospitals.in
Web: fortishealthcare.com/internationalpatients

After 18 years of pioneering clinical achievements at its first heart hospital on Bangalore's Cunningham Road, Fortis Hospital Bangalore opened the doors to its new state-of-the-art, 400-bed, super-specialty hospital in August 2006. JCI accreditation was awarded in 2008, and the center was re-accredited by JCI in 2011.

Formerly known as Wockhardt Super-Specialty Hospital, specialties include cardiovascular surgery, cardiology, orthopedics, neurosciences, minimal access surgery, and women's and children's services.

Wockhardt Super-Specialty Hospital was designed in consultation with Partners Harvard Medical International (PHMI), the global arm of Harvard Medical School. PHMI worked with selected healthcare providers across the globe to improve excellence in clinical medicine, medical education, and biomedical research.

Accreditation: Joint Commission International

Leading Specialties: Cardiology and heart surgery, orthopedics

Fortis Hospitals Mumbai

Mulund Gurgaon Link Road
Mumbai, INDIA
Tel: +91 22 6799.4187
Email: enquiries@fortishealthcare.com
Web: fortishealthcare.com/internationalpatients/index.php

Known throughout Asia and the rest of the world for its specialty centers, Fortis Mumbai is one of India's shining healthcare stars, particularly in the area of heart disease management and surgery. The hospital group, headquartered in Mumbai, first set up a heart hospital in Bangalore in 1990.

Formerly Wockhardt Hospital, Fortis Mumbai boasts several centers of excellence, including centers for cardiac care, orthopedics, neurosurgery, and oncology. Fortis's Mumbai location also offers its world-renowned Hip Resurfacing Clinic, where hundreds of patients from America and Europe have been treated in the last few years.

In 2005 Fortis in Mumbai became the first super-specialty hospital in South Asia to receive JCI accreditation.

Accreditation: Joint Commission International

Leading Specialties: Cardiology and heart surgery, cosmetic and reconstructive surgery, fertility and reproductive medicine, oncology, orthopedics, spine surgery, weight loss surgery

Max Healthcare and Super Specialty Hospitals

1 Press Enclave Road
Saket, New Delhi 110017, INDIA
Tel: +91 11 2651.5050
Email: international@maxhealthcare.com
Web: maxhealthcare.in

Twelve specialty centers with 1,800 beds and 1,000 doctors make Max Healthcare one of the subcontinent's most influential health centers. International health travelers usually visit one of Max's two super-specialty centers (both in New Delhi), mostly for cardiac and orthopedic surgeries.

Max Delhi has treated more than 20,000 international patients from 50 countries. The Max Heart and Vascular Institute offers advanced cardiac imaging, interventional cardiology, and electrophysiology.

The Max Institute of Orthopedics and Joint Replacement Surgery, in South Delhi, is a tertiary-care center that prides itself on infection control and specialized physiotherapy services for all its patients.

Main departments include the Institute of Neurosciences (brain tumors, aneurysms, stroke, infectious diseases of the brain, spinal tumors, and chronic spinal pain); the Max Cancer Center (integrated, team-oriented approach to surgical, radiation, and medical oncology); Max Eyecare (vision correction, cataract surgery, and corneal surgery); and the Institute of Aesthetic and Reconstructive Plastic Surgery (correction of birth defects, wide range of cosmetic procedures). Additional specialties include bariatric surgery, obstetrics and gynecology, pediatrics, and dental care.

Max's International Patients Services Department offers telemedicine evaluation and recommendations; travel arrangements to Delhi (including visa, ticketing, airport pickup and drop-off, currency exchange, lodging assistance, and special return journey arrangements if needed); interpreters; lodging assistance; and an exclusive help desk and dedicated relationship manager to ensure quality service.

Leading Specialties: Cardiology and heart surgery, cosmetic and reconstructive surgery, fertility and reproductive medicine, oncology, ophthalmology, orthopedics, spine surgery, weight loss surgery

Rotunda: The Center for Human Reproduction

1st Floor, B Wing 36, Turner Road
Bandra (West), Mumbai 400 050, INDIA
Tel: +91 22 2655.2000; +91 22 2640.5000
Email: info@rotundaivf.com
Web: rotundaivf.in

Fertility treatment is usually a long and emotionally arduous processes. As most couples struggling with fertility issues know, treatments are usually expensive and not covered by health insurance. In addition, fertility treatments conducted in a general hospital can often be an exclusively clincal, somewhat dehumanizing experience. As an alternative to high costs and impersonal care, couples are increasingly choosing to receive treatment abroad, then return to their home countries for ongoing support and, hopefully, prenatal care.

Founded in 1963 and based in Mumbai, Rotunda is one of India's most respected fertility treatment facilities. In-house pathology, endoscopy, and sonography services allow a couple to undergo all tests and procedures under one roof.

In addition to the standard fertility services, Rotunda offers gestational surrogacy services, donor egg in vitro fertilization (IVF), laser-assisted hatching, and a recurrent pregnancy loss clinic. A staff of 10 directors, fertility specialists, embryologists, and researchers has received training in the UK, India, Belgium, and Germany.

Rotunda's Travel Services Department welcomes patients at the airport; helps manage hotel bookings, local transport, ticketing, visa support, and sightseeing; and even selects a last minute gift for family back home. A free online second opinion is available as part of the initial consultation process.

Rotunda is India's only lesbian-gay-bisexual-transsexual-friendly center. Rotunda treats about 100 international patients annually.

Leading Specialties: Fertility and reproductive medicine

Shroff Eye Hospital and LASIK Centre

222, S V Road, Bandra West
Mumbai 400050, INDIA
Tel: +91 22 6692.1000
Email: info@shroffeye.org
Web: shroffeye.org

Established in 1919 and family run since its inception, the Shroff Eye Hospital and LASIK Centre is among the few JCI-accredited vision hospitals in the world. Drs. Ashok C. Shroff, Rahul Ashok Shroff, and Anand Ashok Shroff, along with 12 other physicians and consultants, provide full-service vision diagnosis and treatment, catering to international travelers from more than 90 countries.

The hospital has two centers in Mumbai offering cataract surgery (including micro-incision high frequency ultrasound); vitreoretinal surgery (for treating advanced diabetic retinopathy, retinal detachment, macular hole, and other retinal conditions); LASIK surgery; glaucoma surgery; squint surgery; corneal treatments (including keratoplasty, oculoplastic surgery, and other cosmetic treatments); and pediatric eye care (including squint and lazy eye).

The Shroffs are particularly proud of their LASIK Clinic, which deploys the latest wavefront-guided LASIK technology, including the recent ReLEx, FLEx, and SMILE procedures. Also known as custom LASIK, the treatment involves new technologies that measure distortions in the eye, providing the physician with the information needed to chart a treatment plan customized to each patient. Shroff Eye is also India's first and only facility to deploy WaveLight Concerto 500 Hz LASIK instrumentation.

In 2012 Shroff was awarded full JCI re-accreditation.

Accreditation: Joint Commission International

Leading Specialties: Ophthalmology

Patient Experience

Nancy K., Colorado

Like many Americans, I was unable to qualify for health insurance due to a pre-existing condition (prolapsed mitral valve and atrial septal defect). Traveling for the care I needed started out solely as a financial consideration, but as I learned more, I realized that I would feel more confident about getting high-quality care overseas than I would here. So I traveled to Delhi, India, with my husband. I did research on the internet, and I chose a treatment center that I thought was right for me.

"My diagnosis was that I needed to replace the mitral valve and repair the hole between the chambers of my heart. An extraordinary team performed my surgery. Their English was flawless because most Indian doctors have been trained in either the UK or US. My key surgeon is internationally known for his skill in the technique he used for my surgery.

"I was in the hospital for four weeks. I had no problems there, but my trip home was very difficult, naturally, because the journey was so long and I didn't have a lot of energy. I have had lung issues since my return to the States. I live at an altitude of 7,500 feet, and the thin air here has taken a toll on me. My follow-up care is the same as if I had had my surgery at home because my personal cardiologist looks after me, not the surgeon.

"My total costs (including travel) were about 10 percent of what I would have paid here. I would absolutely travel abroad again for healthcare. The high level of care and supreme cleanliness cannot be found in most of the sadly understaffed hospitals in this country. The main thing for anyone considering healthcare in another country is *do your research!*" ∎

DESTINATION: **ISRAEL**

■ AT A GLANCE

Jerusalem, Tel Aviv

Languages	Hebrew, English, and Russian widely spoken
Time Zone	GMT +2
Country Dialing Code	+972
Electricity	230V, plug type B
Currency	Israeli shekel (ILS)
Leading Specialties	Cardiology and heart surgery, fertility and reproductive medicine, health screening, neurology and spine surgery, oncology, orthopedics, stem cell and regenerative therapy, urology
Typical Savings (over USD retail)	30%–55%
Standards and Affiliations	Academic Council of the Israel Medical Association; Ministry of Health, Israel
International Accreditation	Joint Commission International

■ TREATMENT BRIEF

War, impending war, and other social turmoil may make you think twice about Israel as a health travel destination, but that second thought might be worth the effort—and the money. Although many patients, particularly Westerners, feel uneasy about the political turmoil of the Middle East, Israel has much to offer health travelers.

Israel's international providers, and to a lesser extent its government, are now actively promoting international health travel throughout the region and to its allies in the US, for good reason. Standards are high, doctors are plentiful and well trained, and the medical technology employed in top hospitals is state of the art.

Israel's more than 60 general and acute-care hospitals, 11 of which are JCI accredited, comprise approximately 15,000 beds. Another 14,000 beds are available for chronic-care patients (including geriatric patients) and some 7,000 for psychiatric patients. Nearly half of those beds are in government-

operated facilities. Almost 20 percent are in hospitals run by non-profit and religious organizations. In 2010 more than 25,000 doctors were practicing in Israel—3.3 for every 1,000 Israeli citizens, one of the world's highest doctor-patient ratios.

Israel has five medical schools, each affiliated with a major university: the Hebrew University Medical School associated with the Hadassah Medical Organization, the Tel Aviv University Medical School, the Technion Medical School in Haifa, the Ben-Gurion University Medical School in Be'er Sheva, and the Medical School of the Bar-Ilan University in Safed. Israel also has two schools of dentistry, one of pharmacology, and 20 nursing schools. Courses for physiotherapists, occupational therapists, nutritionists, x-ray technicians, and laboratory technicians are offered at several institutions.

The top Israeli hospitals are equipped with the same state-of-the-art medical instruments routinely used in diagnosis in the US and Europe. Israel is also known for the design and manufacture of medical equipment; Israel's CAT scanners and advanced microcomputer-supported devices are exported widely. The country has pioneered the development and use of laser surgical instruments, computerized monitoring systems, and other life-saving and pain-relieving devices. Chances are Israeli-manufactured devices have been used by your hospital or doctors during the course of a treatment.

ISRAEL AND MEDICAL TRAVEL

In 2014 Israel welcomed some 40,000 medical travelers, most of Jewish descent from Russia and other Commonwealth of Independent States nations, and increasingly from North America and the EU. An important consideration for the English-speaking medical traveler is that English is universally and fluently spoken throughout the country, including by most doctors, surgeons, and administrative staff.

Health and wellness tourism is also on the rise, with tens of thousands seeking the healing waters of the Dead Sea as part of their travel plans. Those planning health travel should not overlook a visit to the Dead Sea's spas and medical centers, where oxygen-enriched air and mineral-rich salt and mud treatments are believed to treat a variety of disorders from psoriasis to arthritis pain.

FERTILITY SPECIALTIES

No overview of healthcare in Israel would be complete without mention of Israel's in vitro fertilization (IVF) centers, which rank among the world's finest. The IVF unit at Assuta Medical Center is the largest in the country. IVF centers at Chaim Sheba, Hadassah, and Rabin are also renowned for their excellent specialists, high number of treatments, and high success rates. Prices for fertility services can total a fraction of those found in North America. At one clinic in Israel, for example, the price of a standard IVF cycle is about US$4,000, excluding medication, whereas couples expect to pay $13,000 to $25,000 or more in the US.

For sightseers and history buffs, Israel offers an abundance of opportunities. Jerusalem and its environs abound with religious and historical sites venerated by three of the world's major religions. In Israel's bustling markets, shoppers will find antiques, rugs, jewelry, and other items. Israel has more than 60 national parks and 230 nature reserves, many of which are historic sites.

SELECTED HOSPITALS AND CLINICS

Assaf Harofeh Medical Center
PO Beer Yaacov
Zerifin, Tel Aviv 70300, ISRAEL
Tel: +972 8977.9500
Email: info@assafharofeh.org
Web: assafh.org

Assaf Harofeh was founded in 1948 on the grounds of an old British military hospital. Today's modern facility belies that humble origin and serves as an academic teaching facility for Tel Aviv University's Sackler Faculty of Medicine. This 850-bed facility in the center of the country is now one of Israel's largest.

Located near Tel Aviv and less than 10 miles from Ben Gurion Airport, the hospital provides general medical, surgical, cardiac, pediatric, neonatal, gynecological, and obstetric services, as well as 24-hour emergency services, intensive care, and ambulatory psychiatric services. Leading procedures include da Vinci robotic-assisted surgery, hyperbaric chamber treatments, cochlear implants, thoracic surgery, and nuclear medicine.

The first and largest academic nursing school and Israel's oldest school of physiotherapy are on the hospital grounds. Assaf Harofeh earned its JCI accreditation in 2014.

Accreditation: Joint Commission International

Leading Specialties: Cardiology and heart surgery, oncology

Assuta Medical Center

20 Habarzel Street Ramat-Hachayal
Tel Aviv 69710, ISRAEL
Tel: +972 3764.4044; +972 3764.3247
Email: touristcenter@assuta.com
Web: en.assuta.co.il

Founded in 1935, Assuta is Israel's largest private healthcare provider network, with 11 clinics and hospitals across Israel. Its main facility, Assuta Medical Center Tel Aviv, provides diagnostics and treatment in nearly all disciplines, focusing on cardiology, oncology, gynecology and fertility, urology, ENT, and complex treatments.

This 350-bed, JCI-accredited facility deploys 1,500 doctors and surgeons and 400 nurses to treat nearly 50,000 inpatients and 130,000 outpatients annually.

Assuta welcomes international patients, mostly from Russia, but increasingly from the EU and North America. English is fluently spoken at Assuta and throughout Israel. Translators are available for Russian-speaking patients.

A good mid-range business hotel, the Leonardo Boutique, is located directly across from Assuta's main entrance. The hotel often serves so many recovering patients it looks like part of the hospital itself.

Assuta enjoys direct billing arrangement with leading global insurance companies, including Allianz, AXA, Bupa, Vanbreda, and Seven Corners.

Founded in 1987, Assuta's IVF Center ranks among the top IVF units worldwide in terms of size and success rates. More than 11,000 IVF procedures are performed annually in the two Assuta IVF clinics in Tel Aviv and Rishon LeZion, Israel's fourth largest city, eight kilometers (five miles) south of Tel Aviv.

The center's leading gynecologists and infertility experts deploy a range of advanced techniques to treat both female and male infertility, including testicular sperm extraction and injection of a single sperm into the oocyte using micro-manipulation and assisted hatching.

The center's on-site laboratory is the largest of its kind in Israel, staffed by a team of biologists and other specialists and, not surprisingly, equipped with the latest technologies.

Accreditation: Joint Commission International

Leading Specialties: Cardiology and heart surgery, fertility and reproductive medicine, oncology, ophthalmology, orthopedics, spine surgery

Chaim Sheba Medical Center

Tel Hashomer 52621, ISRAEL
Tel: +972 3530.3100
Email: med-tour@sheba.health.gov.il
Web: eng.sheba.co.il

With 1,900 beds, Chaim Sheba Medical Center is the largest and most comprehensive tertiary medical center in the Middle East. It is affiliated with the Sackler Faculty of Medicine of Tel Aviv University.

Along with a major acute-care hospital and a rehabilitation hospital, Sheba's specialty centers include a Heart Institute, Eye Institute, Diagnostic Imaging Institute, and Oncology Institute. Additional leading departments include cardiac surgery, orthopedics, genetics and fertility, child development, burn unit, maxillofacial, interventional radiology and radiosurgery, pediatric hemato-oncology, and bone marrow transplantation.

Sheba's efforts to attract medical travelers date back to 1990, when the hospital began to establish official agreements with health ministries in nearby countries and to treat patients from Russia, the Ukraine, Turkey, Greece, Italy, and Jordan.

Sheba's Department for Medical Tourist Services is staffed by nurses and an administrative aide who assists patients during their medical visits. The staff in this department is fluent in English, and all medical reports are provided in English.

For those who wish to remain close to a patient during his or her stay at the hospital, Sheba offers guest accommodations. The Apropo Hotel is in the General Hospital's shopping mall. The Rehabilitation Hotel is located near the Rehabilitation Center.

Accreditation: Joint Commission International

Leading Specialties: Cardiology and heart surgery, fertility and reproductive medicine, oncology, ophthalmology, orthopedics, spine surgery

Hadassah University Medical Center
Kiryat Hadassah
Jerusalem 91120, ISRAEL
Tel: +972 2677.7111
Email: shivuk@hadassah.org.il
Web: hadassah-med.com

Established in 1912 and nominated for a Nobel Peace Prize, Hadassah University Medical Center is one of Israel's oldest and largest medical institutions. Some 850 doctors and surgeons in 130 departments and clinics treat more than 90,000 inpatients and 600,000 outpatients annually.

Specialties on its two campuses, both in Jerusalem, run the gamut: oncology and hematology; transplantation (bone marrow); general surgery (specializing in laparoscopic, robotic-assisted, and minimally invasive surgeries); ophthalmology; pediatrics; and cardiovascular surgeries.

Hadassah is known throughout Israel and the region for taking on complex conditions. Israel's first successful heart transplant and first robotics-assisted surgery were performed there, as was the first robotic-assisted surgery. Hadassah claims to have also performed the world's first computer-guided hip replacement surgery.

A us$75 million charitable contribution in 2007 from Jewish American billionaire William Davidson allowed Hadassah to construct the impressive Sarah Wetsman Davidson Hospital Tower, which opened in 2012 with 500 beds and 20 operating theaters.

Hadassah welcomes 5,000 international patients annually, with translators on hand for English, Russian, Arabic, and French. A 100-bed hotel within the hospital provides easy access to doctors and services for recovering patients and companions. A mall within the hospital offers a supermarket, clothing, shoes, toys, and household items.

For the artistically inclined, 12 original Marc Chagall stained glass windows grace the medical center's Abbell Synagogue.

Leading Specialties: Cardiology and heart surgery, fertility and reproductive medicine, oncology, ophthalmology, orthopedics, stem cell and regenerative therapy

Herzliya Medical Center
7 Ramat Yam
Herzliya On-Sea 46851, ISRAEL
Tel: +972 9959.2458
Email: inter@hmc-ims.com
Web: hmc.co.il

This private 93-bed hospital is on the Herzliya Promenade, about 15 minutes north of Tel Aviv. It has been in operation since 1982. The center includes over 20 clinics, providing outpatient treatment in a variety of medical fields. Its special services include diagnostic imaging, gastroenterology, cardiology, dialysis, cytogenetics, in vitro fertilization, and executive checkups.

Frequently performed operations include cardiothoracic surgery (more than 20,000 cardiac catheterizations and 5,000 heart operations have been done at HMC); general and endoscopic surgical procedures; laser surgery, microsurgery, computer-guided orthopedic and arthroplasty procedures; gynecological surgery; urological procedures; and plastic surgery.

Staff members in Herzliya's International Department speak 11 languages and assist health travelers with obtaining an entry visa, traveling to and from the airport, arranging meetings with doctors, billing overseas insurance carriers, and even sightseeing. They accompany patients during all stages of treatment and provide medical reports in English and other languages. Patients and guests typically stay at one of the hotels on the beachfront near the hospital.

Leading Specialties: Cardiology and heart surgery, cosmetic and reconstructive surgery, orthopedics, urology

Rabin Medical Center
Jabutinski Street 39
Petah-Tikva 49100, Israel
Tel: +972 3937.6991
Email: info@imcs-4u.com
Web: clalit.co.il/rabin/

The Rabin Medical Center (RMC) is located 20 minutes outside Tel Aviv. Composed of the Beilinson and

Golda-Hasharon campuses, RMC is the largest medical center in Israel. This tertiary-care facility is affiliated with the Tel Aviv University Sackler School of Medicine.

RMC's Department of Organ Transplantation performs organ transplants, including kidney, liver, and pancreas. It is the only place in Israel where multi-organ and live-donor liver transplants are performed.

The Department of Cardiothoracic Surgery is the country's largest, performing more than 1,300 procedures annually. One quarter of the operations are performed on children hospitalized in the adjacent Schneider Children's Medical Center of Israel, and an additional 300 operations are performed at Kaplan Hospital in Rechovot. A heart and lung transplant unit is an integral part of the department.

The Davidoff Center, opened in 2005, is the largest cancer facility in Israel, treating patients referred from hospitals throughout the country and abroad. Some 15 percent of Israel's cancer patients are seen there. Hematology (blood, lymph, and bone marrow) is a top specialty. Outpatient services include treatment for breast and lung cancer, head and neck tumors, and urological problems (prostate, bladder, kidney, and testicular).

The Integrative Medicine Unit for Cancer Patients offers cancer patients an array of alternative and complementary medicine therapies in parallel with the medical care provided. Treatments include traditional Chinese medicine (acupuncture and Chinese herbs); massage and body therapies (shiatsu, reflexology); integrative pain management; mind-body therapies (health psychology, medical hypnosis, interactive guided imagery); naturopathy (nutrition and Western herbs and supplements); and group disciplines (yoga, taichi, mindfulness-based stress reduction, healthy lifestyle).

The Cardiac Catheterization Unit in the department of cardiology assists thousands of patients in avoiding surgical procedures with the help of specialists in interventional heart catheterization. The Pulmonary Institute treats complex respiratory diseases and critical patients before and after lung transplants. The Women's Comprehensive Health Center provides a full range of medical services for women, from puberty through menopause.

RMC provides patients with private accommodations while hospitalized, including single rooms with adjacent bathroom and shower. RMC helps find accommodation for patients' companions in nearby facilities. The center also provides patients with an escort during the entire length of their hospitalization.

A medical summary report is provided in English and in other languages as needed at the end of the patient's stay.

Accreditation: Joint Commission International

Leading Specialties: Cardiology and heart surgery, oncology, orthopedics, spine surgery

Tel Aviv Sourasky Medical Center

6 Weizmann Street
Tel Aviv 64239, ISRAEL
Tel: +972 3697.3426
Email: ichilov-int@tlvmc.gov.il
Web: tasmc.org.il/sites/en/Pages/default.aspx

The Tel Aviv Sourasky Medical Center (TASMC) is a full-service healthcare center, with comprehensive medical, surgical, and diagnostic units. It earned its JCI accreditation in its centennial year, 2014. It is the national referral center for both adults and children for various specialties, including surgical oncology, gastroenterology, neurosurgery, orthopedic oncology, orthopedics, surgical oncology, organ transplantation, plastic surgery, and microsurgery. TASMC annually logs more than 103,000 new hospital admissions, 34,600 surgical procedures, 1,500,000 outpatient clinic visits, 200,000 emergency room visits, and 11,000 deliveries.

Children are treated at the Dana-Dwek Children's Hospital, which offers diagnostic, inpatient, and outpatient care in all pediatric subspecialties. Women receive specialized care at the Lis Maternity Hospital. Lis provides up-to-date services in obstetrics/gynecology, high-risk pregnancy, neonatal intensive care, in vitro fertilization (IVF), and infertility treatments.

Accreditation: Joint Commission International

Leading Specialties: Orthopedics, oncology

DESTINATION: **MALAYSIA**

■ AT A GLANCE

Kuala Lumpur, Subang Jaya, Georgetown

Languages	Malay, English, Chinese widely spoken, some Bahasa Indonesia
Time Zones	GMT +7, GMT +8
Country Dialing Code	+60
Electricity	240V, plug type D
Currency	Malaysian ringgit (MYR)
Leading Specialties	Cardiology and heart surgery, cosmetic and reconstructive surgery, dentistry, health screening, neurology and spine surgery, oncology, ophthalmology, orthopedics, transplant, weight loss surgery, wellness and prevention
Typical Savings (over USD retail)	60%–80%
Standards and Affiliations	Association of Private Hospitals of Malaysia; Malaysian Society for Quality in Health; Malaysia Healthcare Travel Council
International Accreditation	Joint Commission International

■ TREATMENT BRIEF

Because Malaysia was a longtime British colony until 1957, Western culture is ingrained throughout the country. English is universally and comfortably spoken. Tourist attractions abound, particularly in the squeaky-clean, ever-evolving capital of Kuala Lumpur and on the islands of Penang and Malacca, two favorite international beach resorts and health travel destinations.

All private medical facilities in Malaysia are required to be licensed under the Private Healthcare Facilities and Services Act 1998 and work closely with the Ministry of Health, which monitors compliance and establishes benchmarks and regulations for quality assurance.

Malaysia now has ten JCI-accredited hospitals, with aggressive plans for private facility expansion over the next five years.

■ MALAYSIA AND MEDICAL TRAVEL

Though most Asia-bound health travelers think of heading to India or Thailand for treatment, Malaysia is now firmly on the medical travel map. Patients are responding: in 2012 more than 600,000 medical travelers sought treatment in Malaysia. Those numbers continue to grow at a 35 percent rate. The country's facilities and expertise are on par with those in India and Thailand, with comparable costs on most procedures, particularly for the more complex cardiovascular and orthopedic treatments. A comparative skip from neighboring Singapore, Malaysia offers excellent facilities and care, with prices 30–50 percent lower.

More than 80 percent of Malaysia's cross-border patients visit from Indonesia, where healthcare infrastructure has yet to catch up with the rising middle class. Patients also visit from China (30 percent of Malaysia's citizenry is of Chinese descent) and the Middle East (as a moderate Muslim country, Malaysia offers cultural compatibility to the Islamic patient). Similarly, Australians fleeing rising healthcare costs find comfort in Malaysia's prevalent use of the English language.

Over the years, Malaysia has managed to continue improving its healthcare infrastructure and quality while keeping prices low. Malaysia now competes with India for the value-seeking patient, as well as the affluent patient seeking specialties in the region. Healthcare consumers from the EU and North America are beginning to accept Malaysia as a medical travel destination and embrace its many attributes.

Around 40 of Malaysia's 113 private hospitals, including the giant KPJ and Sime Darby networks, now serve international patients.

■ COMPREHENSIVE, INEXPENSIVE HEALTH SCREENINGS

While visiting for treatment, many international patients take advantage of the thorough, inexpensive physicals offered by most Malaysian private hospitals. A dazzling array of tests and exams—including blood work, bone density scans, chest x-ray, and cardiac stress testing—are available for around us$500. Malaysian hospitals were the creators of "well-man" and "well-woman" packages: comprehensive, low-cost physicals, screenings, and other tests promoting preventive care. Packages include pre-employment, executive screening, and maternity. Health travelers can also choose from a wide array of diagnostic packages, including heart, stroke, and cancer.

■ SELECTED HOSPITALS AND CLINICS

Beacon International Specialist Centre
No. 1, Jalan 215, Section 51, Off Jalan Templer
46050 Petaling Jaya, Selangor, MALAYSIA
Tel: +603 7620.7979
Email: info@beaconhospital.com.my
Web: beaconhospital.com.my

A collaborative approach to treatment is paramount for Beacon's multi-disciplinary doctors and surgeons, best known for their expertise in oncology,

CyberKnife radiosurgery, radiotherapy, chemotherapy, and PET/CT scanning. Many of Beacon's oncologists trained in the United Kingdom and United States. The facility has treated more than 10,000 cancer patients and performed approximately 1,000 CyberKnife surgeries since the hospital opened its doors.

Beacon's second medical opinion service is offered free of charge to international patients. Patients are provided advice on what is considered the best option for treatment. Beacon commonly treats brain, spine, breast, lung, colorectal, and throat and nose cancer.

Estimated pricing is available before all treatments. A PET/CT imaging package includes the scan, reports, and refreshment after the scan. For radiotherapy, the all-inclusive package includes treatment planning, doctor's procedure fees, and weekly treatment reviews.

Beacon reviews approximately 200 international patients annually. Most come from Indonesia, New Zealand, Australia, Iran, Singapore, and the UK. Most staff speak English, and translators are available for Indonesian, Persian, Hokkien, Mandarin, Cantonese, Hakka, Hindi, Punjabi, and Tamil upon request before arrival. Beacon assists international patients with arrangements for accommodations and transportation.

Leading Specialties: Oncology

Dentalpro Dental Specialist Centre
263 Jalan Maarof, Bangsar
59000 Kuala Lumpur, MALAYSIA
Tel: +603 2094.3333
Email: thedentist@dentalpro.org
Web: dentalpro.org

Dentalpro Dental Specialist Centre opened its doors in 2003 and is located within a few minutes of downtown Kuala Lumpur and 40 minutes from the international airport. Its team of 10 dental surgeons and specialists provides a wide range of dental treatments, including general dentistry. Dentalpro's principal expertise lies in restorative and cosmetic procedures.

Treatments include extractions, crowns, bridges,

implants, and veneers. More complex procedures include bone grafting, oral maxillofacial surgery, orthodontics, endodontics, and periodontics.

Dentalpro has seen international patients from more than 100 countries. Services for cross-border patients include airport pickup and drop-off (for a minimal fee), free transportation to and from hotel, assistance with dental records, and preferred price bookings at nearby partner hotels.

Languages spoken include Malay, English, Hindi, and Mandarin, with translators available on request for Arabic, Japanese, and other languages. Dentalpro is accredited by the Malaysia Society for Quality in Health, Malaysia's largest healthcare accreditation agency.

Leading Specialties: Dentistry

Gleneagles Kuala Lumpur

286 Jalan Ampang
Kuala Lumpur 50450, MALAYSIA
Tel: +603 4141.3086
Email: inquiry@gleneagleskl.com.my
Web: gleneagleskl.com.my

Opened in 1996, Gleneagles Kuala Lumpur (GKL), formerly known as Gleneagles Intan Medical Center, is located in the heart of metropolitan Kuala Lumpur. This 330-bed, tertiary-care hospital provides a complete range of medical specialties, with more than 100 physicians, state-of-the-art facilities, and multilingual staff.

Centers of excellence at GKL are the Women and Children Center, Cardiology Center, Orthopedic Center, Neurology Center, and Oncology Center. Specialized programs at GKL include the Cardiac Diagnostic and Interventional Laboratory, Health Screening Center, Endoscopy Center, Diabetes Care Center, and Women's Wellness Center.

GKL welcomes more than 15,000 international patients each year and has served patients from more than 30 countries from the US to the UK, Korea to Japan, and the Middle East to Indonesia. Its international business development department provides a broad range of assistance for the specific needs of an ever-increasing number of medical travelers.

GKL was accredited by JCI in 2010 and by the Malaysian Society for Quality in Health in 2003.

Accreditation: Joint Commission International

Leading Specialties: Cardiology and heart surgery, oncology, orthopedics, spine surgery

Gleneagles Medical Centre (Penang)

Pulau Pinang Clinic Sdn Bhd
1, Jalan Pangkor
10050 Penang, MALAYSIA
Tel: +604 2229.111
Email: enquiry@gleneaglespg.com.my
Web: gleneagles-penang.com

Established in 1973 and now a subsidiary of the giant Parkway Group Healthcare, Gleneagles Medical Centre was the first private hospital in Penang and the northern region to be awarded three years' full accreditation by the Malaysian Society for Quality in Health.

Gleneagles operates specialty centers for cardiac catheterization, cardiac diagnosis, ESWL/stone treatment, hemodialysis, hematology, oncology, transplants, minimally invasive surgery, rehabilitation, and cystoscopy/endoscopy.

Its International Patients Center offers assistance with accommodation arrangements, complimentary airport transfers (depending on availability), and making referrals and appointments.

Leading Specialties: Cardiology and heart surgery, cosmetic and reconstructive surgery, oncology

International Specialist Eye Centre Malaysia

Level 7 & 8, Centrepoint South, The Boulevard, Mid Valley City
59200 Kuala Lumpur, MALAYSIA
Tel: +603 2284.8989; +603 2284.0070
Email: lasikinfo@isec.my
Web: isec.my

Established in 2000 by a small group of internationally recognized eye specialists, the JCI-accredited International Specialist Eye Centre (ISEC) has grown into one of Southeast Asia's most popular destinations for ophthalmology. Each year ISEC conducts more than 50,000 patient consultations and performs more than 5,000 eye operations.

A staff of 14 vision specialists and five optometrists work from 15 consultations rooms, five laser suites, and four operating theaters offering patients an array of specialties, including cornea and anterior segment, cataract and intraocular lens implants, glaucoma treatment, pediatric ophthalmology, strabismus (squint) therapy, retinal diseases (medical and vitreous), LASIK and LASEK, and optometry.

ISEC sees patients from the region and around the world. The staff are fluent in English, Chinese, Bahasa Indonesia, and Tamil.

For those with travel and lighter treatments in mind, an ISEC facility in Penang re-opened in early 2014.

ISEC was awarded its initial JCI accreditation in 2009, with re-accreditation in 2012.

Accreditation: Joint Commission International

Leading Specialties: Ophthalmology

KPJ Ampang Puteri Specialist Hospital

1, Jalan Mamanda 9, Taman Dato' Ahmad Razali
68000 Ampang, Selangor Darul Ehsan, MALAYSIA
Tel: +603 4270.2500
Email: apsh@apsh.kpjhealth.com.my
Web: apsh.kpjhealth.com.my

Just five minutes from downtown Kuala Lumpur, KPJ Ampang Puteri Specialist Hospital (APSH) is one of Malaysia's leading specialist hospitals, with a long list of national and regional awards for safety and quality of care. Ampang Puteri is part of the KPJ Healthcare Group, one of the leading private healthcare providers in the region with more than 26 years of experience in the healthcare industry.

In 2009 alone, KPJ Healthcare Group facilities treated nearly 207,000 inpatients and two million outpatients. APSH, which opened in 1995 and has 230 beds, is one of five KPJ hospitals in Malaysia serving international health travelers.

APSH is a state-of-the-art private medical center with extensive diagnostic and therapeutic resources that reflect the comprehensive range of APSH's specialties. The hospital has several centers of excellence, including those dedicated to cardiology and cardiothoracic surgery, comprehensive health screenings, neurosurgery, orthopedics, and reconstructive surgery. The hospital has performed more than 15,000 reconstructive surgeries of which one-third were for patients from other countries.

In 2008 APSH opened a Pain Management Center, treating back and neck pain, trigger-point pain, myalgia, fibrositis, fibromyalgia, cancer pain, and complex regional pain syndrome.

Holistic care-based home nursing services also are available for patients recently discharged and staying within a ten-kilometer (six-mile) radius of the hospital. Emergency and outpatient services operate 24/7 and are staffed by a medical officer and teams of experienced nurses and aides.

APSH received its most recent JCI accreditation in 2012.

Accreditation: Joint Commission International

Leading Specialties: Cardiology, and heart surgery cosmetic and reconstructive surgery, orthopedics, spine surgery, weight loss surgery

KPJ Damansara Specialist Hospital

119, Jalan SS20/10, Damansara Utama
47400 Petaling Jaya
Selangor Darul Ehsan, MALAYSIA
Tel: +603 7722.2692
Email: dsh@dsh.kpjhealth.com.my
Web: kpjdamansara.com

KPJ Damansara Specialist Hospital (DSH) is conveniently located in an upscale area of Kuala Lumpur that has become a center for expatriates and young urban executives. The 158-bed hospital offers an array of centers of excellence focusing on severe obesity, oncology, health promotion and wellness, neurosurgery, orthopedics and joint replacement, ophthalmology, and cardiac medicine.

KPJ Damansara offers extensive diagnostic and therapeutic resources, such as endoscopic suites, hemodialysis centers, cardiac catheterization, and MRI facilities. Its medical specialists hold international qualifications and are supported by a well-trained paramedical staff.

In 2006 KPJ Damansara opened an Obesity Specialty Center, the first of its kind in Malaysia and Southeast Asia, dedicated to helping significantly obese patients through surgical and nonsurgical procedures.

The hospital's Premier Screening and Wellness Center offers a comprehensive array of health assessment packages that can be tailored to meet individual needs for maintaining overall health and well-being. Packages include basic and premier general executive screenings as well as Premier Well Man and Well Woman Heart Screening packages, all conducted by professional wellness experts who ensure treatment is provided in a setting of confidence, personalized attention, and privacy.

Accreditation: Joint Commission International

Leading Specialties: Health screening, oncology, ophthalmology, weight loss surgery

National Heart Institute

145 Jalan Tun Razak
Kuala Lumpur 50400, MALAYSIA
Tel: +603 2600.6336; +603 2600.6337
Email: info@ijn.com.my
Web: ijn.com.my

Institut Jantung Negara (IJN), also known as the National Heart Institute, is Malaysia's premier heart center and the national referral center for cardiovascular disease, treating adult and pediatric patients from all over the country and abroad.

Established in 1992, IJN is an integrated, one-stop center for comprehensive cardiology care and cardiothoracic surgery. Its variety of treatment options range from surgery for a hole in the heart to transplantation for complex heart failure. Post-treatment, the institute's complete rehabilitation programs incorporate physical and emotional support and dietary counseling.

IJN is affiliated with Papworth Hospital NHS Foundation Trust, Cambridge, England; Kansai University Medical Center, Osaka, Japan; the Heart and Diabetes Center, Bad Oeynhausen, Germany; Hanoi Heart Center, Vietnam; Liverpool John Moores University, England; and the University of South Australia, Adelaide.

IJN's team of physicians has introduced innovations in interventional procedures for diagnosis and treatment as well as in surgeries. The array of

cardiovascular and thoracic procedures performed includes electrophysiology; endoscopic vein harvesting; angiogram and angioplasty via radial artery; multi-slice computed tomography (MSCT); calcium scoring and coronary angiogram; minimally invasive surgery; off-pump surgery; "awake" bypass surgery; automatic internal defibrillator implantation; stent implantation; and implantation of a heart-assist device as a bridge to transplantation for heart failure patients.

The institute also offers heart screening and executive screening programs with emphasis on the prevention of heart disease. Doctors discuss the findings with the patient within one day and provide a comprehensive report usually within two weeks.

IJN recently established an International Patient Center offering visa and immigration assistance (including visa extensions if necessary); medical coordination (including pre-departure and post-treatment consultation, assistance with medical devices, and special therapies); assistance with bill estimation; fund transfers; insurance claims; and transfer of medical records.

Accreditation: Joint Commission International

Leading Specialties: Cardiology and heart surgery

Nilai Medical Centre

PT 13717, Jalan BBN 2/1
71800 Nilai, Negeri Sembilan
Darul Khusus, MALAYSIA
Tel: +606 8500.999; +606 7990.999
Email: enquiry@nilaimc.com
Web: nilaimc.com

Nilai Medical Centre (NMC) first opened in 1999 as Nilai Cancer Institute, focusing on clinical research. In 2013 the hospital was renamed Nilai Medical Centre and has become one of Malaysia's leading cancer treatment facilities. The 86-bed hospital treats not only cancer but also other specialties, including bariatrics and weight management, orthopedics, otolaryngology (ear, nose, and throat surgery), and interventional radiology.

Nilai's NCI Cancer Center and NCI Clinical Research Center treat patients, using immunotherapy, including cell and vaccine therapy. NMC's doctors

tend to favor treating patients with minimally invasive surgery and other less invasive strategies for
certain procedures, including removal of uterine fi-
broida, thyroid surgery, appendectomy, breast lump
removal, discectomy, nucleoplasty, knee meniscus
repair, anterior cruciate ligament reconstruction,
shoulder arthroscopic repair, ovarian cyst removal,
and tubal ligation

NMC's International Patient Center offers appointment scheduling with specialist consultants,
free pickup and drop-off at Kuala Lumpur International Airport or KTM Train Station, assistance with
financial arrangements, travel arrangements from
home country, specially prepared meals upon request, coordination of day trips and tours, and translation services.

Leading Specialties: Oncology, orthopedics,
weight loss surgery

Pantai Hospital Kuala Lumpur
8, Jalan Bukit Pantai
Kuala Lumpur 59100, MALAYSIA
Tel: +603 2296.0888
Email: phkl@pantai.com.my
Web: pantai.com.my

Pantai Hospital Kuala Lumpur (PHKL) is owned by the
giant Pantai Group, which operates nine hospitals
throughout Malaysia. More than 14,400 foreign
patients journeyed to Pantai Hospitals in 2013,
making it one of Malaysia's top destinations for international health travel. Prices are advertised as about
50 percent lower than in the US, Europe, Australia,
and Hong Kong.

The Pantai Group maintains overseas referral
offices in Indonesia and Vietnam to facilitate patient
inquiries. Pantai has forged relationships with a
dozen insurance providers worldwide, including
Prudential/Cigna and Bupa.

Established in 1974 in the heart of Kuala Lumpur,
PHKL is Pantai's flagship hospital, with 292 beds and
more than 130 specialists. A general hospital, PHKL
offers nearly every type of diagnostic and treatment, including specialties in urology, cardiology,
orthopedics, gastroenterology, endocrinology, and
ophthalmology.

The Pantai Executive Screening program is a
comprehensive medical examination for early detection of common disorders, such as hypertension,
diabetes mellitus, and heart disease. Through these
tests, doctors can detect abnormalities in the heart,
lungs, liver, kidneys, and urinary tract.

Centers of excellence within the Pantai Group
focus on oncology, cardiology and cardiothoracic
surgery, orthopedics, obstetrics and gynecology,
urology, neurology and neurosurgery, cosmetic and
reconstructive surgery, gastroenterology, and pain
management. PHKL's Hemodialysis Unit provides
inpatient and outpatient treatment for chronic and
acute kidney ailments.

Pantai in Kuala Lumpur received its JCI accreditation in 2009.

Accreditation: Joint Commission International

Leading Specialties: Cardiology and heart surgery,
endocrinology, health screening, orthopedics,
ophthalmology, urology

Prince Court Medical Centre
39 Jalan Kia Pong
Kuala Lumpur 50450, MALAYSIA
Tel: +603 2160.0000
Email: ibl2@princecourt.com
Web: princecourt.com

Forbes named Prince Court Medical Centre
(PCMC) one of its 10 best destinations for medical
travel—and with good reason. Affiliated with the
Medical University of Vienna, PCMC opened its doors
in 2006 with over a million square feet of floor space.
Funded by Petronas, Malaysia's largest petroleum
company, this 277-bed facility offers the atmosphere
and service of a five-star hotel, with several food and
beverage outlets, a florist, a pharmacy, and free Wi-Fi
in every room.

International patients, including expatriates,
make up 25–30 percent of the total patient count
at Prince Court. That percentage grows even
larger—approaching 50 percent—for health screenings and checkups. Most international patients are
from Indonesia, the Middle East, Bangladesh, and
Africa. Top treatments include various cancer

treatments, hip and knee replacements, robotic-assisted surgery, heart surgery, and women's health.

Key clinical services include burn management, gastroenterology, interventional cardiology, nephrology, occupational health, orthopedics, and rehabilitation.

Leading Specialties: Cardiology and heart surgery, cosmetic and reconstructive surgery, fertility and reproductive medicine, health screening, nephrology, orthopedics

Ramsay Sime Darby Ara Damansara Medical Centre

Lot 2, Jalan Lapangan Terbang Subang
Seksyen U2, 40150 Shah Alam
Selangor Darul Ehsan, MALAYSIA
Tel: +603 5639.1212
Email: healthcare@simedarby.com
Web: ramsaysimedarby.asia

Opened in 2012, Ara Damansara Medical Centre (ADMC) is a full-service, 220-bed hospital with a wide array of specialties and three centers of excellence dedicated to the diagnosis and treatment of heart, brain, spine, and joint diseases. Located in Selangor, 20 minutes outside Kuala Lumpur and 45 minutes from Kuala Lumpur International Airport, ADMC offers cutting-edge diagnostic and treatment technologies and a sophisticated hospital management information system.

ADMC's Brain Center features a full range of treatments and services designed to meet the needs of adult and pediatric patients with brain and nervous system disorders. The center offers sophisticated technologies that enhance early diagnosis and treatment of stroke, brain tumor, epilepsy, dementia, migraines, sleep disorders, neuromuscular diseases, and other neurological disorders. The center uses a Flash Dual-Source CT scanner to provide high-definition images with the lowest possible radiation exposure.

The Heart Center provides a full spectrum of services in the diagnosis and treatment of cardiovascular diseases for adults and children, specializing in congenital heart disease, coronary artery disease, irregular heartbeat, palpitations, and heart failures. In addition to interventional cardiology, treatments

offered include radiofrequency ablation, permanent pacemaker insertion, cardiothoracic surgeries, and cardiac rehabilitation, as well as psychological and nutritional counseling.

ADMC's Spine and Joint Center uses advanced medical technology in combination with a dedicated team of doctors and medical professionals to offer a holistic approach to the diagnosis and treatment of spine and joint diseases. The center provides a wide range of specialized services, such as minimally invasive spinal surgeries and computer-assisted total joint replacements. The center is complemented by a fully equipped rehabilitation facility, including a hydrotherapy pool. Rehabilitative services are tailored to meet the needs of each patient and support the best possible treatment outcome.

The full-service Health Screening Center supports Malaysia's long-standing reputation for preventive health offerings, with comprehensive executive health checks that detect abnormalities early and enable clinicians to stop the possible progression of disease. Screenings include general, men's, women's, cardiac, and digestive.

The team at the Medical Coordination Unit (MCU) serves as the first contact for international patients seeking care at ADMC. Services include appointment scheduling, assistance with travel arrangements and visas, accommodation arrangements at special rates, airport pickup and drop-off, medical referrals, and translation for a variety of languages. The MCU team can also help to arrange for in-country medical concierge services to accompany patients from arrival at the airport through check-in at the pre-arranged hotel.

MCU staff helps convert visa on arrival status for international patients entering Malaysia for emergency medical treatment and helps expedite approvals for visa extensions. Staff at the center also help patients plan a relaxing recovery vacation at any Malaysian destination.

Leading Specialties: Cardiology and heart surgery, health screening, neurology and spine surgery, orthopedics

Ramsay Sime Darby Subang Jaya Medical Centre

1, Jalan SS 12/1A, 47500 Subang Jaya
Selangor Darul Ehsan, MALAYSIA
Tel: +603 5639.1666
Email: sdhipc@simedarby.com
Web: ramsaysimedarby.asia

Established in 1985 in the heart of the Subang Jaya district in Selangor, the Subang Jaya Medical Centre (SJMC) is the area's largest provider of healthcare. This tertiary-care hospital, with 393 beds and 14 operating theaters, has a staff of 170 physicians and surgeons and 650 nurses, all of whom speak English, as well as other languages, including Mandarin, Japanese, Korean, Arabic, and Spanish.

Offering all major specialties, the hospital management and staff pride themselves on the use of revolutionary medical technologies and their international reputation for clinical excellence. As a result, SJMC is among the top referred hospitals of choice in Malaysia for blood and marrow transplants, cancer treatment, computed-assisted joint replacement, comprehensive epilepsy management, and minimally invasive surgeries.

SJMC averages 1,500 outpatients and 100 inpatients each day, with more than 5,000 international patients treated each year (3,600 from Japan; 1,200 from European nations; and 300 from US, Canada, and Australia).

SJMC leads the country in development of expertise for some of the most advanced medical procedures. In 1985 the hospital was the site of Malaysia's first open-heart surgery. In 1995 it performed its first liver transplants on pediatric patients, its first stem cell transplant in 1999, its first adult bone marrow transplant in 2000, its first pediatric bone marrow transplant in 2002, and its first awake craniotomy in 2009.

SJMC's Nuclear Medicine and PET/CT Center is a major regional referral center for cardiology, endocrinology, neurology, and oncology. The Vascular and Interventional Radiology Center combines a specialized branch of radiology with new catheterization and imaging technologies to enable precise diagnosis and minimally invasive treatment of blood vessel disorders and diseases of the internal organs. Accident, emergency, and outpatient services operate 24/7 and are staffed by a medical officer and teams of experienced nurses.

A 2013 merger with Australia's Ramsay Health Care expands the hospital network into Indonesia, with plans for additional facilities in Vietnam, China, and Myanmar. Subang Jaya Medical Centre remains the flagship hospital within the network.

Accreditation: Joint Commission International

Leading Specialties: Cardiology and heart surgery, cosmetic and reconstructive surgery, fertility and reproductive medicine, health screening, neurology and spine surgery, oncology, orthopedics, weight loss surgery

Smile Arts Dental Clinic

No. 55-1, Jalan PJU 5/20 The Strand Kota Damansara
47810 Petaling Jaya
Selangor, MALAYSIA
Tel: +603 6142.6055; +601 2964.8830
Email: smileartsclinic@gmail.com
Web: smileartsdentistmalaysia.com

Established in 2012 and located 30 minutes from Kuala Lumpur, Smile Arts Dental Clinic logs approximately 1,200 patient visits per year. Its five main specialties are cosmetic dentistry (porcelain veneer and teeth whitening), prosthodontics (crown and bridge), endodontics (root canal treatment), implants, and general dentistry. The most frequently performed procedures are root canal treatments, crowns and bridges, porcelain veneers, and fillings.

Other dental services available at Smile Arts include oral hygiene counseling; scaling and prophylaxis; application of dental sealants (cavity prevention); fluoride treatments; re-contouring and bonding; whitening; veneers (porcelain and composite); extractions; removal of cysts; braces; periodontal screening; surgical and nonsurgical periodontal treatment (root planning, flap surgery); implants; and construction and fitting of bite guard appliances.

Approximately 120 international patients, including both expatriates and tourists, are treated annually at this clinic.

Leading Specialties: Dentistry

Patient Experience

Debra M., New Zealand

In searching the internet for alternatives to high-priced cosmetic surgeries at home, Debra located information directing her to KPJ's Ampang Puteri Specialist Hospital for cosmetic surgical procedures. Realizing the package price was approximately one-third what she would pay for the procedures in her home country, Debra decided to combine a nose job, breast implants, facelift, neck lift, brow lift, and eye-bag removal with a holiday in Malaysia. Debra spent about US$16,000 for a package that would have cost her two and one-half times more in New Zealand.

"I was looking for affordable treatments, but I didn't want to compromise on quality. I found this to be the obvious choice. I feel like I've undergone a renewal, and I'm very happy with the results."

Debra plans to use her transformation to promote the same services to her family and friends. "They can't wait to see the new me, and I'm looking forward to telling them about the whole trip." ■

DESTINATION: **MEXICO**

■ AT A GLANCE

Cancun, Los Algodones, Mexico City, Monterrey, Puerto Vallarta, Tijuana

Languages	Spanish, some English
Time Zones	GMT –6, GMT –5
Country Dialing Code	+52
Electricity	127V, Plug type A
Currency	Mexican peso (MXN)
Leading Specialties	Cardiology and heart surgery, cosmetic and reconstructive surgery, dentistry, oncology, orthopedics, weight loss surgery
Typical Savings (over USD retail)	40%–60%
Standards and Affiliations	Mexican Academy of Dermatology; Mexican Academy of Neurology; Mexican Association of Neurological Surgery; Mexican Association of Plastic, Reconstructive, and Aesthetic Surgery; National Institute of Public Health of Mexico
International Accreditation	American Association for Accreditation of Ambulatory Surgery Facilities; Joint Commission International

■ TREATMENT BRIEF

Since research began on the first edition of *Patients Beyond Borders*, Mexico has made great strides in healthcare. No longer known only for border-town dentistry and cosmetic surgery, Mexico has in recent years come into its own as a global healthcare hub, offering patients an array of specialties and procedures that now begin to rival its competitor nations in Asia.

Although estimates vary widely, researchers place the number of patients traveling to Mexico between 200,000 and one million, with undocumented Hispanics returning home for care forming much of the discrepancy.

The lion's share of medical travelers to Mexico are regional—from Texas, Nevada, Arizona, and Southern California—seeking easy access to affordable dental care and cosmetic surgery. Patients from Canada and the UK are also drawn to the region because of the lack of waiting times and the lure of the warm waters of the Pacific and Gulf of Mexico.

With new facilities and services has come increased international recognition. In 2006 Mexico had no JCI-accredited facilities; in 2013 it had eight.

Some medical institutions in Mexico have cross-border ties and operate as part of larger international conglomerates. For example, Christus Muguerza Alta Especialidad is now part of CHRISTUS Health in the US, a group serving eight US states, mostly along the US-Mexican border. The merger has made Christus Muguerza the largest healthcare provider in Mexico.

■ MEXICO AND MEDICAL TRAVEL

Other hospitals in Mexico enjoy affiliation with major educational institutions. Hospital San José Tec de Monterrey, for example, is sponsored by the internationally recognized Tecnológico de Monterrey, a premiere educational institution that boasts more than 18,000 full-time students and operates 32 campuses across Mexico. Through its medical school, Center for Biotechnology, and Center for Innovation and Technology Transfer, Tecnológico de Monterrey educates health professionals while developing new models for clinical care and research.

Not all of Mexico's medical offerings are in major medical centers. Mexico-bound health travelers often seek out smaller clinics run by two or three physicians, some of them second- and even third-generation family enterprises. Unassuming yet clean and efficient, these clinics are often led by either expatriate US physicians or practitioners trained in the US or Europe. Such clinics reliably treat tens of thousands of medical travelers each year, with many of their patients returning annually for checkups, dental cleanings, and a host of other treatments that can be had far less expensively than in the US, Europe, and even many Asian countries.

■ SOME CAUTIONS

While the unrest related to Mexico's drug trade appears to be calming, stories of drug-cartel violence in Mexico persist. Is Mexico safe for the medical traveler? The short answer is yes, if you use your head and follow the new rules of the road. Trust only established travel service providers. Don't head off on your own. Don't rent cars or take your own tours. Use only official taxis. Use guides and tour leaders recommended by your hospital's international patient staff. Stay in a well-regarded international hotel. Ask the concierge there to arrange transportation and sightseeing for you. Before travel, check advisories about unrest in destinations of choice. Exercise the usual cautions when in country.

Although quality clinics are located in nearly every major city and resort in Mexico, finding a

good one can be frustrating. Many websites remain in Spanish, and English-speaking physicians are not always available, nor are translation services. In smaller Mexican clinics, the health traveler is likely to encounter fewer English speakers than in Malaysia or Thailand, tens of thousands of miles away. Unless you're fluent in Spanish, you may want to enlist the assistance of a good health travel agency when arranging care in Mexico.

These challenges aside, geographical convenience is the big motivation for many Mexico-bound health travelers who reside in North, Central, and South America, and the Caribbean. More than 70 percent of Mexico's US patients travel from the border states of California, Texas, and Arizona. Nearby patients from San Diego, Los Angeles, Phoenix, Tucson, Dallas, and Houston make the two- to six-hour trek across the border to their clinic of choice, stay a night or two in a hotel, and then drive back. As one veteran cross-border patient commented, "A three-hour drive across the border saves me US$700 in physicals and dental work every year. That's a no-brainer."

■ SELECTED HOSPITALS AND CLINICS

Alamo Dental Clinic
Suite #3, 167 Alamo Alley
Los Algodones, MEXICO
Tel: +52 658 517.3304; 866 973.7360 (US toll free)
Email: info@alamodentalgroup.org
Web: alamodentalgroup.org

Located in Los Algodones, Mexico, only seven miles west of Yuma, Arizona, Alamo offers specialty services in endodontics, periodontics, and implants, as well as the full range of general dentistry services. The clinics four treatment rooms are staffed by four Mexican-educated dentists and two dental assistants, all of whom can be emailed directly using their personal addresses on the clinic's website. Most Alamo employees speak both Spanish and English.

Alamo advertises savings of 75 percent or more on standard dental services. Specially priced procedures include crowns (metal or porcelain starting at us$220 to gold at us$550), implants (starting at $1,500), extractions (starting at $50), and root canals (starting at $200). Prices on partial dentures begin at $500.

Consultations are free, and appointment times are flexible.

Leading Specialties: Dentistry

La Casa del Diente

Avenida Revolucion 3780, L-1 Colonia Torremolinos
Monterrey, Nuevo Leon 64850, MEXICO
Tel: +52 818 348.5500
Email: cvillarreal.lcdd@gmail.com
Web: lacasadeldiente.com

La Casa del Diente comprises six clinics in the Monterrey metropolitan area. Established in 1984, "the Home of Teeth" has 110 certified dentists and dental surgeons. The clinic welcomes some 24,000 patients every year, of which 130 are international (110 of them from the US and Canada).

Most frequently performed procedures include cosmetic treatments, dental implants, and porcelain veneers. Notably, the dentists there use a computer-controlled anesthesia wand, eliminating the need for syringes. Most of the dentists and staff members speak English. Special packages for medical travelers include treatment, accommodations, transfers, and the services of a bilingual assistant.

Leading Specialties: Dentistry

Cosmed

Vida-Calle Brasilia #1, Col. El Paraíso
Tijuana, B.C. 22106, MEXICO
Tel: +52 664 608.6464; 877 235.1968 (US toll free)
Email: cosmed@cosmedclinic.com
Web: cosmedclinic.com

Despite its relatively small size, Cosmed is among Mexico's most respected cosmetic surgery clinics, with its six surgeons seeing more than 400 international patients monthly for consultations and surgery.

Surgical and non-surgical treatments for women include weight loss plastic surgery; facial rejuvenation (cheek and chin enhancements, collagen injections, facelifts); cosmetic dermatology (chemical peels, dermabrasion, laser skin resurfacing, and wrinkle and scar improvement); body contouring (breast enlargement, lift, and reduction, buttock implants, ultrasonic liposuction, tummy tucks, and spider vein therapy); and hair transplants.

Procedures for men include weight loss plastic surgery; facial rejuvenation (face and neck lifts, brow and eye lifts, rhinoplasty, chin liposuction, Botox); body enhancement (abdominal etching, pectoral implants, lower body lifts, liposculpture); and hair transplants.

Cosmed's surgeons are board certified, with training or certification in the US. Cosmed is a member of the American Society of Aesthetic Plastic Surgery, the International Society of Aesthetic Plastic Surgery, and the San Diego Plastic Surgery Society. Cosmed is one of the only cosmetic surgery clinics in Latin America accredited by the American Association for Accreditation of Ambulatory Surgery Facilities International.

A partnership with Recovery Boutique, a hotel adjacent to Cosmed, allows patients to recuperate nearby with immediate access to doctors. A 24/7 nurse staff attends to patients post-op.

Accreditation: American Association for Accreditation of Ambulatory Surgery Facilities International

Leading Specialties: Cosmetic and reconstructive surgery

Dentalia

Durango no 263 Piso 9 Col. Roma Norte. Del Cuauhtemoc
Mexico D.F. 06700, MEXICO
Tel: +52 552 623.2323; 855 282.4912 (US toll free)
Email: info@dentalia.com
Web: en.dentalia.com

With 42 clinics in 12 cities throughout Mexico, Dentalia is the largest chain of dental clinics in the country. All are located in shopping malls and are open seven days a week. Specialties include cosmetic dentistry, dental implants, restorative dentistry, endodontics (root canal treatment), dental surgery, periodontics, orthodontics (braces), and a special kid-friendly program for pediatric dentistry.

All clinics are managed directly by Dentalia and are not franchises. The network has treated more than 100,000 patients since opening its doors.

Dentalia's international patient services are focused in four cities: Tijuana, Playa del Carmen, Mexico City, and Guadalajara. Services include pickup at the airport and at hotels. All dental providers speak both Spanish and English; interpreters for other languages are available if needed. Dentalia offers dental travelers a free diagnosis and tentative quote before travel.

The website features live chat and a price list.

Leading Specialties: Dentistry

Dentaris

Av Tulum #232 int 5C, SM 4, Cancun
Quintana Roo, MEXICO
Tel: +52 998 887.2579; +1 504 324.1490 (US)
Email: info@dentaris.com.mx
Web: dentaris.com.mx

Established in Cancun in 1992, Dentaris's offices expanded in 2003 to nearby Playa del Carmen. Clinics are staffed with five practicing dentists at each location.

Specialties include cosmetic dentistry and prosthodontics, implant dentistry, endodontics (including root canals), pediatric dentistry, orthodontics (including dental braces), and restorative dentistry. English is spoken by all the dentists, and translators are available for French, German, and Italian, for additional fees. Both clinics offer discounts and are partnered with numerous hotels in these two popular beach resorts. Dentaris provides complimentary transportation to and from the airport and hotel.

Dentaris maintains memberships with the American Dental Association, American Academy of Cosmetic Dentistry, American Academy of Implant Dentistry, and the International Congress of Oral Implantologists.

Each clinic welcomes around 2,000 patients annually.

Leading Specialties: Dentistry

Hospital Angeles Tijuana

Avenida Paseo de los Heroes #10999, Zona Río
Tijuana, Baja California 22010, MEXICO
Tel: +52 664 635.1900; +1 866 668.9263 (US toll free)
Email: info@angeleshealth.com
Web: angeleshealth.com

Hospital Angeles Tijuana is a subsidiary of Grupo Angeles, which owns Angeles Health, Mexico's largest private hospital network, including 23 hospitals, more than 2,000 beds, and 11,000 physicians. The five-story Hospital Angeles hosts 97 patient rooms and 12 operating theaters in addition to specialty operating areas.

Hospital Angeles Tijuana has more than 120 specialist physicians, most of whom have completed fellowships or are board certified in the US or Europe. Specialties and procedures include weight loss (gastric bypass surgery, gastric band surgery); oncology; stem cell therapy; CCSVI treatment; dental surgery; and orthopedics (hip replacement, hip resurfacing).

The facility is an hour drive from San Diego and around three hours from Los Angeles.

Leading Specialties: Cardiology and heart surgery, cosmetic and reconstructive surgery, oncology, orthopedics, weight loss surgery

Hospital San José Tec de Monterrey

Avenida Ignacio Morones Prieto #3000 Pte.,
Colonia Los Doctores
Monterrey, Nuevo Leon 64710, MEXICO
Tel: +52 818 389.8390; 866 475.6334 (US toll free)
Email: international@hsj.com.mx
Web: hsj.com.mx

Founded in 1969 and only 150 miles from the US border, Hospital San José Tec de Monterrey is a comprehensive medical specialty campus with five internationally recognized centers in cardiology, oncology, neuroscience, organ transplantation, and liver disease.

San José Tec has 200 beds (11 master suites and 96 junior suites in tower), 38 ICU beds, and 21 emergency beds. More than 1,500 affiliated physicians and about 500 nurses treat approximately 15,000 inpatients and 92,000 outpatients annually, including 1,400 international patients (800 from the US and Canada).

The affiliated Zambrano Hellion Medical Center opened in 2010, with centers for oncology, cardiology, and vascular medicine. The Salvador Sada Gomez Center for Geriatrics and Alzheimer's disease combines research, teaching, and patient care. Tecnologico de Monterrey School of Medicine has reciprocal training programs with Johns Hopkins Medicine and Baylor College of Medicine in Houston.

Leading Specialties: Cardiology and heart surgery, oncology, spine surgery, weight loss surgery

Imagen Dental

Avenida Gonzalitos #3036 Norte, Col. Mitras Norte
Monterrey, Nuevo Leon, MEXICO
Tel: +52 818 370.1415
Email: patients@imagendental.com
Web: imagendental.com/english

Despite its name, Imagen Dental does more than dentistry. In business since 1994, Imagen has 19 clinics (18 in Monterrey and one in Nuevo Laredo) and more than 200 physicians and surgeons who provide comprehensive dental, optical (glasses and lenses), and auditory (hearing aid) services. Eye surgeries are performed in the operating rooms of JCI-accredited Christus Muguerza Hospital.

Most of Imagen's dental work is cosmetic and includes implants, veneers, crowns, bridges, gum surgeries, and root canals. Imagen uses digital x-ray system, which emits 80 percent less radiation than traditional radiology. The dental clinics employ patient education systems in both English and Spanish and an intraoral camera to show patients pictures and videos of their mouths and teeth.

Tailored to the needs of the medical traveler, Imagen's audiology laboratory can deliver a hearing aid in two days.

Leading Specialties: Dentistry

Just Smiles

Basilio Badillo 311
Col. Emiliano Zapata
Puerto Vallarta, Jalisco 48380, MEXICO
Tel: +52 322 223.0505; +1 213 291.2369 (US)
Email: atencionaclientes@justsmiles.com.mx
Web: justsmiles.com.mx

Established in 1987 in central Puerto Vallarta, Just Smiles has eight dentists who specialize in cosmetic and restorative dentistry, periodontics, orthodontics, and general dentistry. All Just Smiles doctors and hygienists speak English. French is also spoken (check with clinic for details).

Just Smiles reports 85 percent of its patients are international, mostly from the United States and Canada. An impressive roster of case studies includes a male model in New York and a voice instructor in Chicago; both underwent extensive dental restoration.

Initial dental examinations are free, and financing is available.

Leading Specialties: Dentistry

Tijuana Clinic for Cosmetic Dentistry

Torre Zentrum Dr. Atl 2084 Suite 308 Zona Río
Tijuana, MEXICO
Tel: +52 664 634 2276; +1 619 971.2297 (US)
Email: tdentalspa@gmail.com
Web: tccdentistry.com

Tijuana Clinic for Cosmetic Dentistry is located in an upscale office facility in the Zona Río district of Tijuana, just a short distance from the US border crossing at San Ysidro. This busy practice employs specialists in endodontics, oral surgery, periodontics, and orthodontics.

Its director, Dr. Shirley Baker, maintains active memberships in the American Dental Association, the American Cosmetic Dental Association, and the Academy of General Dentistry. Dr. Baker graduated third in her class, with honors and distinction, from the National Autonomous University of Mexico, sometimes lauded as the Harvard of Latin America.

Dental travelers will find a full range of dental services there, including fillings; Zoom2 bleaching; braces; implants; root canal therapy; bridges; partial and full dentures; simple and complicated extractions; treatment of gum disease; and crowns, bonding, veneers, and Lumineers (a brand-name veneer that is thinner and requires little to no removal of the tooth structure).

This clinic provides a pickup service at the Mexico–US border crossing, and the telephone contact number is a San Diego area code—convenient and inexpensive for US-based dental travelers.

Prospective patients can request a free personalized quote. Also free to those who bring a friend are transportation to and from the border, Wi-Fi, and teeth cleaning.

The clinic runs monthly specials. Reduced prices are advertised on the website.

Leading Specialties: Dentistry

DESTINATION: **SINGAPORE**

■ AT A GLANCE

Singapore City

Languages	English, Mandarin, some Malay and Bahasa Indonesian
Time Zone	GMT +8
Country Dialing Code	+65
Electricity	230V, plug type G
Currency	Singapore dollar (SGD)
Leading Specialties	Cardiology and heart surgery, cosmetic and reconstructive surgery, fertility and reproductive medicine, health screening, neurology and spine surgery, oncology, ophthalmology, orthopedics, stem cell and regenerative therapy, transplant, weight loss surgery, wellness and prevention
Typical Savings (over USD retail)	25%–40%
Standards and Affiliations	Optometrists and Opticians Board; Singapore Dental Council; Singapore Medical Council; Singapore Ministry of Health; Singapore Nursing Board; Traditional Chinese Medicine Practitioners Board; Specialists Accreditation Board
International Accreditation	Joint Commission International

■ TREATMENT BRIEF

By nearly any measure, Singapore is a leader in world healthcare. Its well-established health system is composed of 12 private hospitals, eight government hospitals, and several specialist clinics—14 are JCI accredited. The Health Manpower Development program, sponsored by the Ministry of Health, sends Singapore doctors to the best medical centers around the world, and they return bringing with them a quality of services to match international standards.

Singapore's healthcare system is consistently ranked among the world's leading—usually higher ranked by far than the US or Canada and most EU countries. Singapore has one of the lowest infant and maternal mortality rates in the world. As of 2011, life expectancy averages 81.9 years; males live an

average of 79.6 years and females, 84.3 years.

A joint venture with Duke University Medical School has created the Duke–NUS Medical School, based in Singapore, which has admitted hundreds of post-baccalaureate students into its research-oriented, four-year medical school program. Students attend this global initiative from National University of Singapore; Peking University; Chinese University in Hong Kong; University of Mumbai; and Oxford, Cambridge, Yale, Duke, and Harvard universities. Many of the best graduates remain in Singapore to establish their own practices.

■ SINGAPORE AND MEDICAL TRAVEL

Inbound patients are critical to keeping specialists employed in a nation of only five and a half million.

Through aggressive regional and international promotion, Singapore welcomes around 550,000 health travelers annually, mostly from nearby Indonesia, Philippines, and Australia, although increasingly from North America and the EU. Nearly every specialty and sub-specialty is offered to international patients, including cardiovascular, orthopedics and sports medicine, oncology, neurology, reproductive medicine, and cosmetic surgery.

In 2003 the government of Singapore launched the Singapore Medicine Initiative to develop and maintain Singapore as a top medical travel destination and to consolidate its considerable medical offerings. Research partnerships with US universities, such as Johns Hopkins, along with formal relationships with GlaxoSmithKline and Novartis, underscore Singapore's sustained commitment to cutting-edge healthcare.

Singapore as a medical destination is uniquely supported by a multi-faceted medical hub, with research and development, medical conferences and training, pharmaceutical and medical device manufacturing, and headquartering of multi-national healthcare corporations.

Health travelers enjoy the widespread use of English as the preferred business language. Because Singapore is one of Asia's wealthiest nations and has Southeast Asia's highest standard of living, medical travelers are spared the cultural and economic contrasts sometimes experienced in India, Central American, and South America. An ultra-modern skyline reflects a true city-state megalopolis, shopper's paradise, and, more recently, tourist attraction (ResortsWorld Singapore on nearby Sentosa Island offers a newly opened Universal Studios theme park, casinos, and the world's largest aquarium).

Still, Singapore remains one of Asia's more expensive medical travel stops, catering increasingly to patrons from adjacent countries, mainland China, the Middle East, Europe, and Africa who are seeking higher quality care and willing to pay for it.

■ SELECTED HOSPITALS AND CLINICS

Changi General Hospital

2 Simei Street 3
529889 SINGAPORE
Tel: +65 6788.8833
Email: international@cgh.com.sg
Web: www.cgh.com.sg

Changi General Hospital is only 10 minutes from Singapore International Airport. With 790 beds, it offers a comprehensive range of medical, surgical, and paramedical specialties and serves as a medical center for international travelers. Specialties featured for international patients include accident and emergency, otolaryngology, orthopedic surgery, breast surgery, gastroenterology, respiratory medicine, cardiology, general surgery, sports medicine/sports orthopedics, dermatology, health screening, and urology.

The hospital has received awards for its use of advanced information technology to improve patient care. It has been JCI accredited since 2005.

Accreditation: Joint Commission International

Leading Specialties: Cardiology and heart surgery, health screenings, orthopedics

Gleneagles Hospital Singapore

6A Napier Road
258500 SINGAPORE
Tel: +65 6575.7575
Email: gpac@parkway.sg
Web: gleneagles.com.sg/en/

Established in 1957, Gleneagles Hospital is now owned by the giant Parkway Pantai Group Healthcare network. This 272-bed, private, acute-care hospital with more than 300 specialists provides an extensive range of medical and surgical services and has achieved Singapore Quality Class certification.

Gleneagles is a leading center for the care and treatment of cardiac patients. It is also a regional referral center with strong technology resources for imaging and robotic-assisted surgery. Gleneagles was the first hospital in Southeast Asia to use a robotic-assisted SurgiScope for neurosurgery; spinal surgery; and ear, nose, and throat surgeries.

Parkway Healthcare set up the Asian Center for Liver Diseases and Transplantation (ACLDT) at Gleneagles in 1994. ACLDT is the first private center in Asia dedicated to the treatment of all types of liver diseases, including liver cancer, hepatitis, alcoholic cirrhosis, and pediatric liver diseases. Gleneagles was the first hospital in Southeast Asia to perform a living-donor liver transplant.

Other Gleneagles specialties include cancer treatment, cardiology, cardiothoracic and vascular surgery, gastroenterology and hepatology, hematology, lithotripsy (shock waves to break up kidney stones), neuroscience, oral and maxillofacial surgery, neonatology, obstetrics and gynecology, ophthalmology, orthopedics, pediatrics, sports and exercise medicine, and urology.

Gleneagles welcomes the medical traveler, with 35 international patient assistant centers worldwide. Most physicians and staff are fluent in English and Mandarin, with interpreters available for Arabic, Bahasa Indonesia, Bengali, Burmese, Cambodian, Hindi, Russian, Urdu, and Vietnamese. Gleneagles was awarded its initial JCI accreditation in 2006, with re-accreditations in 2009 and most recently in 2012.

Accreditation: Joint Commission International

Leading Specialties: Cardiology and heart surgery, fertility and reproductive medicine, oncology, orthopedics, spine surgery

Healthway Medical Group

2 Leng Kee Road, #02-07
159086 SINGAPORE
Tel: +65 6323.4415
Email: care@healthwaymedical.com
Web: healthwaymedical.com

Healthway Medical Group (HMG) operates the largest network of private general practice and specialty clinics in Singapore. Focused on family medicine, health screening, specialist services, and aesthetics, HMG opened a centralized international patient services center in 1995, giving patients access to a wide array of facility resources and affiliated specialists.

Through its service center, HMG serves more than 4,000 international patients each year by making medical referrals and appointments, providing assistance with travel arrangements, and offering translation and local support services. English is spoken everywhere in Singapore, and translation is available for Russian, Indonesian, Japanese, Burmese, Cambodia, Thai, Mandarin, French, and Spanish.

Of HMG's many clinics and services, Nobel Group, Island Orthopedics, Healthway Dental, and NeuGlow are of particular interest to international patients.

With 12 locations and eight areas of specialty, Nobel Group of Specialists (NGS) offers a wide range of surgical services, including gastrointestinal and colorectal surgery, urological surgery, and vascular surgery. NGS Eye and Vision Center offers a wide range of diagnostics and treatment services from cataract surgery and corneal transplantation to LASIK. NGS also offers specialists in cardiology, ENT, psychiatry, and pediatrics. Two of the 12 NGS clinics are based in and share resources with the JCI-accredited Gleneagles Medical Centre and Mount Alvernia Medical Centre.

Island Orthopedics Consultants (IOC) is one of the largest and most established orthopedic groups in Singapore. With clinic locations in Gleneagles Medical Centre, Mount Elizabeth Medical Centre, Mount Alvernia Medical Centre, and Novena Medical Centre, IOC's orthopedic and sports medicine group emphasizes minimally invasive surgery techniques and provides treatment for a wide range of orthopedic conditions and sports injuries, including knee and hip replacement, arthritis management, reconstructive spine surgery, and musculoskeletal cancer and tumor surgery.

Healthway Dental offers general and specialized dental services through its subsidiary dental groups: Aaron Dental, Universal Dental, Popular Dental, and NeuGlow Dental.

In operation for more than 10 years, NeuGlow is a fully integrated medical aesthetic group with a comprehensive range of services, including dentistry, plastic surgery, medical aesthetics, and hair restoration. NeuGlow's hair center offers the latest permanent hair restoration options, including laser hair rejuvenation and Omnigraft hair transplantation technology. NeuGlow's dental clinics have specialists in orthodontics, endodontics, periodontics, and oral surgery and provide aesthetic dental and smile makeover services. With one of the largest patient bases in Singapore, NeuGlow's aesthetics team provides high-tech beauty and anti-aging solutions under the care of doctors and registered nurses. Services range from Botox and laser hair removal to Vaser LipoSelection and laser tattoo removal.

Healthway's Medical Assessment Centre offers several levels of health screening packages customized by gender and age. Prices range from us$350 to us$1,000, and services can be provided by appointment or walk-in. Available diagnostics and screening tools include MRI, CT scan, mineral bone densitometry, ultrasound, audiometry, EKG, mammography, and comprehensive blood and urine analysis.

Leading Specialties: Cosmetic and reconstructive surgery, dentistry, health screening, ophthalmology, orthopedics

Johns Hopkins Singapore

11 Jalan Tan Tock Seng
308433 SINGAPORE
Tel: +65 6880.2236
Email: iploffice@imc.jhmi.edu
Web: www.imc.jhmi.edu

Established in 2000, Johns Hopkins Singapore (JHS) is the first clinical facility Johns Hopkins established outside the US. Physicians from Johns Hopkins in Baltimore collaborate with local medical institutions and specialists to provide outpatient diagnostic services, screening programs, and second opinions. Inpatient care focuses on the management and treatment of a wide range of adult cancers, including bladder, breast, cervical, colon, kidney, liver, lung, lymphoma, myeloma, nasopharynx, ovarian, prostate, stomach, throat, and uterine.

Research and educational activities are carried out by the Division of Biomedical Sciences, an academic division of the medical school, with a focus on cellular and immunotherapies and a specific interest in stem cell, virology, and cancer research. This emphasis on research gives the medical team at JHS access to advanced therapies and the latest clinical trials.

In 2005 the medical center relocated to its current premises in Tan Tock Seng Hospital, Singapore's second largest hospital with more than 1,400 beds and 17 clinical specialties.

Johns Hopkins Singapore was the first private hospital in Singapore to be awarded Joint Commission International accreditation in August 2004. JHS was re-accredited in 2007, 2010, and most recently in 2013.

JHS's International Patient Liaison Office is staffed with multi-lingual patient coordinators who help provide translation services, appointment coordination, and assistance with travel arrangements.

Accreditation: Joint Commission International

Leading Specialties: Oncology

Mount Elizabeth Hospital

3 Mount Elizabeth Road
228510 SINGAPORE
Tel: +65 6250.0000
Email: ppac@parkway.sg
Web: mountelizabeth.com.sg

Mount Elizabeth Hospital (MEH) is one of Singapore's medical crown jewels, a 345-bed, private, tertiary, acute-care hospital. Known particularly for cardiology and cardiac surgery, Mount Elizabeth has performed the largest number of cardiac surgeries and neurosurgeries in the private sector in the region.

Cancer care is also big there. The Mount Elizabeth Oncology Center (MEOC) provides comprehensive facilities for treating a wide range of conditions. MEOC was the first center in Asia to provide TomoTherapy radiation treatments for cancer.

Other technologies now deployed by MEOC in treating cancer tumors include intensity-modulated radiation therapy, which is beneficial in cases where a tumor occurs very close to a critical organ; external radiation therapy; radiosurgery or stereotactic radiotherapy; and brachytherapy for cancers of the cervix, lung, esophagus, bile ducts, nose, and throat.

MEH's Hematology and Stem Cell Transplant Center was the first facility in Southeast Asia to offer stem cell transplant therapy. The center specializes in treating blood disorders, such as leukemia, thalassemia, and sickle cell anemia, and advanced cancers, such as those of the kidney, pancreas, and ovary.

Accreditation: Joint Commission International

Leading Specialties: Cardiology and heart surgery, neurology and spine surgery, oncology, orthopedics

National Heart Centre Singapore

5 Hospital Drive
169609 SINGAPORE
Tel: +65 6704.8000
Email: nhcs@nhcs.com.sg
Web: www.nhcs.com.sg

National Heart Centre Singapore (NHCS) is a national and regional referral center for cardiovascular medicine. JCI accredited since 2005, NHCS handles more than 100,000 outpatient consultations, 7,000 interventional and surgical procedures, and 10,000 inpatients annually. Its outcomes for heart attack treatment, balloon angioplasty with stenting, and coronary bypass surgery meet international standards. In 2013 NHCS surgeons implanted Singapore's first third-generation heart pump, the Heart-Ware HVAD, for advanced heart failure patients.

In 2014 NHCS opened its new 12-story building, which houses 38 specialist outpatient clinic consultation rooms and laboratories for cardiac diagnostic tests. The new building boasts six cardiac catheterization labs, three operating rooms, and a new 24-bed short-stay unit for patients requiring cardiac procedures or surgeries, such as coronary angioplasty and heart bypass surgery. Besides providing patient care, the new building houses expanded research facilities to enhance interaction between researchers and clinicians.

Accreditation: Joint Commission International

Leading specialties: Cardiology and heart surgery

National Skin Centre

1 Mandalay Road
308205 SINGAPORE
Tel: +65 6253.4455
Email: nscqa@nsc.gov.sg
Web: www.nsc.com.sg

The National Skin Centre (NSC) is an outpatient center that provides specialized dermatology services and conducts research in dermatology. NSC opened in 1988 after taking over the treatment of skin diseases from Middle Road Hospital. It is now the national and regional referral center for treatment of complex skin diseases. It is also a training center for local and international skin specialists and paramedical personnel. NSC dermatologists treat about 1,000 patients daily.

The center offers clinics for contact dermatitis, occupational dermatoses, cutaneous infection, dermatological and laser surgery, hair and nail disorders, immunodermatology, pediatric dermatology, psoriasis, acne, eczema, pigmentation disorders, skin cancer, urticaria, phototherapy, and the treatment of wounds and ulcers. It has been JCI accredited since 2007.

Accreditation: Joint Commission International

Leading Specialties: Dermatology

KK Women's and Children's Hospital

100 Bukit Timah Road
229899 SINGAPORE
Tel: +65 6394.8888
Email: international@kkh.com.sg
Web: www.kkh.com.sg

KK Women's and Children's Hospital has evolved over the decades, since its founding in 1858, into a regional leader in obstetrics, gynecology, pediatrics, and neonatology. Today the 830-bed hospital deploys more than 400 specialists adept in the latest diagnostic and treatment innovations while embracing a holistic approach to women's medicine.

Specialties and procedures include colorectal surgery, dental, dermatology, general obstetrics and gynecology, orthopedics, and women's sports medicine. Centers of excellence include a Breast Center, Endometriosis Center, Gynaecological Cancer Center, IVF Center, Women's Pain Center, and Women's Wellness Center.

The Minimally Invasive Surgery Center is a specialized gynecological center with expertise in endoscopic surgery. A highly qualified team of laparoscopic surgeons performs minimally invasive surgery for uterine fibroids, ovarian cysts, endometriosis, sterilization, reversal of sterilization, and tubal surgery. The KK Children's Hospital offers a wide range of pediatric medical and surgical services, including pediatric allergies, cardiology and cardiothoracic surgery, ENT, dental, pediatric dermatology, and child development.

The Cleft and Craniofacial Center is the only dedicated, comprehensive craniofacial service in Singapore. KK's Children's Cancer Center is one of the largest pediatric children's cancer centers in Southeast Asia.

KK has been JCI accredited since 2005 and received its most recent re-accreditation in 2011.

Accreditation: Joint Commission International

Leading Specialties: Cardiology and heart surgery, cosmetic and reconstructive surgery, dentistry, oncology, orthopedics

National Cancer Centre Singapore
11 Hospital Drive
169610 SINGAPORE
Tel: +65 6236.9433
Email: foreign_patient@nccs.com.sg
Web: www.nccs.com.sg

The National Cancer Centre Singapore (NCCS) is a national and regional center dedicated to the prevention and treatment of cancers, including thoracic, hepatobiliary (liver and bile ducts), pancreatic, head and neck, lung, breast, and ovarian cancers. NCCS sees more than 50 percent of the cancer patients in Singapore.

As a one-stop specialist center housing Singapore's largest pool of oncologists, NCCS uses advanced equipment and employs the latest therapies, including mini-transplants and targeted therapies that maximize outcomes and minimize undesirable side effects.

Designed to provide integrated, holistic, patient-centered clinical services, the center promotes cross-consultation among oncologists of different specialties. NCCS also conducts clinical research and develops public cancer education programs directed toward prevention and treatment.

The Cancer Genetics Service (CGS) is an interdisciplinary department that deploys human genetics and genomics in the cellular treatment of cancer. CGS staff are all oncologists with advanced specialization in cancer genetics and are internationally renowned for genomic work with breast, gastrointestinal, and urological cancers.

English is spoken throughout the facility, with translators available for Bahasa Indonesia, Chinese, Mongolian, Burmese, Russian, and Vietnamese. The facility's international services center serves mostly affluent patients from the region, with increasing admissions from North American and EU patients seeking diagnostic and financial alternatives.

NCCS received initial JCI accreditation in 2011 and was re-accredited in 2013.

Accreditation: Joint Commission International

Leading Specialties: Oncology

National Dental Centre Singapore
5 Second Hospital Avenue
168938 SINGAPORE
Tel: +65 6324.2215
Email: appointment@ndc.com.sg
Web: www.ndc.com.sg

With 92 dental treatment rooms and six surgical suites, National Dental Centre Singapore (NDCS) is the largest dental facility in Singapore. Treating more than 600 patients daily and 160,000 annually, NDCS is primarily a referral center for patients requiring specialty treatments.

Specialty services are delivered through its three clinical departments: oral and maxillofacial surgery, orthodontics, and restorative dentistry. The latter comprises units specializing in endodontics, pediatric dentistry, periodontics, and prosthodontics. Additional complex diagnoses and procedures are performed in the Prosthetic, Speech, and Swallowing Clinic. NDCS also offers sub-specialty services in facial deformity management and maxillofacial implants.

In 2000 NDCS became part of Singapore Health Services, or SingHealth, a consortium of four hospitals, five specialist centers, and eight polyclinics. International patients are served through SingHealth's international medical services department, which handles appointments and referrals, accommodations, local transportation, cost estimates, interpreters for non-English-speaking patients, and other services.

Accreditation: Joint Commission International

Leading Specialties: Dentistry

National University Hospital
5 Lower Kent Ridge Road
119074 SINGAPORE
Tel: +65 6779.2777
Email: iplc@nuhs.edu.sg
Web: nuh.com.sg/iplc

A part of Singapore's National University Health System, National University Hospital (NUH) is an referral center for a wide range of medical and dental specialties. Its departments include cardiology, gastroenterology and hepatology, obstetrics and gynecology, oncology, ophthalmology, pediatrics, and orthopedic surgery.

NUH was chosen by the Ministry of Health in 2007 to develop two new national specialty centers, the National University Heart Centre and the National University Cancer Institute. The Heart Center is staffed by a dedicated team of cardiologists, specialty trained nurses, and medical and radiology technologists. The Angiography Center specializes in complex, minimally invasive cardiac procedures and provides three cardiac laboratories capable of performing diagnostic and coronary, peripheral, valvuloplasty, and congenital interventional procedures.

Organized as clinical divisions and multi-division departments, NUH's Cancer Institute uses a multidisciplinary approach to provide services, from screening and early diagnosis to treatment and long-term care. Using a combination of surgery and chemo-radiotherapy, the institute's two-year survival rate for patients with high-risk stomach cancer is 69 percent, compared to 60 percent in the US and 40 percent in Australia.

The hospital's International Patient Liaison Center offers medical travelers assistance with flight reservations and visa applications; accommodations and ground transportation; treatment cost estimates; language interpretation (Arabic, Bahasa Indonesia, Burmese, Cambodian, Chinese, English, Russian, and Vietnamese); and outpatient medical appointments.

In 2004 NUH became the first Singapore hospital to receive Joint Commission International accreditation. NUH was most recently re-accredited in 2013.

Accreditation: Joint Commission International

Leading Specialties: Cardiology and heart surgery, dentistry, neurology and spine surgery, oncology, ophthalmology, orthopedics

Raffles Medical Group
585 North Bridge Road
188770 SINGAPORE
Tel: +65 6311.1666
Email: rafflesipc@raffleshospital.com
Web: rafflesmedicalgroup.com

Raffles Medical Group (RMG) is one of the largest private healthcare providers in Singapore. RMG consists of an extensive network of 81 Raffles Medical Clinics island-wide and a flagship hospital, Raffles Hospital. RMG's holistic approach to healthcare led to the inception of Raffles Health, a preventive care unit that offers a full range of nutraceuticals, supplements, vitamins, and medical diagnostic equipment.

Raffles Hospital is a full-service, private hospital that offers the full range of specialist services combined with some of the most advanced medical technology. The hospital also offers several outpatient specialty clinics, including Raffles Cancer Center, Raffles Children's Center, Raffles Dental, Raffles Diabetes and Endocrine Center, Raffles Heart Center, Raffles Skin and Aesthetics, Raffles Orthopaedic Center, Raffles Surgery Center, and Raffles Women's Center.

As an alternative or complement to Western medicine, Raffles Chinese Medicine Centre offers services in herbal medicine, acupuncture, and acupressure.

Its International Patients Centre offers medical referrals and appointment making, airport pickup and drop-off to hospital or hotel, travel planning and visitor information, interpreters and concierge services.

Raffles Hospital received initial JCI accreditation in 2008 and was re-accredited in 2011.

Accreditation: Joint Commission International

Leading Specialties: Cardiology and heart surgery, cosmetic and reconstructive surgery, dentistry, fertility and reproductive medicine, oncology, orthopedics, wellness and prevention

Singapore National Eye Centre

11 Third Hospital Avenue
168751 SINGAPORE
Tel: +65 6100.9393
Email: ips@snec.com.sg
Web: snec.com.sg

Opened in 1990, the Singapore National Eye Centre (SNEC) is Singapore's designated national center for specialized ophthalmological care and research. SNEC physicians see 250,000 outpatients each year and perform 14,000 major eye surgeries and 13,000 laser procedures. In partnership with the affiliated Singapore Eye Research Institute, SNEC is actively involved in clinical trials and research into the causes and treatments of major eye conditions, such as myopia and glaucoma.

The center provides a full range of eye treatments with nine subspecialties: cataract and comprehensive ophthalmology, corneal and external eye disease, glaucoma, neuro-ophthalmology, ocular inflammation and immunology, oculoplastic and aesthetic eye surgery, pediatric ophthalmology and strabismus correction, refractive surgery, and vitreoretinal surgery.

SNEC's facilities have grown to include an eight-floor tower with three floors of outpatient clinics, making SNEC one of the world's largest vision facilities. SNEC has operating theaters with newly expanded day recovery suites.

SNEC's clinical audit department has six full-time staff dedicated to the review and evaluation of treatment outcomes and clinical performance against international standards. This department audits more than 10,000 surgical procedures annually and tracks 30 indicators across seven specialties. Cataract surgeries performed at SNEC have a consistently high overall visual success rate of 97 percent to 98 percent, compared to 93 percent in the US and 92 percent in the UK.

SNEC's International Patients Service team provides interpreters for non-English-speaking patients; a private nursing service; a business center for emailing and photocopying medical records; and assistance with hotel accommodations.

SNEC received JCI accreditation in 2009 and was re-accredited in 2012.

Accreditation: Joint Commission International

Leading Specialties: Ophthalmology

Specialist Dental Group

3 Mount Elizabeth
2285103 SINGAPORE
Tel: +65 6734.9393
Email: info@specialistdentalgroup.com
Web: specialistdentalgroup.com

Specialist Dental Group opened at the Mount Elizabeth Medical Centre in 1979. Today a specialized team of 10 dentists provides comprehensive dental services at four locations: three dental clinics at the Mount Elizabeth Medical Centre–Orchard and a new clinic at Gleneagles Medical Centre. Specialties include prosthodontics, orthodontics, periodontics, oral and maxillofacial surgery, pedodontics, and endodontics.

Specialist's international patients come from Australia, the US, the UK, Russia, Mongolia, Fiji, the Maldives, Bangladesh, Indonesia, and Malaysia. Expatriates in Singapore and in nearby countries make up a considerable part of the clinic's patient base. Clinic staffers speak English, Mandarin, Cantonese, Malay, Bahasa Indonesia, Thai, Burmese, Korean, Tamil, Norwegian, and Tagalog. Interpreters are available for Russian, Japanese, Indonesian, Myanmar, Vietnamese, Mongolian, and Middle Eastern patients. Online appointment booking is available.

Leading Specialties: Dentistry

Tan Tock Seng Hospital

11 Jalan Tan Tock Seng
308433 SINGAPORE
Tel: +65 6357.1590
Email: plc@ttsh.com.sg
Web: ttsh.com.sg/IPLC

Established in 1844, Tan Tock Seng Hospital (TTSH) is Singapore's second largest acute-care hospital, with 1,400 beds.

With strengths in geriatric medicine, infectious diseases, rehabilitation medicine, respiratory medicine, rheumatology, allergy, and immunology, TTSH is also a major referral center for diagnostic radiology, ophthalmology, gastroenterology, otolaryngology, and orthopedic surgery.

Other specialties include cardiology, endocrinology, geriatric medicine, medical oncology (through its on-site Johns Hopkins clinic), and urology. Specialty centers include Complementary and Integrative Medicine Center, Dental Clinic, Health Enrichment Center, Johns Hopkins International Medical Center, Pain Management Clinic, Sports Medicine and Surgery Center, and Breast Clinic. Two major specialty centers, one in rehabilitation medicine and communicable diseases and the other in research on treatments for emerging diseases, round out Tan Tock Seng's clinical offerings.

The TTSH International Patient Liaison Center assists with appointment bookings, consultations with doctors and surgeons, translation services, hotel accommodations, visa applications and extensions if needed, and bill and claims resolutions.

TTSH received its initial JCI accreditation in 2005 and was most recently re-accredited in 2011.

Accreditation: Joint Commission International

Leading Specialties: Cardiology and heart surgery, dentistry, oncology, ophthalmology, orthopedics

DESTINATION: **SOUTH AFRICA**

■ AT A GLANCE

Cape Town, Johannesburg, Pretoria

Languages	Afrikaans and 12 other languages, English widely spoken
Time Zone	GMT +2
Country Dialing Code	+27
Electricity	230V, plug types M and C
Currency	South African rand (ZAR)
Leading Specialties	Cardiology and heart surgery, cosmetic and reconstructive surgery, dentistry, ophthalmology, orthopedics
Typical Savings (over USD retail)	25%–40%
Standards and Affiliations	South African Medical Association; Health Professions Council of South Africa; Council for Health Service Accreditation of Southern Africa; Association of Plastic and Reconstructive Surgeons of South Africa; International Society of Aesthetic Plastic Surgery
International Accreditation	American Association for Accreditation of Ambulatory Surgery Facilities International

■ TREATMENT BRIEF

Since Dr. Christiaan Barnard performed the world's first heart transplant operation in 1967, South Africa has been known as the continent's medical hub. Capitalizing on its medical reputation as one way of overcoming the stigma of apartheid, South Africa has emerged as a strong destination for health travelers.

Because of South Africa's long travel times and relatively high treatment costs, most health travelers choose this country for its privacy, unique sightseeing opportunities, or both. For those who do not wish friends and family to know about their cosmetic and other elective procedures, what better excuse for a month's absence than an African safari? Or for patients with a more charitable bent, South Africa and its neighboring nations offer opportunities for a few weeks' volunteer work. Either option is a con-

venient way to pass a month or two and then return home rested and healed.

English-speaking Westerners sensitive to cultural and language differences may prefer South Africa over some South American, Asian, or European countries because they are more likely to be greeted in English. Cape Town and Johannesburg—South Africa's two main medical cities—are distinctly Anglocentric within a melting pot of cultures and social classes.

Long known as a center of high-quality cosmetic surgeries coupled with first-rate surgeons, South Africa has nearly as long a history of excellent dental care, particularly restorative and cosmetic. More recently, orthopedic surgery—primarily hip and knee surgeries—is attracting European health travelers willing to pay higher treatment costs to avoid the cultural rigors of India or Brazil.

South Africa also boasts an enviable stable of

well-established health travel agents whose services can be a godsend to any prospective international patient. The Medical Tourism Association of South Africa helps to maintain quality standards and service and to foster excellent relationships among patients, treatment centers, and international partners.

Note: If you're thinking "exotic far-flung vacation" when you think South Africa, you're on the right track. You need to remember, however, that most cosmetic surgery protocols specifically caution against exposure to the sun after treatment. Because there is no shortage of sun in that part of the world, plan to take your safari, bush trip, or beach getaway before your procedure.

■ SELECTED HOSPITALS AND CLINICS

Cape Town Mediclinic
PO Box 12199, Mill Street 8010
21 Hof Street, Oranjezicht
Cape Town 8001, SOUTH AFRICA
Tel: +27 21 464.5500
Email: hospmngrcapet@mediclinic.co.za
Web: www.capetownmc.co.za

Located in an elegant, historic building in the quiet Cape Town suburb of Oranjezicht, this 150-bed hospital is only a five-minute drive or a 15-minute stroll from Cape Town's central business district, with easy access to Cape Town International Airport. It is one of 49 private hospitals that form the Mediclinic Southern Africa group. Specialties include neuroscience, orthopedics, obstetrics, neonatal intensive care, arthroscopic surgery, joint replacements, aquatherapy and rehabilitation, scoliosis, shoulder disorders, and ophthalmology.

Leading Specialties: Ophthalmology, orthopedics

Christiaan Barnard Memorial Hospital
181 Longmarket Street
Cape Town 8001, SOUTH AFRICA
Tel: +27 21 480.6111
Email: customer.service@netcare.co.za
Web: https://netcare.co.za/139/netcare-christiaan-barnard-memorial-hospital

Named after South Africa's famed heart transplant pioneer, Christiaan Barnard Memorial Hospital is most noted for cardiac and kidney transplant surgeries, although it provides a variety of medical services, especially in other forms of heart surgery, urology, orthopedics, and dental care.

The hospital treats many heads of state, partly because of its reputation for confidentiality. This hospital is part of the giant Netcare Group, which operates the largest private hospital group, primary care network, and emergency service in South Africa. Netcare is also the biggest private trainer of emergency medical personnel and healthcare workers in the nation.

Leading Specialties: Cardiology and heart surgery, transplant (heart and kidney), urology

Life Bay View Private Hospital
Corner Alhof & Ryk Tulbach Streets
Mossel Bay 6500, SOUTH AFRICA
Tel: +27 44 691.3718
Email: susan.oosthuizen@lifehealthcare.co.za
Web: lifehealthcare.co.za

One of South Africa's finest hospitals occupies one of the world's most beautiful settings for a treatment center. Set along the Garden Route, a three-hour eastward coastal drive (or 40-minute flight) from Cape Town, Life Bay View Private Hospital overlooks the Indian Ocean, where porpoises can be seen frolicking outside patients' rooms.

Established in 1995 and purchased in 2010 by Life Healthcare Group, Bay View now has 108 beds. The hospital prides itself on the high-profile care administered in the center's geographical remoteness.

Twenty-three physicians and surgeons and a staff of 300 have seen thousands of international patients over the past decade. Life Bay View performs more than 200 cardiac surgeries and 1,800 orthopedic surgeries annually.

The hospital is best known for its Cardiac Cath Lab, founded in 1999 by Christiaan Barnard. At Life Bay View the full gamut of heart diagnostics and surgeries is performed at less than half the cost of comparable treatments in the US.

Two of Bay View's five operating theaters are equipped with laminar flow technology. Other operating rooms include a digital urology theater and a gastroenterology suite. Its radiology unit includes x-rays, CT scanner, MRI scanner, bone densitometry scanner, and sonar equipment.

In addition to the full range of orthopedic surgeries, Life Bay View's Orthopedics Clinic offers the Birmingham hip resurfacing procedure. This popular alternative to traditional hip replacement costs about US$10,000 at Bay View. Patients specifically seeking this procedure may consider South Africa a more convenient destination than India or Southeast Asia.

Other specialties include urology, gastroenterology, general and endoscopic surgery, neurology and neurosurgery, and ophthalmology.

The hospital's international clientele hails mostly from the UK and Germany. Life Bay View's international services director helps patients with bookings, hotels, and transportation. Bay View pays for the 40-minute flight from Cape Town to the clinic.

Leading Specialties: Cardiology and heart surgery, ophthalmology, orthopedics, urology

The Netcare Rosebank Hospital

14 Sturdee Avenue
Johannesburg 2196, SOUTH AFRICA
Tel: +27 11 328.0500
Email: customer.service@netcare.co.za
Web: netcare.co.za

The Rosebank Hospital is owned by Netcare Limited, South Africa's largest hospital network. Located in the ritzy northern suburbs of Johannesburg, this 116-bed private hospital offers a variety of disciplines, including dentistry and maxillofacial surgery, neurology, oncology, ophthalmology, and urology.

The Rosebank facility has earned an international reputation for excellence in plastic and reconstructive surgery. Its Center of Excellence for Plastic and Reconstructive Surgery specializes in breast augmentation, liposuction, and abdominoplasty

(tummy tucks). Reconstructive surgeries include delicate work on hand injuries and high-acuity congenital abnormalities. Rosebank uses the latest instrumentation for these procedures, including lasers and endoscope and microscope cameras.

Rosebank's Center for Sports Medicine and Orthopedics places the hospital in a unique position to meet the medical needs of both professional and leisure sportsmen and sportswomen. Specialties range from general orthopedics to specialized knee and shoulder procedures. Surgeons are trained in, and tend to favor, minimally invasive surgery. Supporting services include sports medicine, physiotherapy, biokinetics, and podiatry.

Each self-contained ward at Rosebank has an in-suite bathroom, satellite television, and telephone.

Leading Specialties: Cardiology and heart surgery, cosmetic and reconstructive surgery, dentistry, ophthalmology, orthopedics

Pretoria Eye Institute

630 Schoeman Street/Francis Baard Street
PO Box 56184
Arcadia, 0007 Pretoria, SOUTH AFRICA
Tel: +27 12 427.0000
Email: info@eyeinstitute.co.za
Web: www.eyeinstitute.co.za

Pretoria Eye Institute (PEI) was Africa's first private eye hospital. Twenty-five ophthalmologists cover all branches of medical and surgical ophthalmology, corneal surgery, glaucoma treatment, laser and refractive surgery, oculoplastic and orbit surgery, strabismus surgery, vitreoretinal surgery, uveitis services, neuro-ophthalmology, and ocular oncology. PEI serves international travelers, including patients from the UK, who come to take advantage of the considerable cost savings.

Leading Specialties: Ophthalmology

DESTINATION: **SOUTH KOREA**

■ AT A GLANCE

Seoul, Daejeon, Incheon

Languages	Korean, English spoken by most health professionals
Time Zone	GMT +9
Country Dialing Code	+82
Electricity	110V and 220V, plug types A and B
Currency	South Korean won (KRW)
Leading Specialties	Cardiology and heart surgery, cosmetic and reconstructive surgery, dentistry, health screening, neurology and spine surgery, oncology, ophthalmology, orthopedics, transplant, weight loss surgery, wellness and prevention
Typical Savings (over USD retail)	30%–45%
Standards and Affiliations	Korea Health Industry Development Institute; Ministry for Health, Welfare, and Family Affairs
International Accreditation	Joint Commission International

■ TREATMENT BRIEF

Like many Asian nations, South Korea has developed economically and culturally far more quickly than the average American may realize. After many years of post-war governmental strife, Korea launched one of the planet's fastest growing economies—now the third largest economy in Asia (behind Japan and China) and the eleventh largest in the world.

Korea is also one of the world's most technologically and scientifically advanced countries; it is the only one in the world with nationwide 100 mbit/s broadband internet access and full HDTV broadcasting. Some 90 percent of all Korean homes are connected to high-speed broadband internet. A bullet train network zips travelers around the country at speeds exceeding 220 kilometers (136 miles) an hour. Hyundai and Samsung are located there, a reminder of Korea's formidable ability to compete in major industry sectors.

Healthcare is no exception, and Korea's star as a

health travel destination is rapidly rising. Although language and cultural barriers persist, Korea boasts a network of 20 modern international hospitals, including Severance Hospital, the world's largest JCI-accredited hospital, with more than 2,000 beds.

The Korean penchant for technology is revealed in its hospitals, where most are fully digitized and electronic health records are the rule. Visitors can even watch their granny's colonoscopy on a television monitor in the hospital lobby (optional!).

Korea's foray into international health travel began with service to Japanese patients, and despite a sometimes uneasy political relationship between the two countries, patients flock from Japan to take advantage of the huge cost savings and excellent care Korea has to offer. The Korean government has initiated a set of measures to promote international health travel by aiding hospitals in their marketing and by easing regulations. The government is also pushing to simplify the process of issuing visas for overseas patients, especially those from Asian nations.

In addition to the usual range of general surgeries, Korea's hospitals and clinics are known for cosmetic surgeries and treatments for spinal disorders and cancer. In the center of the country, Daegu hosts the most famous herbal medicine market in South Korea, dating from 1658. On the southern coast, Busan is one of Asia's seashore hot spots, where medical travelers flock to Hanyang University Medical Center for its low-cost comprehensive health screenings.

Medical travelers who react adversely to the heat and humidity of Southeast Asia will find Korea's northern mountainous climate more to their liking. And Korean Air offers non-stops from at least a dozen US and Canadian cities. Its northern geography shortens flights to a long, but manageable, 11 to 14 hours.

■ SELECTED HOSPITALS AND CLINICS

Asan Medical Center

88, Olympic-ro 43-gil, Songpa-gu
Seoul 138-736, SOUTH KOREA
Tel: +82 2 3010.5001; +82 2 3010.7942 (International Office)
Email: int@amc.seoul.kr
Web: eng.amc.seoul.kr

Asan Medical Center (AMC) is Korea's largest medical institution, with 1,400 physicians and surgeons, 3,000 nurses, more than 3,000 beds, and 67 operating rooms, occupying more than 372,000 square meters (four million square feet). A typical day sees more than 2,400 inpatients and 10,000 outpatients treated. AMC's mission is to look "beyond medicine toward good health." Staff support patients through a multi-disciplinary medical approach, patient-oriented facilities, cooperative treatment systems, simplified administrative processes, and reduced waiting times.

AMC was established in 1989 by the founder of the Hyundai Motor Company, Chung Ju-Yung, also known as "Asan." He started the Asan Foundation based on the conviction that gains from business

should be returned to society for the people's welfare. His mission was "to help the least privileged members of our society." Today his eponymous medical center is one of Korea's top healthcare organizations and serves as the parent to seven regional hospitals.

AMC offers a number of centers of excellence and a full range of medical and dental specialties. The center ranks No. 1 in Korea in the number of surgeries performed for 13 of the top 30 diseases, and is particularly renowned for organ transplantation and complex cancer-related surgeries.

Established in 1991, the Organ Transplantation Center performed Korea's first heart transplant and first simultaneous transplantations of the kidney and pancreas, as well as the world's first modified right lobectomy and liver transplant, helping to make AMC a world leader in the field. AMC's success rate for one-year survival of patients receiving a liver transplant is 96 percent, compared to the US average of 88 percent. Over the years, American physicians have worked with AMC's liver transplant team to learn the advanced technology that enables AMC to achieve such a high success rate.

Opened in 1989, the Asan Heart Institute is a world leader in heart disease treatment and research. The institute specializes in the latest technology and techniques, including minimally invasive robotics-assisted da Vinci surgery, hybrid operations, and stent-graft applications. Institute doctors have been innovators in left main coronary artery intervention, with a one-year survival rate of 98 percent. More than 120 international physicians attend AMC's cardiology training program each year.

AMC established Korea's first multi-disciplinary cancer clinic in 2006, with specialists in diagnosis, surgery, medical oncology, and radiation therapy collaborating to develop customized treatment plans for each patient. Opened in 2009, the Asan Cancer Center comprises 14 sub-centers for treating lung, stomach, colon, breast, esophageal, urologic, and brain cancers. The center emphasizes international collaboration and maintains an academic exchange and personnel training program with the Dana Farber Cancer Institute of Harvard Medical School.

Opened in 1990, AMC's Health Screening and Promotion Center (HSPC) provides convincing evidence that early detection and treatment enhance disease prevention and cure, leading to reduced healthcare costs and increased life expectancy and quality. HSPC offers individually tailored screenings for stroke, heart disease, and arteriosclerosis, as well as many types of cancer (liver, kidney, pancreatic, gastric, colon, prostate, lung, thyroid, breast, ovarian, and uterine). The center is a top international program at Asan, receiving 950 international patients from 34 countries for health checkups in 2009.

Asan's International Clinic was opened in 1989 to meet the medical needs of expatriates, business people, and tourists. The Asan International Office was established in 2009 to meet the growing demands of global healthcare and medical travel. Together they create a foreigner-friendly, customer-centered system for medical care, helping international patients take full advantage of Asan's services, regardless of home country or language. Asan's International Clinic staff includes full-time physicians and nurses fluent in English and Japanese.

Fast-track medical exams with no waiting time are available to foreign visitors. International Clinic doctors review cases (medical records, images, and pathology slides can be sent ahead of time), discuss them with appropriate specialists, and provide a second opinion on treatment within 48 hours. A dual attending system between Asan specialists and International Clinic staff minimizes potential conflicts due to language barriers or cultural differences. There is a hotline for patients who speak other languages.

Leading Specialties: Cardiology and heart surgery, health screening, oncology, orthopedics, spine surgery, transplant

Cheongshim International Medical Center

460 Songsan-Ri, Sorak-Myeon, Gapyeong-Gun
Gyeonggi-Do 477-855, SOUTH KOREA
Tel: +82 31 589.4641
Email: alexander@cheongshim.com
Web: eng.csmc.or.kr

Established in 2003, Cheongshim Hospital of Western and Oriental Medicine changed its name to Cheongshim International Medical Center (CIMC) in 2006. This 250-bed hospital employs 15 physicians and surgeons and 200 additional staff. All of the doctors and most of the nurses and administrative personnel speak English. In 2007 CIMC saw more than 60,000 outpatients and more than 50,000 inpatients, roughly 20 percent of them medical travelers.

One of the hospital's main strengths continues to be the close collaboration between its department of Eastern medicine and its Western clinical departments, which include internal medicine, general and orthopedic surgery, obstetrics and gynecology, diagnostic radiology, rehabilitation medicine, and anesthetics/pain management.

CIMC's combined Western and Eastern treatment methods have proven particularly effective for stroke recovery, palsy, arthritis, lumbago, allergic disease, obesity, and post-natal recuperation.

CIMC operates a health screening center utilizing the latest diagnostic equipment. The hospital's rehabilitation center is the largest in Korea and offers patients numerous therapeutic modalities, including modern exercise rooms and hydrotherapy pools for supervised exercise therapy, thermal and electrical treatment devices, a spa, and even a beauty therapy center.

Located in a picturesque resort area east of Seoul, CIMC was conceived as a place for both medical treatment and recreation. Its VIP lodging features comfortable rooms with a view of Cheongpyeong Lake, and the various amenities include boat tours, aesthetic skin care, and massage.

Leading Specialties: Health screening, orthopedics, weight loss surgery, wellness and prevention

Inha University Hospital

7-206, 3-GA, Sinheung-Dong, Jung-Gu
Incheon 400-711, SOUTH KOREA
Tel: + 82 32 890.3200
Email: uhia@inha.com; hyungji25@hotmail.com
Web: inha.com/eng/

A tertiary and acute-care hospital and one of Korea's largest, the 804-bed Inha University Hospital boasts 450 physicians and surgeons and 2,000 additional staff. Its nine specialty centers offer specialized medical examinations and treatments, including high-quality, affordable, personalized health screenings that have garnered Inha an international reputation. Near Incheon International Airport, Inha is easily accessible by cross-border patients.

Inha's Health Promotion Center offers patients pre-designed screening packages as well as the opportunity to choose from a checklist of more than 100 items in consultation with a coordinator for an individually customized examination. Screening takes only about two and a half hours, unless overnight sleep observation is conducted. Airport pickup service and an overnight stay in a private room are provided for international patients, who come to the center from 17 countries.

The Cancer Center is staffed by experts in a variety of disciplines; is equipped with multi-channel CT/PET, and CyberKnife; and boasts a prestigious blood and marrow transplant (BMT) unit. Its innovative treatments include donor mesenchymal stem cells (engineered through a unique culturing method invented by the BMT team) for life-threatening refractory graft-versus-host disease; tandem autologous and allogeneic BMT for selected blood cancers; and bone marrow transplants to effect cures for multiple myelomas considered incurable by conventional methods. Inha's recently opened Women's Cancer Center treats most conditions, including breast, ovarian, thyroid, and uterine cancer.

The Digestive Disease Center has a team of 15 doctors and 15 nurses. The latest narrow band imagining system (Olympus Evis Lucera 260) is used for upper and lower gastrointestinal endoscopy. Endoscopic retrograde cholangiopancreatography (a procedure that combines upper GI endoscopy and x-rays) and the newest ultrasound system (Aloka ProSound Alpha 10) enable sophisticated diagnosis and treatment of gastrointestinal and pancreatobiliary disease. Gastrointestinal tests include manometry, 24-hour pH monitoring, and biofeedback.

Inha's International Healthcare Center assigns each medical traveler a healthcare coordinator who handles travel and clinical tasks, including coordinating consultations and appointments, transfer of medical records, assistance with Korea visa application (if required), airport pickup and drop-off, and assistance with financial arrangements for self-pay patients.

Inha received its initial JCI accreditation in 2010 and was re-accredited in 2013.

Accreditation: Joint Commission International

Leading Specialties: Cardiology and heart surgery, oncology, weight loss surgery

Jaseng Hospital of Oriental Medicine
635 Shinsa-Dong, Gangnam-Gu
Seoul 135-896, SOUTH KOREA
Tel: +82 2 3218.2167; +82 2 3218.2105
Email: enjaseng@jaseng.co.kr
Web: jaseng.net

Jaseng Hospital of Oriental Medicine treats all kinds of musculoskeletal conditions, including serious spinal disorders, without surgery—even in cases when patients can no longer walk because of severe back pain. Jaseng has amassed vast clinical experience since it opened in 1999, providing more than 500,000 treatments every year. It is a leader in the globalization of Korean traditional medicine.

Jaseng's main facility has 174 inpatient beds and 120 doctors and nurses. Its specialized centers include more than 30 clinics for spinal disorders, bone and joint ailments, temporomandibular joint (TMJ) dysfunction, internal medicine, and gynecology. Jaseng has also launched a non-surgical spinal treatment branch hospital in the city of Bucheon and branch clinics in Bundang, Ilsan, Mokdong, and Jangchungdong.

Jaseng has expanded into the US with four centers in California (Fullerton, Los Angeles, San Diego, and San Jose). The group is looking to open additional hospitals throughout the US and Europe.

For optimal healthcare using the best non-surgical methods from Western and Eastern medicine, the hospital employs state-of-the-art diagnostic equipment in addition to traditional therapies. Chuna spine manipulation, for example, utilizes a push-and-pull technique for spinal alignment. Acupuncture (including injections of herbal extract and bee venom) releases tightened muscles. Chuna herbal medicine strengthens degenerated bones, discs, and ligaments. Its core ingredient, a compound called Shinbarometin, is patented in Korea, the US, and Japan.

Physical and exercise therapy are implemented to prevent recurrence. These therapies are attracting worldwide attention. Many Western doctors have visited Jaseng to learn about its treatment system and techniques, and the hospital has conducted collaborative research with Harvard Medical School's Osher Research Center and the University of California Irvine School of Medicine.

In a recent study with Harvard, 95 percent of 128 patients diagnosed with severely herniated discs were fully recovered after six months of Jaseng's nonsurgical treatment with Chuna medication, Chuna manipulation, and herbal/bee venom acupuncture; 77 percent of them experienced dramatic pain relief within two months.

The hospital's International Clinic has now treated more than 2,600 foreign patients, including more than 20 ambassadors. Staff members speak English, German, Japanese, and Chinese, and language interpretation services are provided. International services include airport transport, assistance with medical documents, travel and accommodations, insurance claims, and local travel.

Leading Specialties: Orthopedics, spine surgery

Kyung Hee University Medical Center

1 Hoegi-Dong, Dongdeamun-Gu
Seoul 130-702, SOUTH KOREA
Tel: +82 2 958.9644
Email: abroad@khmc.or.kr
Web: khmc.or.kr/eng

Kyung Hee University Medical Center (KHMC) was established in 1971 with the aim of integrating Eastern and Western medicine in patient care and medical education for the first time in Korea. It is the nation's only institution offering colleges of medicine, Eastern medicine, dentistry, nursing, pharmacology, and Eastern pharmacology.

The medical center comprises five large-scale facilities and three additional branches, with 15 operating rooms and a total inpatient capacity of 1,170 beds. It boasts modern equipment that includes CT, PET/CT, and MRI scanners; angiography systems; Gamma Knife; and TomoTherapy. KHMC treated nearly 200,000 outpatients and more than 32,000 inpatients in 2007.

KHMC's hospital has 171 doctors and 371 residents practicing in 31 specialties. In the Dental Hospital, 38 specialists and 90 residents practice in eight specialized fields of dentistry. Forty-three Eastern medical doctors and 90 residents treat patients in eight specialties in the Korean Medical Hospital. This facility also collaborates in patient care with the staff of the East-West Neo Medical Center.

In the Cancer Center and Center of Gastroenterology, patients are treated by a doctor of Western medicine and a doctor of Eastern medicine from the East-West Neo Medical Center. The East-West Health Examination Center utilizes both Western and traditional Korean medicine in its screening examinations and in its health-maintenance guidelines for patients.

KHMC's East-West Medical Research Institute has been appointed by the World Health Organization as its traditional medical research collaborative center every four years since 1988.

Leading Specialties: Dentistry, health screening, oncology, wellness and prevention

Kyung Hee University East-West Neo Medical Center

149 Sangil-Dong, Gangdong-Gu
Seoul 134-727, SOUTH KOREA
Tel: +82 2 440.7000; +82 2 440.7304 (International Health Care Center)
Email: glove@khnmc.or.kr
Web: inter.khnmc.or.kr/eng2/

As its name indicates, Kyung Hee University East-West Neo Medical Center (KHNMC) merges the strengths of Western and Eastern medicine. It opened in 2006 on a foundation of more than 50 years' experience in healthcare and medical education, starting with the College of Oriental Medicine in 1953 and later establishing schools of pharmacy, dentistry, medicine, and nursing.

KHNMC has since developed into a complete healthcare complex, with more than 130 doctors supported by 300 nurses and 20 coordinators in an 800-bed facility. A large percentage of the medical staff has practiced, trained, and conducted research abroad, and many staff members speak English.

KHNMC offers expertise in all areas of orthopedics, including rheumatology, spine and joint surgery, sports medicine, and acupuncture. Additional specialties include Eastern medicine and dental implants. The hospital is organized around numerous disease-specific and organ-specific centers, as well as integrative centers in which doctors collaborate to combine the advantages of Western and Eastern medical treatment.

In 2007 alone, KHNMC treated 440,000 outpatients and 194,000 inpatients and performed more than 2,500 orthopedic surgeries. The hospital has also conducted five kidney transplants and three liver transplants. Its state-of-the-art equipment includes MRI, multi-detector CT, systems for robotic-assisted surgery, videoconference surgery, and a picture archiving and communication system.

KHNMC offers four centers of excellence. The Arthritis and Rheumatism Center, specializes in hip and joint resurfacing and replacement, with a particular specialization in treating patients with hemophilia. The center also uses a variety of traditional Eastern treatments in rehabilitation and pain management. The Spine Center offers spinal surgery, chiropractic treatment, and Eastern medicine.

The Dental Hospital, provides customized treatment options for dentofacial problems. Dental services range from scaling, aesthetic dentistry, and implants to oral and maxillofacial surgery.

The Health Promotion Center, provides a wide range of comprehensive screening programs. A diverse selection of medical examination packages is specifically designed to cover the areas of patients' greatest concern and help patients understand how to control their risk for various diseases, such as diabetes, stroke, and cancer.

KHNMC's International Health Care Center has English-speaking staff and provides foreign patients with full access to all of the medical center's services.

Leading Specialties: Dentistry, health screening, orthopedics, spine surgery, wellness and prevention

Seoul St. Mary's Hospital, Catholic Medical Center

505 Banpo-Dong Seocho-Gu
Seoul 131-701, SOUTH KOREA
Tel: +82 2 2258.5745
Email: ihcc@catholic.ac.kr
Web: cmcseoul.or.kr/global/eng/

Seoul St. Mary's Hospital is a part of Catholic Medical Center (CMC) founded in 1962 to oversee medical education, research, and healthcare conducted and provided by the Catholic Church in Korea. CMC is the largest medical network in the country, with eight affiliated hospitals and the Catholic University of Korea College of Medicine, for a total of 5,000 beds attended by 1,200 physicians, 900 residents, and 250 interns.

As part of its commitment to top-notch care, CMC sends 35 to 40 doctors annually to renowned universities in the US, Canada, Germany, and Japan to pursue further studies, conduct research, and build clinical collaborations. CMC also strives to advance the medical sciences and find cures for disease through its nine research institutes.

CMC's newest member, Catholic University of Korea Seoul St. Mary's Hospital, opened in 2009. St. Mary's is the single largest hospital in Korea, with 2,000 beds, 25 specialty departments, and six core centers: Hematopoietic Stem Cell Transplantation Center, Cancer Center, Organ Transplantation Center, Cardiovascular Center, Women's Cancer Center, and Eye Center. The facility's state-of-the-art technology includes MRI, PET/CT, and single photon emission computed tomography (SPECT) CT, as well as an angiography unit, TomoTherapy Hi-Art system, x-ray therapy unit, magnetic navigation surgery system, and CyberKnife robotic-assisted surgery system.

Seoul St. Mary's International Health Care Center serves mostly patients from the region, with staff fluent in English, Russian, Japanese, French, and Chinese. Medical reports and insurance forms can be generated in English, Russian, Japanese, and French. The hospital created a ward for international patients only to reduce language and culture barriers between patients and the medical teams.

St. Mary's received its first JCI accreditation in 2010 (just one year after opening its doors), and was fully re-accredited in 2013.

Accreditation: Joint Commission International

Leading Specialties: Cardiology and heart surgery, oncology, ophthalmology, orthopedics

Severance Hospital, Yonsei University Health System

250 Seongsanno (134 Sinchon-Dong), Seodaemun-Gu
Seoul 120-752, SOUTH KOREA
Tel: +82 2 2228.5800
Email: ihcc@yuhs.ac
Web: yuhs.or.kr/en

Part of Korea's giant Yonsei University Health System, Severance Hospital was established in 1885. Severance is one of the world's largest JCI-accredited hospitals, accommodating more than 2,000 beds and boasting 970 physicians and surgeons (many English speaking) plus 4,170 additional staff. Supported by the latest equipment and an advanced information technology infrastructure, Severance and Yonsei have become a hub for medical services in East Asia.

As an annual average, Severance performs more than 44,000 surgeries and sees approximately one and a half million outpatients and 660,000 inpatients. With its five adjoining specialty centers, Severance offers services to international patients through more than 60 clinical departments and divisions. Best known for oncology, cardiology, ophthalmology, and orthopedics, the hospital is of particular interest to international patients for da Vinci robotic-assisted surgery and complex plastic and reconstructive surgery cases. Severance also offers comprehensive VIP health screenings for risk factors and early disease detection.

Severance's Cancer Center was Korea's first and the center has played a crucial role in treatment development, including whole-body radiation examination for marrow transplant patients, a heat remedy to kill cancer cells, and radiation neurosurgery options for cerebral tumors. TomoTherapy has been utilized since 2006. The center continues to produce groundbreaking research results through a sister institution relationship with the renowned MD Anderson Cancer Center in the US.

The Rehabilitation Hospital, provides multi-disciplinary services in physical, occupational, and speech therapy, including the production of auxiliary devices, such as artificial limbs. Specialized rehabilitation programs are offered for stroke, spinal cord injury, brain injury, pediatric patients, amputees, and chronic pain. The hospital also offers a variety of specialized diagnostic procedures, such as motion analysis, urodynamics, functional electrical stimulation, and computerized infrared thermographic imaging.

Severance's Cardiovascular Hospital, provide comprehensive and advanced care through its three departments (cardiology, pediatric cardiology, and cardiovascular surgery), 10 specialized clinics, and an outpatient clinic. Procedures offered include open-heart surgery, off-pump coronary artery bypass grafting, valve repair, heart transplantation, minimally invasive cardiac surgery, robotic-assisted cardiac surgery, and aorta and peripheral vascular surgery.

An average of 900 patients are treated daily at the Eye, Ear, Nose, and Throat Hospital which offers a wide range of day-surgery programs. The hospital has set many Korean precedents, including the country's first artificial cochlear implant, and has been recognized for developing a myopia eyeball-fixation device. Treatment is provided for Behçet's disease, cataracts, glaucoma, vitreoretinal disorders, deafness rehabilitation, allergies, snoring, dizziness, head and neck tumors, and speech disorders.

The Children's Hospital is the second of its kind in Korea. Utilizing a multi-disciplinary diagnosis and treatment system, this 200-bed hospital specializes in complicated cases transferred from local hospitals. Its clinics include the Epilepsy Clinic and Pediatric Cancer Clinic. The hospital has a sister institution relationship with the world-renowned Children's Hospital of Philadelphia.

Severance has been operating an International Healthcare Center since 1962 to coordinate international patients' primary care and referrals to specialists throughout the hospital. All of the center's doctors and staff speak English, and interpretation in other languages can be arranged. The staff manages pre-visit consultations, transportation, accommodations, and tourism services for patients from overseas.

In 2007 the center welcomed more than 2,000

incoming patients from the US and Canada. Additionally, Severance serves as the referral hospital for US military personnel in Korea and the on-call hospital for US presidential visits.

Severance received initial JCI accreditation in 2007 and renewals in 2010 and 2013.

Accreditation: Joint Commission International

Leading Specialties: Cardiology and heart surgery, dentistry, oncology, ophthalmology, orthopedics, spine surgery

Sun Dental Hospital

394-1 Jungchon-dong, Jung-gu
Daejeon, SOUTH KOREA
Tel: +82 10 8637.5995
Email: jhkwon@sunhospital.co.kr
Web: sundentalhospital.com

For dental patients wishing to take in the spectacular Korean countryside, a 50-minute high-speed train ride will get you to Daejeon, Korea's fifth largest city and Seoul's sister governing body. Located downtown is the JCI-accredited Sun Dental Hospital, one of the largest dental clinics in the country and one of the few internationally accredited dental facilities.

Thirty-two dental specialists and more than 100 staff members treat around 600 patients a day. Specialties include implantology; orthognathic surgery (corrections of the jaw and face); orthodontics (braces and retainers); prosthodontics (aesthetic and restorative treatments); periodontics (gums, bones, and ligaments); and pediatric dentistry.

Sun Dental operates more like a hospital, with an in-house ICU and access to emergency care through its sister facility, Sun Hospital, also in Daejeon.

Sun's international services include shuttle to and from the airport and train station, 24/7 concierge, and assistance with travel. English, Russian, Mongolian, and Chinese are spoken, with translators available for other languages.

Sun received its initial JCI accreditation in 2012.

Accreditation: Joint Commission International

Leading Specialties: Dentistry

Wooridul Spine Hospital

445, Hakdong-ro, Gangnam-gu
Seoul 135-951, SOUTH KOREA
Tel: +82 2 513.8450
Email: ipc@wooridul.com.kr
Web: wooridul.com

Since its establishment in 1982, Wooridul Spine Hospital (WSH) has emerged as one of the world's leading spine-specialty treatment facilities. With more than 1,130 neurospine specialists and other professionals, its staff provides services ranging from neurospinal, spinal thoracic, and anterior spine surgery to spinal medicine, orthopedics, and rehabilitation within the hospital's Spine Total Care system.

The hospital follows a philosophy of minimally invasive surgery and technique, striving for the least possible destruction of healthy tissue, and endeavors to provide treatment without surgery whenever possible. WSH has developed an endoscopic surgery method that reduces the area of skin laceration, resulting in faster recovery, a high success rate, a reduced relapse rate, and a high rate of patient satisfaction. New surgical methods for spinal disc treatment are currently in development.

Wooridul Hospital currently manages 10 hospitals throughout Korea and has expanded into Indonesia (Jakarta), the UAE (Dubai and Abu Dhabi), Turkey (Istanbul), and China (Shanghai). The main Seoul WSH facility, opened in November 2007, boasts the latest high-tech equipment for treating spinal cancer and arthritis.

WSH has taught its treatment methods to more than 530 neurospine specialists from more than 60 countries. A one-year training program for foreign doctors was launched in 2003. The hospital exchanges current surgery techniques with institutions in the US and France through conference and live-surgery video feed, hosts an annual international neurospine forum, and publishes research results in world-renowned medical journals.

The Wooridul International Patient Center, established in 2006 in the Gangnam district of Seoul, prides itself on one-stop care and administrative support. Through the 24-hour call center and online, prospective patients receive remote diagnostic examination and consultation, including detailed discussions of procedures, costs, and hospitalization.

International services include online and offline medical consultations, assistance with visas and medical visas, airport pickup and drop-off, interpreters (Japanese, English, Russian, and Arabic spoken in most Wooridul facilities), assistance with insurance, and assistance with local tourism.

Wooridul has partnered with an extensive international network of large health plans, including Allianz, Bupa, Cigna, GeoBlue, HTH Worldwide, MetLife, Tricare, and UnitedHealthcare.

Leading Specialties: Spine surgery

Patient Experience

Conor M., Ireland

In more than four decades as a diplomat, I have had occasion to visit and stay in a number of hospitals throughout the world. Recently, I had to undergo a very serious open-heart operation at Severance Hospital in Seoul, and the experience made a lasting impression on me.

"From the moment my condition was diagnosed, I was given sound and frank advice on the options before me. Great care was also taken to explain the progress of my treatment in laymen's language. I had often found previously that doctors tended to be aloof from their patients, but this was not the case at Severance. And it was not only the senior professional staff whose attitude was admirable. All the support staff, from the nurses to the orderlies who wheeled me to the x-ray room each morning, were unfailingly friendly and cheerful.

"And the operation itself? Well, as I am writing this, it was obviously a success, perhaps due in part to my overall health condition, but in greater part due to the superb competence and expertise of my doctors, to whom I owe my life.

"Nobody is happy to undergo an open-heart surgery. I was lucky in more ways than one that mine was taken care of by the doctors and staff of Severance Hospital. I will forever be in their debt." ■

DESTINATION: **TAIWAN**

■ AT A GLANCE

Taichung City, Taipei, Kaohsiung City

Languages	Mandarin Chinese, Taiwanese, Hakka, English spoken by health professionals
Time Zone	GMT +8
Country Dialing Code	+84
Electricity	110V, plug type A
Currency	Taiwan dollar (TWD)
Leading Specialties	Cardiology and heart surgery, cosmetic and reconstructive surgery, health screening, neurology and spine surgery, oncology, orthopedics, transplant, wellness and prevention
Typical Savings (over USD retail)	40%–65%
Standards and Affiliations	Taiwan Joint Commission on Hospital Accreditation; Taiwan Hospital Association; Public Hospital Association; Taiwan College of Healthcare Executives
International Accreditation	Joint Commission International

■ TREATMENT BRIEF

One of the original four Asia Tigers, Taiwan has grown by leaps and bounds over the past 50 years to become a fully modernized, industrialized nation and a top player in the global economy. Situated on the southeast of the Asian continent, Taiwan is in the center of the East Asian island arc, bordering Japan to the north and the Philippines, Hong Kong, and Vietnam to the south. This central location makes Taiwan a well-traveled regional tourism and healthcare hub, linking the Pacific Ocean, East China Sea, and South China Sea.

Taiwan's beautiful and wild mountainous region on the east side of the island provides an array of luxury recovery accommodations, vacation attractions, sightseeing opportunities—and increasingly—healthcare options. Listed as "One of the top 10 best countries to visit in 2012" by travel guidebook publisher Lonely Planet, Taiwan is a top tourism destination offering a rich culture, beautiful natural landscapes, robust economy, and established tourism infrastructure.

In 2013 Taiwan welcomed more than six million tourists, including more than two million visitors from Mainland China. Western culture and art thrive in Taiwan—from baseball to billiards and karaoke. Taiwanese film director Ang Lee brought us *The Life of Pi* and produced the Oscar winners *Crouching Tiger, Hidden Dragon*, and *Brokeback Mountain*.

Although suffering from pollution and traffic snarls, Taiwan's principal cities are modern, friendly, and safe, with bullet trains connecting the island's major industrial and population centers.

■ TAIWAN HEALTHCARE AND MEDICAL TRAVEL

Taiwan applies some of the world's highest healthcare standards, so much so that Nobel Laureate Paul Krugman has praised Taiwan's healthcare and national health insurance as among the best in the world.

Dozens of newly constructed hospitals and clinics dot the densely populated landscape, mostly in or near Taipei, its capital. Nineteen facilities are now JCI accredited, including hospitals, ambulatory centers, and clinical care facilities.

Though medical travelers from nearby China and Japan are major markets, centralized efforts have long been aimed at westernizing Taiwan's health centers and promoting international health travel from the US, UK, Australia, and other English-speaking nations.

Mainland Chinese travelers visiting Taiwan for a health screening, cosmetic procedure, or medical treatment benefit from a shared language and cultural background. Visiting patients receive high-quality care comparable to care in Western countries while enjoying much shorter travel times and more reasonable prices. Since 2007, Taiwan has also welcomed thousands of medical travelers from Hong Kong, Macao, and Singapore and patients from the Chinese diaspora.

While US healthcare languishes in an expensive, often counterproductive "heal the sick" mind-set, Taiwan's focus is clearly preventive. Comprehensive healthcare screenings abound, and Taiwan's close cultural ties to China have produced a wealth of alternative and complementary therapies and procedures.

Still, for the English-speaking patient, language and cultural barriers make the medical travel journey more challenging than counterparts in Southeast Asia. When English can be found, customer service is excellent, at times over the top. One example is Chang Bing Show Chwan Health Care Center Park, which boasts a modern art gallery, a children's museum, and a 200-seat movie theater for patients.

Taiwan's specialties include cardiology, orthopedics, weight loss surgery, neurosciences, cosmetic medicine, and fertility treatments. Costs savings are generally on par with Thailand and Mexico—with savings of 40–65 percent over comparable care in countries such as the US and Australia.

■ SELECTED HOSPITALS AND CLINICS

Bair's Eye Clinic

No. 192-4 Beitun Road, Beitun District
Taichung City 406, TAIWAN
Tel: +886 4 2234.8222
Email: mail@eyelasik.com.tw
Web: www.eyelasik.com.tw

Bair's Eye Clinic in Taichung City performs LASIK surgery on 20 to 30 foreigners each month. Specialists at Bair formulate a treatment plan custom designed for each patient.

LASIK is the most common type of laser vision-correction procedure. It corrects nearsightedness, farsightedness, and astigmatism. The clinic offers custom wavefront LASIK procedures (also known as custom ablation). For patients with thin corneas or large pupils, Bair offers photorefractive keratectomy. LASEK is an effective procedure for patients who have thin or flat corneas.

For nearsighted or farsighted patients, an implant called a phakic intraocular lens is inserted under the surface of the eye to serve as an internal contact lens. In a procedure utilizing intrastromal corneal ring segments, two slim half-rings are inserted around the edges of the cornea to adjust the vision of myopic patients by flattening the curvature of the cornea.

Potential candidates for treatment at Bair's must meet certain requirements for general and eye health. Visit its website to review criteria.

Leading Specialties: Ophthalmology

Chang Bing Show Chwan Memorial Hospital

No. 6 Lugong Road, Lugang Town
Changhua County 505, TAIWAN
Tel: +886 4 781.2012; +886 9 2197.5153
Email: showimc@gmail.com
Web: www.cbshow.org.tw

The hospital opened in 2006 with 1,000 beds and nearly 400 physicians and surgeons. JCI accredited in 2009, it is affiliated with Johns Hopkins University, Tokyo Women's Hospital, Vancouver General in Canada, and Garfield Medical Center in Los Angeles.

Chang Bing Show Chwan Memorial Hospital is a new concept in health facilities design: a health park that integrates treatment facilities, an art gallery, a movie theater, and a museum, along with restaurants, retail stores, recreational facilities, and convenient transportation into what its planners call "a unique and holistic healthcare experience."

Show Chwan staffers work to integrate a patient-centered philosophy with the latest medical technology, including PET/CT scanning, robotic-assisted arm (minimally invasive) surgery, and Gamma Knife radiosurgery.

Show Chwan's treatment specialties include orthopedics, cardiovascular surgery, gastroenterology, neurology and neurosurgery, and cosmetic procedures.

Accreditation: Joint Commission International

Leading Specialties: Cardiology and heart surgery, cosmetic and reconstructive surgery, neurology and spine surgery, orthopedics

E-Da Hospital
No. 1 Jiau-Shu Tsuen Road, Yan-Chao Shiang
Kaohsiung County 824, TAIWAN
Tel: +886 7 615.0011
Email: ed103221@edah.org.tw
Web: edah-hospital.com

E-Da Hospital opened its doors in 2004. Two hundred physicians and surgeons at this regional teaching hospital treat patients in a 1,246-bed facility that boasts impressive modern architecture and luxurious interior decor complete with pianists performing in the lobby, light and water shows, art exhibits, and numerous cultural activities.

E-Da's doctors specialize in minimally invasive surgeries; esophageal and voice reconstruction; total joint replacement; brachial plexus injury; hyperhidrosis (excessive sweating); Gamma Knife radiosurgery; prostate laser surgery; sleep assessments; and cardiac catheterization. E-Da employs technologically advanced equipment, including Gamma Knife, 64-slice CT, and MRI.

Chin-Kun Huang International Endoscopic Obesity Center is part of E-Da Hospital. Surgeons there perform mostly gastric bypass operations, with smaller numbers of LAP-BAND and sleeve gastrectomies. The center is a member of the Asia Pacific Metabolic and Bariatric Surgery Society and the International Federation for the Surgery of Obesity and Metabolic Disorders.

E-Da's International Service Center team offers advice on physicians and procedures, assistance with visa applications, and arrangements for local accommodations. Case managers offer email and teleconferencing communication with physicians and assistance with local and international travel. An internet platform is provided for web-conferencing once patients return home.

E-Da received initial JCI accreditation in 2008 and was re-accredited in 2011.

Accreditation: Joint Commission International

Leading Specialties: Cosmetic and reconstructive surgery, orthopedics, weight loss surgery

National Taiwan University Hospital
No. 7, Chung (Zhong) Shan South Road, Zhongzheng District
Taipei 10002, TAIWAN
Tel: +886 2 2356.2900
Email: ntuhimsc@ntuh.gov.tw
Web: www.ntuh.gov.tw

Established in 1895, National Taiwan University Hospital (NTUH) is affiliated with the National Taiwan University College of Medicine. NTUH provides a comprehensive range of specialty and sub-specialty services with more than 2,300 beds in the main hospital and five branch hospitals throughout the island. This JCI-accredited facility treats more than 13,000 international patients each year.

NTUH employs more than 1,300 full-time physicians, surgeons, attending doctors, and medical residents. All physicians are certified; many have received advanced training in Europe, the US, or Japan. In recent years, NTUH has accomplished a number of groundbreaking clinical achievements, including

Asia's first successful positive cross-matched living donor kidney transplant in 2005 and Asia's first robotics-assisted kidney transplant in 2012.

NTUH is the leading hospital for cardiovascular treatment in Taiwan, treating around 3,400 cardiac catheterization cases every year. It has carried out more than 400 heart transplants, with a success rate exceeding 90 percent. NTUH's Cardiovascular Center opened in 2012.

NTUH has several transplant teams that perform heart, liver, lung, kidney, and bone marrow transplants. Its three-year survival rate for kidney transplant is 96 percent; for living donor liver transplant, 82 percent.

NTUH's hepatology (liver, gallbladder, pancreas) service center is one of the leading medical and research units in the world. It provides continuous screening, management, and outcome monitoring services for patients with chronic liver diseases and hepatocellular carcinoma.

NTUH's oncology team specializes in treating HCC, non-small cell lung cancer, nasopharyngeal cancer, and advanced gastric cancer. All NTUH departments have extensive expertise treating diseases common to ethnic Chinese.

NTUH established its International Medical Service Center in 2005 to support patients from overseas and from Mainland China. The center offers appointment scheduling, billing coordination, doctor referrals, assistance with travel planning, medical visa application, transportation, and translation.

Accreditation: Joint Commission International

Leading Specialties: Cardiology and heart surgery, oncology, transplant

Taipei Medical University Shuang Ho Hospital
No. 291, Zhongzheng Road, Zhonghe District
New Taipei 23561, TAIWAN
Tel: +886 2 2249.0088
Email: 12340@s.tmu.edu.tw
Web: www.shh.org.tw

Opened in 2008, Taipei Medical University Shuang Ho Hospital offers outpatient, inpatient, and emergency services, plus 36 specialties and subspecialties, including oncology, cataract surgery,

joint replacement, minimally invasive surgery, peritoneal dialysis, radiosurgery, stroke treatment, and health screenings.

Shuang Ho is equipped with state-of-the-art equipment for diagnosis and treatment, including PET/CT, 3T-MRI, Gamma Knife, and TomoTherapy. The hospital has 10 specialty centers: Aesthetic Laser Center, Cancer Center, Dialysis Center, Health Management Center, Hyperbaric Oxygen Therapy Center, PET/CT Center, Radiation Therapy Center, Sleep Center, Stroke Center, and Disabled Patient Oral Health Center.

The Cancer Center integrates 13 functional groups and 11 medical teams including, nutritionists, pharmacists, social workers, religious practitioners, and community resources to provide comprehensive care. The Radiation Therapy Center offers image-guided volumetric modulated arc therapy, TomoTherapy, Gamma Knife, and brachytherapy.

With the only medical heliport permitted in New Taipei City, Shuang Ho offers emergency medical air transportation for patients visiting or living in remote areas, islands, or other countries, including Mainland China.

Services for international patients include appointment scheduling; document coordination; language translation; daily inpatient support; transportation; and support before, during, and after hospitalization.

Shuang Ho received JCI accreditation in 2009 and was re-accredited in 2012.

Accreditation: Joint Commission International

Leading Specialties: Oncology, orthopedics

Taipei Medical University Wan Fang Hospital
No. 111, Hsing-long Road, Sec 3, Wenshan District
Taipei 116, TAIWAN
Tel: +886 2 2930.7930
Email: ims@wanfang.gov.tw
Web: www.taiwanhealthcare.com

Located beside a major transit station in Taipei, Taipei Medical University Wan Fang Hospital has been operating since 1997 as Taiwan's first publicly owned and privately operated hospital. Wan Fang Hospital has 730 beds, more than 350 full-time physicians, and more than 2,000 additional staff members.

Because it is affiliated with Taipei Medical University, many doctors in training from the university complete internships at Wan Fang.

Wan Fang has 43 medical departments with specialists in every major category. Wan Fang is especially well known for its neurosurgery, cardiology, and orthopedics departments; its Health Examination Center; and its specialty medical care centers, such as its CyberKnife Center, Cancer Center, Obesity Prevention Center, Infertility Treatment Center, Laser Cosmetic Center, and Burn Center.

The hospital has established the International Liaison Center for assisting foreign visitors. Available services include an international medical service website; travel planning; lodging arrangements; direct admission; billing coordination; and assistance before, during, and after hospitalization.

In 2006 Wan Fang received its initial JCI accreditation, the first medical center in Taiwan to receive the award. JCI re-accredited the hospital in 2009 and 2012.

Accreditation: Joint Commission International

Leading Specialties: Cardiology and heart surgery, neurology and spine surgery, oncology, orthopedics

Taipei Medical University Wan Fang Hospital

No. 252, Wu Hsing Street
Taipei 110, TAIWAN
Tel: +886 2 2737.2181
Email: ipc@tmuh.org.tw
Web: www.tmuh.org.tw/tmuh_en/

Taipei Medical University Wan Fang Hospital was founded in 1976. By 2012 the JCI-accredited facility had expanded to 833 beds, with 28 specialty medical departments. Thirty-nine sub-specialty medical departments provide a broad range of clinical services.

The facility's main specialty centers include the Center for Reproductive Medicine; Cardiovascular Center; da Vinci Surgery Center; Joint Replacement Center; Health Management Center; Breast Health Management Center; Comprehensive Weight Management Center; Esthetic Medical Center; Stereotactic Radiosurgery Center; and Traditional Chinese Medicine Center.

All specialty centers take an integrated approach to patient care and treatment. The Center for Repro-

ductive Medicine has helped tens of thousands of infertile couples conceive. The Joint Replacement Center annually performs 500 arthroscopic surgeries, 200 joint replacement surgeries, and 150 spinal surgeries—all using minimally invasive surgery techniques.

The Comprehensive Weight Management Center integrates traditional Chinese medicine and Western medicine emphasizing diet control, medication, exercise, intragastric balloon, and laparoscopic bariatric surgery.

Emphasizing cutting-edge technology, the Stereotactic Radiosurgery Center uses highly accurate laser equipment, including image-guided volumetric modulated arc therapy and TomoTherapy.

The International Patient Center supports patients with travel planning, accommodation arrangements, medical visa application, translation, cost estimates, billing, and appointment coordination.

Accreditation: Joint Commission International

Leading Specialties: Cardiology and heart surgery, cosmetic and reconstructive surgery, fertility and reproductive medicine, orthopedics, weight loss surgery, wellness and prevention

Taipei Nobel Eye Clinic

No. 13, 5th floor, Gongyuan Road, Zhongzheng District
Taipei 10046, TAIWAN
Tel: +886 2 2370.5666; +886 2 6630.2226
Email: debbie@nobelgroup.com.tw
Web: nobelgroupeng.com.tw

Established in 2001 under the management of Taiwan Nobel Medical Group, Taipei Nobel Eye Clinic specializes in laser vision correction surgery and cataract refractive surgery. Both are outpatient procedures with short recovery times. The clinic is known in Taiwan for its top team of ophthalmologists and state-of-the-art medical equipment.

Procedures include femtosecond IntraLase and iris location wavefront LASIK operation; femtosecond laser presbyopia therapy; strabismic amblyopia treatment; treatment of cornea diseases; and ultrasonic lens emulsification surgery for cataracts.

Leading Specialties: Ophthalmology

DESTINATION: **THAILAND**

■ AT A GLANCE

Bangkok, Phuket, Chonburi

Languages	Thai, English widely spoken in business and medical circles
Time Zone	GMT +7
Country Dialing Code	+66
Electricity	220V, plug types A, B, and C
Currency	Thai baht (THB)
Leading Specialties	Cardiology and heart surgery, cosmetic and reconstructive surgery, dentistry, fertility and reproductive medicine, gender reassignment, health screening, neurology and spine surgery, oncology, ophthalmology, orthopedics, weight loss surgery, wellness and prevention
Standards and Affiliations	Thailand Health System Research Institute; Institute of Hospital Quality Improvement and Accreditation; National Health Commission Office; Thailand Ministry of Public Health; Society of Plastic and Reconstructive Surgeons of Thailand; Thai Association of Orthodontists
International Accreditation	Joint Commission International

■ TREATMENT BRIEF

Despite social and political unrest over the past few years, Thailand's steadily rising economy has brought this land of 67 million well into the ranks of industrialized nations. Long the world's largest exporter of rice, Thailand now also has a firm foothold in electronics and light manufacturing, tourism, and a host of other sectors contributing to a rising urban middle class.

In response, the Thai government has dramatically overhauled its healthcare system over the past decade, providing 19 million Thais with universal health coverage, along with new hospitals, state-of-the-art instrumentation, technology, and healthcare services.

Thais are known for their exceptional hospitality, one reason why Thailand is one of Asia's top tourism destinations. Service and graciousness extend deep into the clinical experience as well. Western healthcare providers would be prudent to examine Thailand's version of patient-centered care!

Thailand's world-renowned spas and wellness resorts, often set in breathtaking coastal surroundings, make this remarkable land even more appealing to the health traveler, particularly in a world now more conscious of prevention and alternative treatment strategies. Medical spas such as the S-Spa in Bangkok have led the world in combining relaxation with clinical procedures performed under medical supervision.

■ THAILAND AND MEDICAL TRAVEL

Although it now shares the spotlight with India, Singapore, and Malaysia, Thailand is the rightful wellspring of contemporary international health travel.

With the crash of the Thai baht in the late 1990s, business and governmental leaders capitalized on Thailand's excellent medical infrastructure to attract US expatriates and cross-border patients from nearby countries with less robust healthcare choices. Patients from the Middle East, Cambodia, Laos, and Vietnam were rapidly followed by European clients.

As a result, today thousands of Americans and Canadians travel to Bangkok or Phuket, mostly for savings on elective surgeries that more than compensate for the uncomfortably long flight.

Asia's first JCI accreditation went to a hospital in Bangkok. Thirty-two Thai hospitals are now JCI accredited, more than any other country in South or Southeast Asia.

Thailand's huge medical calling card is Bangkok's venerated, JCI-accredited Bumrungrad International Hospital, covering a 93,000-square-meter (one million-square-foot) complex in downtown Bangkok. Over 1,200 full-time and consulting physicians representing every imaginable specialty and subspecialty practice there—more than 200 have been US board certified.

Bumrungrad has set the pace for both the quality and quantity of contemporary international healthcare throughout Asia and the world. Bumrungrad's large presence is not without its competition, and the equally impressive Dusit Medical Group owns and operates a large network of hospitals throughout Thailand, including Bangkok International Hospital, Bangkok Hospital Phuket, Bangkok General Hospital, and Samitivej Sukhumvit Hospital.

Thailand offers the medical traveler far more than the transgender procedures that often occupy the media limelight. Specialties include cosmetic surgery, orthopedics, cardiology, fertility and reproductive medicine, spine surgery, and dentistry. Despite rising standards of living, Thailand remains one of the world's best values, with cost savings on medical procedures ranging from 40–60 percent over out-of-pocket fees found in the US, the EU, and Japan.

Although not Thailand's native tongue, English is becoming more widely spoken in Thai cities and resort centers, and English is taught as a second language in Thai schools. Although extremes of wealth and poverty can be readily witnessed, health travelers may feel more comfortable in Thai culture than in India or South Africa.

■ SELECTED HOSPITALS AND CLINICS

Bangkok Hospital Medical Center
2 Soi Soonvijai 7, New Phetchaburi Road, Bangkapi, Huai Khwang
Bangkok 10310, THAILAND
Tel: +66 2 310.3000
Email: info@bangkokhospital.com
Web: bangkokhospital.com

The flagship of Thailand's largest hospital group (Dusit Medical Group), Bangkok Hospital Medical Center (BMC) has more than 650 full-time and consulting physicians, 700 nurses, and numerous teams of support technicians and specialists. BMC boasts that many of its internationally trained and certified physicians have returned to their homeland committed to improving the quality of national healthcare through advanced treatments and procedures.

BMC is one of the most technologically sophisticated hospitals in Thailand, an expansive, state-of-the-art medical campus providing comprehensive medical care through multi-disciplinary teams of highly trained specialists. With its four hospitals and broad range of specialized clinics, BMC is equipped with diagnostic and treatment facilities not generally available at local hospitals. The center received JCI accreditation in 2013 and is known throughout the world for delivering world-class, award-winning healthcare.

BMC boasts four hospital buildings: Bangkok International Hospital, Bangkok Heart Hospital, Bangkok Hospital, and Wattanasoth Cancer Hospital, with two supporting buildings for dentistry and rehabilitation. The three focuses at BMC are cardiology, oncology, and neurology.

Bangkok International Hospital was the first Thai medical center to serve international patients. Its International Medical Center improved and expanded its services in 2002 and now serves more than 140,000 patients annually from more than 60 countries. Sixteen specialized centers, ranging from orthopedics to neurology to cardiology, have brought together internationally trained physicians and state-of-the-art medical technology to attract visitors from all parts of the world.

Bangkok Heart Hospital is Thailand's first and only dedicated private heart hospital. It is equipped with advanced technology and staffed by dedicated personnel who deal with nearly every heart condition, including diagnostics, interventional cardiology, cardiac surgery, and rehabilitation. It boasts one of Thailand's only da Vinci robotic-assisted systems, used in minimally invasive surgeries. Procedures include cardiac MRI, CT angiogram, adult stem cell therapies, radiofrequency ablation, pacemaker, and an all-artery cardiac bypass surgery.

Wattanasoth Cancer Hospital is the only dedicated private cancer hospital in Thailand. The center is offers PET/CT scanning, NOVALIS for intensity-modulated radiosurgery and radiotherapy, and Gamma Knife for radiosurgery of the brain.

At the Bangkok Neuroscience Center, 12 neurologists and 14 neurosurgeons treat a host of diseases and traumas, including headache; dizziness and vertigo; stroke and its aftermath; seizures; Parkinson's and related diseases; Alzheimer's; brain and spinal cord injury; tumors of the brain and spinal cord; muscle and nerve diseases; paresthesia of the limbs, trunk, or face; developmental disorders; and genetic anomalies.

The Neuroscience Center deploys the Leskell Gamma Knife, a radiosurgical device that enables doctors to treat deep-seated brain lesions without the risks of open-skull surgery. Hundreds of precisely targeted beams of cobalt gamma radiation painlessly "cut" through brain tumors, blood vessel malformations, and other abnormalities, allowing neurosurgeons to correct disorders not currently treatable using established procedures.

BMC's patient wards rival top hospitals in the US. They include a guest sofa bed for a companion, personal telephone for international calls, microwave oven, refrigerator, personal safe, free internet access, free English-language newspaper, and an inpatient library. The BMC campus offers amenities from concierge services and luxury accommodations to translation and visa assistance.

Fixed-price packages can be found on the BMC website in 12 specialty areas, including dental, ENT, urology, LASIK, heart screenings and surgeries, cancer screenings and treatments, and neurology.

Accreditation: Joint Commission International

Leading Specialties: Cardiology and heart surgery, dentistry, neurology and spine surgery, oncology, orthopedics

Bangkok Hospital Phuket

2/1 Hongyok Utis Road, Muang District
Phuket 83000, THAILAND
Tel: +66 7625.4425
Email: info@phukethospital.com
Web: phukethospital.com

Bangkok Hospital Phuket is on Phuket Island near Patong Beach. Since opening its doors in 1995 as a joint venture among Bangkok Dusit Medical Services, Anuphas and Sons, and a group of local investors, the hospital has been offering a full range of services. It runs specialty centers for colorectal diseases, cosmetic surgery, pediatrics, diabetes, endocrinology, kidney diseases, ENT, vision, liver and gastrointestinal disorders, cardiology, rehabilitation, and women's health. Wellness Diamond packages for executives include an array of blood tests, ultrasound, x-ray, MRI, cardiac computed tomography angiography , treadmill test, pulmonary function test, ECG, a dental checkup, and an eye test.

The hospital can serve 1,000 outpatients and 200 inpatients in its 24 specialized care centers, which include five operating rooms, 11 ICU beds, and eight CCU beds. The hospital runs 10 outreach clinics at various locations around Phuket. Bangkok Hospital Phuket earned its first JCI accreditation in 2009.

Accreditation: Joint Commission International

Leading Specialties: Cardiology and heart surgery, cosmetic and reconstructive surgery, orthopedics

Bangkok International Dental Center

157 Ratchadaphisek Road, Din Daeng
Bangkok 10400, THAILAND
Tel: +66 2692.4433
Email: contact@bangkokdentalcenter.com
Web: bangkokdentalcenter.com

A favorite of Thai and regional expats, Bangkok International Dental Center (BIDC) and its Smile Signature dental clinics jointly provide more than 60 treatment rooms and have a team of more than 100 dentists and dental specialists. Parent company Dental Corporation, is one of the largest private dental network groups in Thailand.

Many BIDC dentists have graduated from universities in the UK, the Americas, and Australia, and continue their training through courses conducted at BIDC clinics and at other institutions.

The main BIDC headquarters is a 4,500-square-meter (48,000-square-foot) complex consisting of a seven-story dental clinic, a 30-room hotel, a bank, a restaurant, and a coffee shop. The clinic has its own on-site laboratory specializing in dental implants. BIDC was the first center in Thailand to offer the SLActive Straumann Dental Implant system, as well as the Bone Level Straumann Dental Implant system. BIDC's team of implantologists boasts one of the highest dental implant success rates in the country.

BIDC provides many amenities for its patients, including free high-speed internet, cable television, and private conference and consultation rooms. BIDC also offers special rates for guests at selected hotels near its clinics.

BIDC was recently awarded accreditation by the US-based Joint Commission International Ambulatory Care Division, one of the few dental clinics in Asia currently JCI accredited. BIDC is also the recipient of the prestigious Prime Minister's Export Award Best Service Provider for Hospital/Clinics, the first dental clinic to be so honored. The dental center has also won other numerous private and governmental awards as an outstanding international dental service provider.

Accreditation: Joint Commission International

Leading Specialties: Dentistry

BNH Hospital

9/1 Convent Road, Silom
Bangkok 10500, THAILAND
Tel: +66 2686.2700
Email: info@bnh.co.th
Web: bnhhospital.com

Founded in the ninteenth century, BNH is one of Thailand's oldest healthcare facilities and the first international hospital in Thailand. More than 75,000 international patients visit BNH annually from 150 different countries. The hospital has nearly 440 physicians from every medical service area.

Specialty centers include the Spine Center, Women's Health Center, and the International Travel Medicine Clinic. The renowned Preecha Aesthetic Institute is also housed within BNH.

BNH operates a special center for spinal and orthopedic surgery. Since opening in 2005, the Spine Center has performed more than 200 complex surgeries, nearly half of them for international patients. The surgical team has also implanted more than 100 disc prostheses, a rate higher than some centers in the US or EU. The center's total artificial disc replacement is a minimally invasive surgery, so the patient experiences less blood loss and significantly less pain.

With 60–70 percent cost savings compared to what patients can negotiate from a US and EU hospital for a similar procedure, the success rate runs an impressive 90 percent, well above international averages of 60–70 percent.

Accreditation: Joint Commission International

Leading Specialties: Dentistry, fertility and reproductive medicine, orthopedics, spine surgery

Bumrungrad International Hospital

33 Sukhumvit 3 (Soi Nana Nua), Wattana
Bangkok 10101, THAILAND
Tel: +66 2667.1000
Email: info@bumrungrad.com
Web: bumrungrad.com

Established in 1980, the venerated Bumrungrad International Hospital serves more than one million patients per year, including more than 400,000 international patients who visit from 190 countries.

This 580-bed facility provides a full range of tertiary healthcare services, including 19 operating rooms equipped for most general surgery and surgical specialties. Some are minimally invasive, including cardiothoracic, orthopedic, urological, ophthalmological, laser, transplant, and otolaryngological (ear, nose, and throat) surgeries.

Bumrungrad International was the first hospital in Asia to obtain JCI accreditation, in 2002, and has been re-accredited four times since then. One of Thailand's 32 JCI-accredited hospitals, Bumrungrad was the first Asian hospital to receive JCI disease-specific accreditations for its stroke and heart programs.

Of its 1,200 physicians, surgeons, and consultants, approximately 220 are US board certified, making the facility a favorite of Western medical travelers, expats, and regional business executives.

Bumrungrad Heart Center offers pacemaker implantation, invasive and non-invasive procedures for congenital heart disease, valvoplasty (balloon valve treatment) and valve replacement, and coronary artery bypass graft (CABG).

The hospital's Horizon Regional Cancer Center employs image-guided radiotherapy and HD brachytherapy. Orthopedic procedures, such as hip replacements and resurfacing, are also popular among international patients.

Unlike most hospitals, Bumrungrad's costs are transparent to the patient. The facility posts all-in package pricing for more than 70 procedures in seven specialty areas, including health screenings, cosmetic surgery, women's medicine, and urology. Patients might be surprised to see package pricing available even for complex procedures, such as a hip replacement or a coronary artery bypass.

Similarly, Bumrungrad is one of the only hospitals in the world to post actual costs online through its REALCOST program, which tracks invoices of some 40 procedures performed within the previous year. Patients can find package pricing and specially posted discounts online. US hospitals would do well to note these innovative initiatives.

Accreditation: Joint Commission International

Leading Specialties: Cardiology and heart surgery, cosmetic and reconstructive surgery, dentistry, health screening, neurology and spine surgery, oncology, ophthalmology, orthopedics, weight loss surgery, wellness and prevention

Phuket International Hospital

44 Chalermprakiat Ror 9 Road
Phuket 83000, THAILAND
Tel: +66 7 624.9400
Email: info@phuketinternationalhospital.com
Web: phuketinternationalhospital.com

Founded in 1982 and JCI accredited in 2012, Phuket International Hospital (PIH) was the first private hospital to open in the area. Extensively remodeled during 2007, a new wing of the hospital contains an outpatient facility and additional patient rooms, which have increased the hospital's occupancy to 150 beds.

The hospital runs specialty centers and clinics for cardiology; pediatrics; dentistry; otolaryngology; infertility; neurology; neurosurgery; orthopedics; plastic surgery; rheumatology; sinus disorders and allergies; skin; and women's health. PIH aggressively promotes its medical checkup packages tailored for Western patients. A variety of tests and exam packages are offered at prices well below fees encountered in the US.

For those interested in alternative therapies, the Acupuncture and Alternative Medicine Center offers massage, Chinese herbal medicine, *tui na* (Eastern bodywork therapy), and cupping (the use of suction cups in place of needles at acupuncture points).

The International Office assists health travelers and referring physicians looking for a consultation, second opinion, or treatment for a complex illness or injury. International staff members speak a wide range of languages. They schedule appointments; coordinate activities from admissions through discharge; make transportation arrangements; and assist with financial arrangements.

Accreditation: Joint Commission International

Leading Specialties: Cardiology and heart surgery, cosmetic and reconstructive surgery, dentistry, health screening, neurology, orthopedics

Piyavate International Hospital

998 Rimkhlong Samsen Road, Bangkapi, Huai Khwang
Bangkok 10310, THAILAND
Tel: +66 2 625.6650
Email: imcc@piyavate.net
Web: piyavate.com

Piyavate International Hospital, a publicly owned healthcare services facility, began serving patients in 1993. This 26-story hospital houses nearly 300 inpatient beds and offers numerous medical specialties. Centers of excellence include Neuroscience Center, Oncology and Gene Therapy Center, Eye Center, Perfect Heart Fitness Center, Urology Center, and Internal Medicine Clinic.

Piyavate's Advanced Dental Institute provides services ranging from dental implants and cosmetic dentistry to oral surgery and braces. The hospital's Aesthetic Surgery Institute offers cosmetic plastic surgery and, through its Romrawin Clinic, comprehensive treatment for skin conditions and anti-aging skin care. In Piyavate's Rehabilitation Center, advanced equipment is utilized to provide patients with physical therapy and occupational rehabilitation.

Treatments in the Traditional Chinese Medicine Center include acupuncture, Chinese herbal medicine, and *tui na* massage. Piyavate also offers competitively priced physical exams and checkups, including a blood test, diabetes test, DNA test, and stress test, plus a breast and gynecological examination for women.

Services to international patients include appointment scheduling; financial and billing arrangements; assistance with insurance; airport pickup and drop-off; visa and flight preparation; and interpreter services (Arabic, Italian, Bangladesh, Hindi Urdu, Filipino, Chinese, Vietnamese, and Japanese).

Leading Specialties: Cosmetic and reconstructive surgery, dentistry

Preecha Aesthetic Institute

898/1 Sukumvit Soi 55, Wattana, North Klong Ton
Bangkok 10110, THAILAND
Tel: + 66 2 715.0111
Email: consult@pai.co.th
Web: pai.co.th

Preecha Aesthetic Institute (PAI) is headed by Dr. Preecha Tiewtranon, a leader in modern plastic, reconstructive, and aesthetic surgery. Former chairman of the plastic surgery unit of King Chulalongkorn University Medical School, he has served as president of the Society of Plastic and Reconstructive Surgeons of Thailand and as president of the Society of Aesthetic Surgeons of Thailand.

As of 2005, Dr. Preecha had performed more than 30,000 cosmetic and plastic surgeries. As Bangkok's undisputed authority in gender reassignment, he has trained most of Thailand's qualified gender reassignment surgeons, and his techniques have become standard practice throughout the world. From 1980 to 2005, Dr. Preecha performed more than 3,500 gender reassignment and facial feminization surgeries.

PAI's modern hospital facility, in the heart of Bangkok, houses 10 treatment rooms and offers a full range of dermatological treatments and plastic surgeries in its Aesthetic Plastic Surgery Center and Dermatology and Laser Center. The institute's staff of 30 includes practitioners who hold diplomas from the American Board of Surgery and surgeons board certified in the US, Australia, and Thailand.

PAI's services include cheekbone, facial, and jaw contouring; eye therapies; rhinoplasty; various surgeries of the ear, lips, and chin; hair transplant and laser hair removal; and mammoplasty, labiaplasty, and vaginoplasty. Certain physicians at PAI specialize in body contouring, facial feminization, and gender reassignment surgery.

Leading Specialties: Cosmetic and reconstructive surgery

Samitivej Srinakarin Hospital

488 Srinakarin Road, Suanluang
Bangkok 10250, THAILAND
Tel: +66 0 2378.9000
Email: info.srinakarin@samitivej.co.th
Web: samitivejhospitals.com

Samitivej Srinakarin Hospital is the group's newest addition to the Samitivej Network, located on Bangkok's east side, a few minutes from Bangkok's Suvarnabhumi International Airport. The 400-bed, 17-story main hospital building is surrounded by 8.5 hectares (21 acres) of landscaped gardens and fountains that foster an environment of tranquility.

Specialties include cardiovascular, oncology, reproductive medicine, cosmetic surgery, dentistry, ENT, and ophthalmology. Its Wellness Center focuses on preventive care and executive screenings.

Srinakarin's Cancer Center and Oncology Clinic focus on prevention, screening, diagnosis, and outpatient treatment. A full team of multi-lingual medical, surgical, and radiation oncologists, physicists, and oncology nurses render Srinakarin one of Thailand's most renowned cancer treatment facilities.

The Samitivej Srinakarin Children's Hospital, opened in 2003, remains Thailand's largest dedicated pediatric facility.

A complete range of dental services and oral surgeries is offered at the hospital's Dental Center, including orthodontics, root canal, full and partial dentures, crowns and bridges, implants, extraction, bone graft surgery, and treatment of gum disease. Seven dental units, three x-ray operating suites, a panoramic x-ray machine, a laser system, and an intraoral camera make this center a state-of-the-art, one-stop shop with no need for multiple trips to offsite labs.

Samitivej Srinakarin received its first JCI accreditation in 2009 and was fully re-accredited in 2012.

Accreditation: Joint Commission International

Leading Specialties: Cosmetic surgery, dentistry, health screening, oncology

Samitivej Sriracha Hospital

8 Soi Laemket, Jermompol Rd, Sriracha
Chonburi 20110, THAILAND
Tel: +66 0 3832.0300
Email: infossh@samitivej.co.th
Web: samitivejhospitals.com/Sriracha/en

Samitivej Sriracha Hospital is 100 kilometers (60 miles) southeast of Bangkok. Since its opening more than a dozen years ago, this 150-bed hospital has become a key healthcare provider for corporations and industries on Thailand's eastern seaboard.

Sriracha's proximity to the resort towns of Pattaya and Rayong also attracts many regionals, tourists, and expats seeking quality medical care. The hospital has 15 intensive care units and six operating rooms. Its specialty services include the Children's Clinic, Dental Clinic, and Wellness Center.

Accreditation: Joint Commission International

Leading Specialties: Cardiology and heart surgery, dentistry, health screening, wellness and prevention

Samitivej Sukhumvit Hospital

133 Sukhumvit 49, Klongtan Nua, Vadhana
Bangkok 10110, THAILAND
Tel: +66 2 711.8000
Email: info@samitivej.co.th
Web: samitivejhospitals.com/sukhumvit/en

In operation since 1979, Samitivej Sukhumvit Hospital has 270 beds, 87 examination suites, 400 full- and part-time physicians, and 1,200 caregivers.

Sukhumvit offers five specialty centers. The Eye Clinic specializes in general ophthalmology, pediatric ophthalmology and strabismus, retinal and vitreous conditions, glaucoma, oculoplastic reconstruction, and ocular oncology.

A Hemodialysis department treats patients with acute or chronic renal failure. Certified by the Royal College of Physicians of Thailand, the department is known throughout the country for its success rate in kidney transplantation. Kidneys are received from the Thai Red Cross Organ Donation Center. Artificial kidney machines are also deployed for hemodialysis.

The Liver and Digestive Institute treats liver and digestive diseases, including cirrhosis, fatty liver disease, pancreatitis, and infection of the bile duct and gallbladder. Specialty surgeries include liver transplantation as well as procedures on the liver, bile duct, gallbladder, esophagus, stomach, small intestine, and large intestine.

The Minimally Invasive Bone and Joint Center provides evaluation, diagnosis, and treatment for all bone- and joint-related ailments. The center's orthopedic surgeons treat broken bones, displaced joints, joint inflammation, slipped discs, and congenital malformations. They frequently perform microsurgery for the knee and shoulder as well as hip and knee replacements.

Sukhumvit's Plastic Surgery Clinic offers all types of cosmetic and reconstructive surgery, including rhinoplasty (nose); upper and lower blepharoplasty (eyelids); abdominal lipectomy (tummy tuck); facelift; liposuction; breast augmentation; chin augmentation; scar revision/repair; correction of congenital abnormalities; and breast reconstruction. UltraPulse and Sharplan carbon dioxide lasers are used to remove skin tags, warts, moles, and scars safely and effectively.

The hospital has a full-service International Patient Center. Interpreters assist patients in Arabic, English, French, German, Japanese, and Korean. The hospital's immigration counter assists foreigners with visa and other immigration requirements.

American visitors will feel at home with a 7-Eleven, Starbucks, and ATMs on the ground level of the hospital. Sukhumvit treats nearly 100,000 international patients annually, more than 16,000 of them from the US and Canada.

Samitivej Sukhumvit received its initial JCI award in 2007 and was most recently re-accredited in 2013.

Accreditation: Joint Commission International

Leading Specialties: Cosmetic and reconstructive surgery, dentistry, ophthalmology, orthopedics, spine surgery

TRSC International LASIK Center

968 Rama IV Road, U Chu Liang Building, 6th floor, Silom, Bangrak
Bangkok 10500, THAILAND
Tel: +66 2 733.2020
Email: inter@lasikthai.com
Web: lasikthai.com

Opened in 1997, TRSC International LASIK Center was founded by Dr. Ekktet Chansue and Wanida Chansue with the goal of creating a refractive surgery clinic in Thailand meeting international standards of excellence. Now the largest stand-alone LASIK facility in Asia, TRSC focuses especially on refractive eye surgery, cataract eye surgery, and phakic intraocular lens implantation surgery. The center has performed 44,000 eye surgeries since 1997 and annually manages 3,000 appointments and performs more than 2,000 surgeries.

TRSC's specialized focus on refractive surgery has enabled it to channel its investments into the latest diagnosis equipment and lasers for treatment. The center offers three types of LASIK, including FemtoLASIK (bladeless LASIK) with Wavefront analysis to provide greater surgical accuracy. Center surgeons are US board-certified ophthalmologists trained in refractive surgery in the US, Canada, and Germany.

TRSC provides personal counselors to accompany international patients throughout the treatment process. Counselors are available 24 hours a day and provide a range of additional services, including assistance with hotel arrangements, administrative support, and handling medical documents. Translators are available for Japanese, English, and other languages. The center performs more than 500 surgeries on international patients each year.

Leading Specialties: Ophthalmology

Yanhee International Hospital

454 Charansanitwong Road, Bang-O, Bangplad
Bangkok 10700, THAILAND
Tel: +66 2 879.0300
Email: info@yanhee.net
Web: yanhee.net

What started out as Yanhee Polyclinic in 1984 is today Yanhee International Hospital, a modern, ten-story building with 400 beds, serving 2,000 outpatients daily. The hospital is expanding rapidly: a 15-story addition opened in 2009, and another new building to house outpatient facilities was completed in 2012.

Yanhee employs 95 full-time doctors and 120 part-time health professionals, along with 800 nurses and other staff members. Its facilities include an intensive care unit, dialysis unit, nursery emergency room, laboratory, and 95 examination rooms and delivery rooms.

Among its several specialties, Yanhee is especially well known for low-cost plastic surgery and aesthetic treatments. Its Beauty Center offers services in dermatology, cosmetic surgery, treatment of varicose veins, and weight control, and encompasses a Snoring and Voice Change Center, Hair Center, and Permanent Cosmetic Tattoo Center.

Aesthetic dentistry, laser dentistry, prosthetics, and oral surgery are provided at the hospital's Dental Center. Treatments at the Naturopathic Center include acupuncture, colonic irrigation, and Thai traditional medicine.

Yanhee's website lists prices in US dollars for a large number of individual procedures and treatment packages. First-time visitors are often surprised to see Yanhee orderlies dashing about on roller blades delivering medical documents, lab tests, and other transportables around the busy facility.

Yanhee received its initial JCI accreditation in 2011.

Accreditation: Joint Commission International

Leading Specialties: Cosmetic and reconstructive surgery

Sex and the City: Thai-Style

No discussion of healthcare in Thailand would be complete without at least a mention of gender re-assignment surgery. Difficult to obtain in the US without a good deal of red tape and expense, sex re-assignment treatment options are probably more available in Bangkok than anywhere else on the planet.

Women can choose from a smorgasbord ranging from vaginoplasty (a rejuvenative tightening of the vagina) to full female-to-male gender re-assignment; men are offered single or full orchiectomy (testicle removal), penile width enhancement, penile lengthening, and full male-to-female gender re-assignment.

Partially because of Bangkok's well-publicized sex industry, hundreds of sex change clinics have seized on Thailand's recent successes in medical travel. Unfortunately, many prey on the vulnerable. Thus, as with any other medical procedure, patients should conduct careful investigations, including thorough reference checks and re-doubled research on clinic accreditation and physician experience. ■

DESTINATION: **TURKEY**

■ AT A GLANCE

Ankara, Beşiktaş, Istanbul, Izmir, Kocaeli

Languages	Turkish, English widely spoken
Time Zone	GMT +2
Country Dialing Code	+90
Electricity	220V, plug type B
Currency	New Turkish lira (TRY)
Leading Specialties	Cardiology and heart surgery, cosmetic and reconstructive surgery, dentistry, health screening, neurology, oncology, ophthalmology, orthopedics, transplant, wellness and prevention
Typical Savings (over USD retail)	50%–65%
Standards and Affiliations	Republic of Turkey Ministry of Health; Turkish Board of Healthcare Professionals; Turkish Medical Association; Turkish Society of Plastic, Reconstructive and Aesthetic Surgery
International Accreditation	Joint Commission International

■ TREATMENT BRIEF

With one foot in Europe and the other in the Near East, Turkey is a land of diverse cultures and landscapes, ranging from the bustling commercial centers of Istanbul to the quiet agricultural villages of the eastern provinces. Now a major presence on the world's economic and political scene, Turkey is poised to play its part in the global healthcare arena as well.

The Turkish Cultural and Tourism Ministry has spent millions to spread the word that Turkey welcomes medical and health travelers. The country has much to offer. Turkish cuisine is among the best in the world. And—if you have the time and feel well enough for a vacation—millions before you have enjoyed the port cities of Marmaris and Fethiye, the stone dwellings of Cappadocia, and the hot springs of Pamukkale.

Turkey boasts a thriving network of more than 1,200 public and private hospitals. Many of its 300 private facilities have developed working relationships with prestigious international medical centers, providing opportunities for staff development and information exchange. Affiliations include Harvard Medical International, Johns Hopkins International, Mayo Clinic, Memorial Sloan-Kettering, and NewYork–Presbyterian.

■ TURKEY AND MEDICAL TRAVEL

Turkey is promoting medical travel in a big way; in 2014 Turkish medical institutions welcomed some 165,000 foreign patients. Few medical travelers realize that Turkey has 51 JCI-accredited hospitals—more than any other country.

The leading healthcare groups are largely to be found in Turkey's three largest cities (Istanbul, Ankara, and Izmir), offering one-stop service to foreign patients and often covering all arrangements from the day of request to the day of departure.

Most medical travelers heading to Turkey are from nearby neighboring regions—the Middle East, the Turkic States, Russia, and North Africa—seeking specialized healthcare unavailable or inadequate in their homelands. More recently, patients from North America and Europe escaping high prices or long waits are discovering Turkey's medical merits. Medical costs in Turkey compare favorably with well-traveled international healthcare destinations in Asia, with high healthcare standards dictated by aggressive national and international accreditation, certification, and oversight.

The visiting patient can expect a comprehensive range of medical services. Turkey's specialties include transplantation (bone, kidney, liver, pancreas, stem cell); genetic testing; neurosurgery (brain cancer, degenerative spine disorder, peripheral nerve surgery, epileptic surgery); ophthalmology (one of the world's largest vision clinic networks is headquartered in Istanbul); cardiology; orthopedics (spine, shoulder, knee, sports, and pediatrics); cosmetic surgery; and dentistry.

■ WELLNESS TOURISM FLOURISHES HERE

Turkey has developed a booming trade in vacation tourism over the last three decades; thus, extending the traditional Turkish warmth and hospitality to medical travelers is not a stretch. Health and wellness travelers see Turkey as a popular destination because of its natural thermal spa resorts and mud baths, which alone attract nearly a half million visitors.

Even though Turkey aggressively promotes to the Western medical traveler, English-speaking patients should be cautious of language barriers and first gain comfort in a facility's translation services.

■ SELECTED HOSPITALS AND CLINICS

Acibadem Healthcare Group

Istanbul Cad. No. 82, Yesilköy Bakirköy, 34149
Istanbul, TURKEY
Tel: +90 216 544.4664
Email: international@acibadem.com.tr
Web: acibademinternational.com

Sixteen full-service general hospitals and 11 outpatient clinics operate within the Acibadem network, which is more than a consortium of bricks-and-mortar healthcare facilities. Its business interests include hospital design and construction, mobile clinics, health and life insurance, facilities management, laboratory testing, and medical education.

In 2012 Acibadem became part of the world's second largest healthcare company, International Healthcare Holdings, a global network that operates hospitals and clinics in Malaysia, Singapore, India, China, and Brunei.

Acibadem operates specialty centers for the treatment of cancer (surgery, radiotherapy, and chemotherapy); heart disease (pediatric and adult cardiology and cardiac surgery); infertility (IVF); transplants (liver, kidney, and bone marrow); spine and joints; sports medicine; nuclear medicine; and robotic-assisted surgery. The newly opened Sports Clinic at Acibadem Fulya adds to the mix, along with Turkey's first comprehensive medical wellness clinic (the Acibadem Life Medical Clinic) at the Bodrum facility.

Acibadem Kadiköy Hospital in Istanbul was the first hospital in the group. Renovated twice since its opening in 1991, the hospital boasts the use of Flash CT, the fastest and lowest radiation computed tomography, which can perform angiography and full-body tomography in seconds. Kadiköy is renowned for its specialists in in vitro fertilization (IVF), cardiology and cardiovascular surgery, and the management of high-risk pregnancies. The Orthopedics and Traumatology Clinic is known for excellence in hand surgery.

Acibadem's International Hospital in Istanbul was Turkey's first Western-style private hospital. It opened its doors in 1989 and joined the Acibadem chain in 2005. In 2006 all clinic areas, examination rooms, and inpatient floors were renovated. The hospital offers a modern intensive care unit, dialysis units for renal patients, as well as emergency observation beds and post-coronary angiography observation units. Advanced imaging for cancer patients employs 1.5 Tesla MRI.

Acibadem Maslak Hospital in Istanbul occupies more than 40,000 square meters (430,000 square feet) of covered area, employing both smart building technology and a nearly paper-free electronic record-keeping system. Specialty clinics serve patients seeking treatment for stroke, thyroid disorders, obesity, and infertility.

In addition to Flash CT, the Maslak Cancer Center utilizes Linear Accelerator (LINAC) Trilogy equipment, which minimizes damage to healthy tissue in cancer treatment; RapidArc (Volumetric Modulated Arc Therapy) technology, which reduces 30-minute cancer treatments to two minutes; CyberKnife to treat tumors that cannot be treated with conventional radiotherapy; and the da Vinci SI robot for laparoscopic surgery.

The International Patient Services Center of Acibadem Hospitals assists health travelers with consultations; diagnostic services; billing and insurance; travel and lodging arrangements; and language interpretation. Its staff members provide cost estimates; schedule medical appointments; assist with international insurance arrangements; help with visa procurement; book hotel rooms; arrange ground transportation from the airport; coordinate hospital admissions; provide copies of medical records; assist with discharge and payment; and support continuing communication with physicians after patient departure.

Health travelers seeking a consultation can send their medical history, diagnostic images, and laboratory test results for review by an Acibadem physician, who will advise a recommended course of treatment and assess whether travel to Turkey is warranted.

Accreditation: Joint Commission International

Leading Specialties: Cardiology and heart surgery, fertility and reproductive medicine, oncology, orthopedics

Anadolu Medical Center

Anadolu Caddesi No. 1, Cayirova Mevkii, Gebze, Cikisi Gebze
Kocaeli 41400, TURKEY
Tel: +90 262 678.5513
Email: int.patients@anadolusaglik.org
Web: anadolusaglik.org

Operating since 2005, Anadolu Medical Center (AMC) is a JCI-accredited hospital with 110 physicians and surgeons, 209 beds, eight operating rooms, and a large intensive care unit. Through its affiliation with Johns Hopkins Medicine in Baltimore, AMC's multilingual nurses and staff members receive training from the Johns Hopkins faculty.

The medical center's 17-hectare (42-acre) campus is home to treatment facilities, medical offices, a medi-hotel, and health-related retail stores—all well away from the hustle and bustle of Istanbul. The campus has earned praise for its architecture and location atop a hill bordered by woodlands and olive groves, and a spectacular sea view. Outreach services are also provided at two satellite clinics in Istanbul (AMC Atasehir and AMC Suadiye).

AMC prides itself on its marriage of cutting-edge technology with a patient-friendly environment. CyberKnife and linear accelerators with an IMRT system are available for cancer treatment. The hospital utilizes state-of-the-art imaging technology, picture archiving and communication systems, telemedicine, and electronic record keeping.

AMC engages multi-disciplinary teams of physicians to resolve complicated health problems. The Tumor Board, for instance, concentrates on precise diagnosis and effective treatment of cancer patients. Other teams address back pain, cardiac arrhythmia, diabetes, and stroke.

For patients, physicians, and referring organizations seeking an objective assessment of available treatment options, the hospital provides a medical second opinion program, diagnosis confirmation program, and telemedicine program. International patients can have cases re-evaluated by AMC's specialists without traveling outside of their home country. After receiving the medical data by email, fax, or regular mail, the AMC physicians review the case and typically return a treatment plan and cost estimations within two or three days (sometimes longer in complicated cases). A video conferencing system enables collaboration with consulting physicians from other countries.

Each year AMC's international patient services department facilitates more than 3,000 medical visits for patients from more than 60 countries. The department's staff answer questions and handle all arrangements, from medical consultations to travel arrangements to details of the hospital stay.

AMC provides free transportation from airports to local hotels and to medical appointments and treatment facilities. If arrangements are made in advance, VIP transportation service can be provided for patients and their traveling companions.

Patients and patients' families visiting AMC are welcome to stay at the Anadolu Titanic Comfort Hotel, an on-campus guesthouse comprising 29 standard rooms, two handicapped-access rooms, eight suites, and one executive suite. The hotel is walking distance to AMC, making the lodging ideal for companions and recovering patients.

Anadolu was initially awarded JCI accreditation in 2007 and most recently re-accredited in 2013.

Accreditation: Joint Commission International

Leading Specialties: Cardiology and heart surgery, cosmetic and reconstructive surgery, dentistry, oncology, ophthalmology, orthopedics

CTG Dentalcare

1416 Sok. No: 34 Kahramanlar
Izmir 35230, TURKEY
Tel: +90 232 446.3034
Email: info@ctgdental.co.uk
Web: ctgdental.co.uk

Located in Izmir on the western coast of Turkey, CTG Dentalcare was established in 2004 and specializes in cosmetic dentistry, endodontics, implants, orthodontics, and periodontics. The center moved to a new building in 2010 and is now the largest private dental clinic in the Izmir region. Of CTG's 11 dentists, several are university affiliated and four are PhD level specialists. Staff speak German and English.

CTG uses advanced diagnostic and treatment tools, including dental tomography and laser dentistry. Zirconium crowns and titanium implants are used to ensure high quality, biocompatible results. The center also has experience with the proper removal of mercury fillings. Work is guaranteed with terms and restrictions posted on CTG's website.

Popular with patients in the United Kingdom, CTG offers a wide range of international patient services from translation to development of all-inclusive treatment packages. Free price quotes are available on the center's website. Local consultations are available for patients in London.

Leading Specialties: Dentistry

Florence Nightingale Group

Gayrettepe Mh., Cemil Aslan Güder Sk No:8,
Beşiktaş 34349 TURKEY
Tel: +90 212 375.6161
Email: international@groupflorence.com
Web: groupflorence.com

The Florence Nightingale Group (FNG) traces its history back to 1989, when Sisli Florence Nightingale Hospital was established under the auspices of the Turkish Cardiology Foundation. Three other hospitals have since been added to the group: Gayrettepe Florence Nightingale Hospital in 1997 and Kadiköy Florence Nightingale Hospital and Göktürk Florence Nightingale Medical Center in 2007. Sisli, Gayrettepe, and Kadiköy are accredited by JCI.

The Florence Nightingale hospitals share radiological and other diagnostic images using the latest archiving and communication technology. The group collaborates with several world-renowned medical schools and hospitals, such as Baylor College of Medicine, Houston; Center for Cell Therapy and Cancer Immunotherapy, Tel Aviv; Columbia University Medical Center, New York; Memorial Sloan Kettering Cancer Center, New York; and Weill Medical College of Cornell University, New York.

The international patient department of any hospital in the Florence Nightingale Group can be contacted through a shared inquiry system. Special services for international patients include appointment scheduling; travel arrangement assistance; translation; direct admission; medical referrals; and assistance before, during, and after hospitalization.

Gayrettepe Florence Nightingale Hospital was

first JCI accredited in 2003 and most recently re-accredited in 2012. This 100-bed hospital offers inpatient and outpatient diagnosis and treatment facilities that include a fully equipped radiology department.

Gayrettepe's centers of excellence include an in vitro fertilization unit and infertility treatment unit, providing a full range of assisted reproduction services, from preimplantation genetic diagnosis to embryo freezing. In addition to IVF and microinjection, these units offer testicular sperm extraction and aspiration, epididymal sperm aspiration, microsurgical epididymal sperm aspiration, and percutaneous epididymal sperm aspiration.

Gayrettepe's Oncology Center offers integrated medical, radiation, and surgical oncology. Intensity-modulated radiation therapy is used to deliver higher levels of irradiation to cancerous tissue while avoiding healthy tissue. For some lung cancer cases, the bronchoscopy unit provides radiotherapy from inside the lung, a practice thought to shorten the treatment period, enhance effectiveness, and reduce side effects.

Gayrettepe's robotic-assisted surgery in urology unit utilizes the da Vinci surgical system to perform prostatectomies.

Kadikoy Florence Nightingale Hospital entered service in 2007 and attained JCI re-accreditation in 2012. The 74-bed hospital provides inpatient and outpatient services in all specialties. Among its facilities are diagnostic units, fully equipped radiology and angiography departments, and emergency facilities.

Kadikoy's Cardiology and Cardiovascular Surgery Center is a polyclinic offering blood pressure and Holter monitoring, echocardiography, and treadmill testing. Angiography and bypass surgery are performed.

Kadiköy's Physical Therapy and Rehabilitation Center treats muscular and skeletal disorders, including rheumatoid arthritis and osteoarthritis; herniated discs; neck and back pain; sports injuries; and various problems in shoulders, elbows, hips, knees, and ankles. Kadiköy's Plastic Surgery Center performs aesthetic surgery for obesity, breast reduction and reconstruction, nose and facial reconstruction, and other conditions.

When Sisli Florence Nightingale Hospital opened in 1989, it had a capacity of 50 patient beds and performed 250 open-heart surgeries annually. Today it operates as the largest private hospital in Turkey, where some 2,500 heart surgeries and 3,500 general surgeries are performed each year. The hospital was first JCI accredited in 2004 and most recently re-accredited in 2013.

Sisli's Cardiology and Cardiovascular Surgery, Angiography, and Rhythm Disorders Center deploys a 35-member surgical staff treating patients in 12 operating rooms and three procedure rooms. Over the last 20 years, Sisli has performed about 40,000 heart surgeries and 100,000 angiography, balloon angioplasty, coronary laser, permanent pacemaker, and stent procedures.

Sisli's Organ Transplantation Center is staffed with 30 doctors, nurses, and technicians who perform about 100 kidney and liver transplants annually (from both living and cadaver donors). The team also carries out studies on biliary tract, liver, and pancreatic diseases; removes tumors of the liver and pancreas; and treats tumors with radiofrequency ablation when appropriate.

Accreditation: Joint Commission International

Leading Specialties: Cardiology and heart surgery, cosmetic and reconstructive surgery, fertility and reproductive medicine, oncology, orthopedics

Kent Hospital

8229/1 Sokak No. 56, Çigli
Izmir 35580, TURKEY
Tel: +90 232 386.7070
Email: info@kenthospital.com
Web: kenthospital.com

Kent Hospital was founded in 1999 as one of the largest and most modern hospitals in southeastern Europe. On nearly four hectares (about nine acres) of land, the campus was built following American Institute of Architects guidelines and in consultation with the Mayo Clinic in Rochester, Minnesota, on facility design, medical guidelines, and administrative protocols.

The hospital is a full-service medical complex offering tertiary-care services in a range of specialties. Kent received JCI accreditation in 2006.

With 102 beds, 21 intensive care beds, and six surgery suites, Kent employs 143 full-time physicians, including 60 surgeons, and 240 part-time (visiting) surgeons. Most of the physicians and a number of additional staff members speak English. Other languages spoken include Arabic, Bulgarian, French, German, Greek, Italian, Russian, and Spanish.

Some of the procedures most frequently performed at Kent include coronary angiography, coronary artery bypass surgery, heart valve replacement, hip and knee replacement, IVF, spinal fusion, and vaginal hysterectomy. Kent also offers a full range of minimally invasive and endoscopic surgical procedures.

Kent's cardiology diagnostic unit is equipped for echocardiography, EKG and Holter monitoring, and EKG stress testing. The unit provides angioplasty, coronary angiography, pacemaker implantation, and stenting.

The hospital's other specialty centers include the Diabetes Center, IVF Center, Kidney and Liver Transplant Center, Plastic Surgery Center, Sleep Disorder Center, and Urology Center.

Kent received initial JCI accreditation in 2006 and was most recently re-accredited in 2012.

Accreditation: Joint Commission International

Leading Specialties: Cardiology and heart surgery, cosmetic and reconstructive surgery, fertility and reproductive medicine, oncology

Liv Hospital

Ahmet Adnan Saygun Cd., Canan Sk.
No. 5, Ulus/Besiktas
Istanbul, TURKEY
Tel: +90 530 174.4425
Email: international@livclinics.com
Web: livclinics.com

With 154 beds, eight operating rooms, and 50 specialty departments, Liv Hospital treats about 4,000 international patients annually. Liv is best known for its specialty services in cardiology, oncology, orthopedics and traumatology, neurosurgery, general surgery, and the treatment of eye diseases.

Frequently performed diagnostic procedures include EKG, CT, MRI, and PET scans. Cancer treatment specialists at Liv perform about 500 TrueBeam STx linear accelerator treatments each month. This technology targets radiation on a tumor, destroying cancer cells while sparing healthy tissue.

Da Vinci robotic-assisted surgeries are also performed. Heart patients can share their angiography films online with Liv specialists in cardiology and cardiovascular surgery. Second opinions are free.

Specialized medical testing and packages are offered. The standard women's health checkup includes radiology, chest x-ray, abdominal ultrasound, and thyroid and metabolic testing.

Most health travelers come from Libya, Azerbaijan, Iraq, US, Italy, and the UK. Translators are available for English, Arabic, Russian, Azeri, Persian, Bulgarian, Serbian, Croatian, and other languages.

Liv's international office arranges medical services across all specialties for health travelers. Package prices for weekend checkups include hotel accommodations, local transportation, art show tickets, dinner, and sightseeing tours. Services for international patients include pre-treatment cost estimates, free local transportation, and arrangements for city tours.

Financing is not available, but Liv's list of cooperating insurance companies is long and growing. Some discounts can be arranged, so it pays to ask for price reductions.

Accreditation: Joint Commission International; American Association for Accreditation of Ambulatory Surgery Facilities International

Leading Specialties: Cardiology and heart surgery, oncology, ophthalmology, orthopedics

Memorial Healthcare Group, Sisli Hospital

Piyalepaşa Bulvarı 34385
Okmeydanı Istanbul, TURKEY
Tel: + 90 212 314.6666; +90 212 444.7888
Email: internationalpatients@memorial.com.tr
Web: memorial.com.tr

Memorial Healthcare Group (MHG) serves local and international patients with its network of hospitals and satellite clinics in Istanbul, Antalya, Diyarbakır, and Kayseri. Its specialties include organ transplantation, cardiovascular surgery, cardiology, oncology, and IVF treatments. Group-wide services to health travelers include second opinions; treatment plans; medical appointments; cost estimates; help with airport transfers; travel and accommodation arrangements; airfare discounts; facilitation of admission; discharge and follow-up processes; multi-lingual staff; and English interpreters.

Memorial Sisli Hospital, founded in 1995, was the groups's first project. Opening its doors in 2000, Memorial quickly earned a reputation for quality in cardiology, cardiovascular surgery, organ transplantation, and IVF and genetics. It attained its JCI accreditation in 2002. The facility covers 53,000 square meters (570,000 square feet) and maintains 200 inpatient beds. The website features a virtual tour of the facility. Memorial has its own five-star guesthouse for recovering patients and their families.

Accreditation: Joint Commission International

Leading Specialties: Cardiology and heart surgery, fertility and reproductive medicine, oncology, transplant (liver, kidney)

DESTINATION: **UNITED ARAB EMIRATES**

■ AT A GLANCE

Dubai, Al Ain

Languages	Arabic, Persian, English widely spoken
Time Zone	GMT +4
Country Dialing Code	+971
Electricity	240V, plug type G
Currency	UAE dirham (AED)
Leading Specialties	Cardiology and heart surgery, cosmetic and reconstructive surgery, dentistry, fertility and reproductive medicine, ophthalmology , orthopedics, weight loss surgery, wellness and prevention
Typical Savings (over USD retail)	50%–65%
Standards and Affiliations	Dubai Healthcare City Center for Healthcare Planning and Quality; Dubai Health Authority; General Authority for Health Services; International Pan Arab Critical Care Medicine Society; Ministry of Health UAE
International Accreditation	Joint Commission International

■ TREATMENT BRIEF

The UAE is a federation of seven emirates, or states, bordered by Oman and Saudi Arabia. Once considered a desert wasteland, the UAE has evolved over the past two decades into an international blend of Eastern- and Western-style commerce and tourism. On the healthcare front, the UAE already offers patients some 80 JCI-accredited hospitals and specialty clinics.

The city of Abu Dhabi is the capital of the UAE and the center of government for the state of the same name. Abu Dhabi is home to more than 20 JCI-accredited hospitals. The state of Dubai is the UAE's second largest emirate, also situated on the Persian Gulf. Dubai has grown spectacularly over the past decade into one of the Middle East's largest commercial centers and most visited tourism destination. Dubai boasts more than 40 JCI-accredited hospitals.

■ THE UAE AND MEDICAL TRAVEL

Most cross-border patients are either affluent neighboring Middle Easterners seeking quality care or wounded patients from nearby war-torn countries. Larger facilities—such as the American Hospital, the Johns Hopkins-affiliated Tawam Hospital, and City Hospital—offer a full range of specialties, including cardiology, orthopedics, neurology and spine, reproductive medicine, and ENT.

The UAE's two healthcare hubs, Abu Dhabi and Dubai, carry high costs of living, including healthcare and hospitality. Thus, medical travelers outside the region largely comprise affluent patients attracted to the many specialty and sub-specialty clinics offering cosmetic surgery, vision care, IVF/infertility, and prosthesis. As one of the world's leading tourism destinations, Dubai is beginning to court the more casual healthcare consumer, who might seek to offset the costs of a vacation with a health screening or combine a visit with a cosmetic or dental procedure. The 360-bed Cleveland Clinic Abu Dhabi, scheduled to open in 2014, will bring tertiary and quaternary care to local and international patients alike.

■ RECLAIMING THE MIDDLE EASTERN PATIENT

Over the years, thousands of Middle Eastern nationals have traveled to Thailand, Singapore, India, and other Asian hospitals for healthcare. After a hard look at these costs, the Dubai government acted to reclaim its regional base of patients. More than US$100 million has been raised to realize this vision, which now includes facilities for medical care and wellness, research, and education.

Dubai Healthcare City, founded in 2002, is an example of a healthcare cluster striving to build an infrastructure of quality metrics and excellent patient experience in combination with research and academic affiliations. The 381,000-square-meter (4.1-million-square-foot) campus has attracted a large general hospital (the City Hospital), a JCI-accredited cosmetic surgery hospital (American Academy of Cosmetic Surgery Hospital), and more than 100 specialty clinics and medical centers.

■ SELECTED HOSPITALS AND CLINICS

American Academy of Cosmetic Surgery Hospital
District 1 Building No. 73, PO Box 505099
Dubai Healthcare City
Dubai, UNITED ARAB EMIRATES
Tel: +971 4 423.7600; +971 44 423.7600
Email: info@aacsh.com
Web: aacsh.com

A JCI-accredited institution opened in 2007 as Dubai Healthcare City's (DHCC) first hospital, the American Academy of Cosmetic Surgery Hospital treats more than 5,100 outpatients and nearly 150 inpatients annually. American Academy of Cosmetic Surgery Hospital (AACSH) comprises five units: an anti-aging clinic, surgical clinic, med spa, smile enhancement clinic, and admission unit. Specialties include cosmetic surgery, bariatrics, dentistry, and anti-aging.

As is customary with DHCC facilities, English is spoken throughout at the hospital, and translators are available for numerous languages, including Arabic, Bulgarian, Farsi, French, German, Greek, Italian, Russian, Spanish, Tagalog, and Turkish.

AACSH includes five-star, fully modernized suites built to ensure patient privacy and confidentiality. Staff members can help patients arrange transportation to and from Dubai International Airport, as well as visa and travel itineraries. The hospital's unique in-house Al Shehana ("female falcon") spa offers rejuvenation, beauty, healing, relaxation, and rehabilitation under medical supervision.

For allied healthcare professionals, the hospital hosts a fully equipped modern educational unit and various continuing medical education courses.

AACSH was first accredited in 2009 and received full re-accreditation in 2012.

Accreditation: Joint Commission International

Leading Specialties: Cosmetic and reconstructive surgery

Dr. Sulaiman Al Habib Medical Center Dubai
Building 55, Dubai Healthcare City
PO Box 505005
Dubai, UNITED ARAB EMIRATES
Tel: +971 4 429.7777
Email: infodubai@drsulaimanalhabib.com
Web: drsulaimanalhabib.com

One of seven medical institutions operated by the Dr. Sulaiman Al Habib Medical Group, one of the Middle East's largest providers of comprehensive healthcare services, this medical center opened in 2007 in Dubai Healthcare City.

With 63 physicians on staff, Dr. Sulaiman Al Habib Medical Center is a world-class outpatient facility with comprehensive primary and preventive healthcare services. Specialties include cardiology, diabetes and endocrinology, dentistry, ENT, neurology, orthopedics, ophthalmology, and urology.

Leading Specialties: Cardiology and heart surgery, oncology, orthopedics, spine surgery

Dr. Wafa Gynecology and Fertility Centre

Al Razi Building No. 64, Block A, Unit 3002, Dubai
Healthcare City
PO BOX 505157
Dubai, UNITED ARAB EMIRATES
Tel: +971 4 437.7520
Email: info@drwafagfc.com
Web: wafafertility.com

Established in 2010, this Dubai Healthcare City clinic
joins locations in Abu Dhabi, Muscat, and London
founded by Dr. Khalil Wafa, a fellow of London's
Royal College of Obstetricians and Gynaecologists
with more than 25 years of experience, and who
helped pioneer the use of IVF in the Middle East.

Dr. Wafa's team provides services extending well
beyond fertility treatment into key areas such as
gynecology, sexual health, and wellness issues, including those dealing with polycystic ovary disease,
obesity, and diabetes. Other treatments include
intra-uterine insemination (IUI), intra-cytoplasmic
sperm injection (ICSI), sperm freezing, egg freezing,
and assisted hatching.

The clinic offers some of the most technologically advanced techniques in assisted reproductive
technology and gynecological procedures, including
keyhole laparoscopic and hysteroscopic surgery.
Specialists also provide pre-implantation genetic diagnosis to exclude major genetic abnormalities and
gender selection. Dr. Wafa Center assists patients
with treatment of azoospermia (low sperm count
and other male low fertility conditions) and recurrent IVF implantation failure.

Leading Specialties: Fertility and reproductive
medicine

Dubai Bone and Joint Center

Building No. 64, Block F, 1st Floor, 1020
PO Box 118855
Dubai Healthcare City
Dubai, UNITED ARAB EMIRATES
Tel: +971 4 423.1400
Email: info@dbaj.ae
Web: dbaj.ae

The only specialized, comprehensive center in the
Middle East for musculoskeletal disease, the Dubai
Bone and Joint Center (DBAJ) is the clinical arm of
the Mohammed Bin Rashid Al Maktoum Academic
Medical Center. Its staff is focused on using innovative procedures in joint replacement, back and neck
surgery, pediatric orthopedics, rheumatology, and
physiotherapy.

DBAJ has embarked on a research program with
the University of Amsterdam's Academic Medical
Center to study gene therapy and its potential to
treat rheumatoid arthritis. Its clientele includes
members of Middle East royal families, international
diplomatic corps, and global executives who live and
work in the region.

Leading Specialties: Orthopedics

London Centre for Aesthetic Surgery Gulf

District 1, Building No. 64, Block E, 4th floor, Room
4017
Dubai Healthcare City
PO Box 505085
Dubai, UNITED ARAB EMIRATES
Tel: +971 4 375.2393
Email: gulf@lcas.com
Web: lcas.ae

Opened in Dubai in 2008, the London Centre for
Aesthetic Surgery follows the pioneering meth-
odologies of Drs. Roberto and Maurizio Viel. The
surgeons, identical twin brothers, hold international
certifications in cosmetic surgery and are fellows of
numerous professionals associations throughout
Europe and the US.

The Viel brothers opened their London clinic in
1990. The Dubai clinic offers a full array of traditional
invasive and revolutionary non-invasive procedures.
They specialize in cosmetic eye surgery, facial rejuvenation, anti-aging medicine, breast augmentation,
penoplasty, and liposelection (a fat removal procedure incorporating ultrasound technology).

Leading Specialties: Cosmetic and reconstructive
surgery

Mediclinic City Hospital

Building 37, Dubai Healthcare City
PO Box 505004
Dubai, UNITED ARAB EMIRATES
Tel: +971 4 435.9999
Email: cityhospital@mediclinic.ae
Web: mediclinic.ae/cityhospital

Opened in 2008 as Dubai Healthcare City's first multi-disciplinary hospital, this 229-bed, JCI-accredited hospital contains many of the most advanced technologies available in the region. Mediclinic City Hospital is owned by Mediclinic International, one of the 10 largest listed private hospital groups in the world.

With a staff of more than 140 physicians and surgeons and 270 nurses, the hospital served nearly 20,000 inpatients and 216,000 outpatients in 2013. That year, Mediclinic welcomed more than 20,000 patients from the US and Canada.

This medical center has offers advanced medical technology from around the world, including a 3T MRI and the latest SPECT-CT gamma camera. Key specialties and treatments include breast surgery; cardiac surgery; dentistry; endocrinology; ENT; gastroenterology; nephrology (kidney); neurology and neurosurgery; nuclear medicine; ophthalmology; orthopedics; pulmonology (lung); urology; and vascular surgery. Specialized health screening packages are available for both men and women. A dedicated representative provides patient support during the screening process.

Even though English is the official language for hospital services and communications, more than 40 nationalities are represented among the hospital's staff. A language board is prominently displayed to help patients arrange translation services as needed.

Mediclinic City Hospital was first accredited by JCI in 2010 and re-accredited in 2013. The laboratory is also accredited by the College of American Pathologists.

Accreditation: Joint Commission International

Leading Specialties: Cardiology and heart surgery, orthopedics, spine surgery

Magrabi Eye Hospital

Building No. 64, Block E, 2nd Floor, 2038
Dubai Healthcare City
PO Box 36267
Dubai, UNITED ARAB EMIRATES
Tel: +971 4 437.0606
Email: dubai@magrabi.com.sa
Web: magrabihospitals.com

Since 1955, Magrabi Eye Hospital has been the largest medical network in the Middle East and Africa for specialized eye care. It now serves more than half a million patients and performs 50,000 eye surgeries annually. Magrabi's inpatient and outpatient surgery center in Dubai, with a staff of eight eye specialists and 39 support personnel, joins more than 30 other centers in nine countries, including eight not-for-profit centers.

Services include refractive surgery, treatment of cornea and external eye diseases, cataract, glaucoma, retina- and vitreous-related diseases, oculoplasty, pediatric ophthalmology, and optometry services (contact lenses). The center also is part of the Emirate's Noor Dubai's initiative, which is focused on raising public awareness about eye care and the causes of visual impairment. The campaign includes free treatment of all cases referred directly by Noor Dubai to the Magrabi center.

Leading Specialties: Ophthalmology

Moorfields Eye Hospital Dubai

Building No. 64, Block E, 3rd Floor
Dubai Healthcare City
PO Box 505054
Dubai, UNITED ARAB EMIRATES
Tel: +971 4 429.7888
Email: aqf@moorfields.ae
Web: moorfields.ae

Moorfields Eye Hospital Dubai (MEHD) is the first overseas branch of Moorfields Eye Hospital NHS Foundation Trust in London, the world's oldest and largest ophthalmic facility, and one of the most respected centers for ophthalmic treatment, teaching, and research.

Moorfields NHS is a leading international tertiary-care and training center in ophthalmology;

more than half of all ophthalmologists practicing in the UK have received specialist training at Moorfields NHS. The entire operation employs some 1,200 people in 11 locations, with 24,000 procedures performed every year. MEHD has performed more than 31,000 procedures since opening its doors in 2007.

The Dubai branch hospital follows Moorfields's 200-year-old traditions. The MEHD medical team consists of 10 consultant ophthalmologists, two orthoptists, four optometrists, and a fully trained nursing staff. Services at MEHD include treatment for various eye conditions and disorders, including age-related macular degeneration, cataracts, diabetic retinopathy, and glaucoma. The hospital provides LASIK vision correction and oculoplastic procedures. Eye surgeries include laser refractive, corneal, oculoplastic, strabismus, pediatric, glaucoma, and complex vitreoretinal surgeries.

Basic screenings and eye examinations are also offered. MEHD has access to more than 100 doctors in Moorfields London should the need arise.

MEHD staff and support staff are multi-lingual and speak Arabic, English, French, German, Italian, Portuguese, Farsi, Hindi, Urdu, and Tagalog.

Support for international patients includes assistance with travel, accommodations, and local transport.

Leading Specialties: Ophthalmology

Sharif Eye Center, Dubai
Dubai Healthcare City
Ibn Sina Bldg. 27, Block D, Unit 101
Dubai, UNITED ARAB EMIRATES
Tel: +971 4 423.3664
Email: dubai@sharifeyecenter.com
Web: sharifeyecenter.com

One of three locations for the Sharif Eye Center in the Middle East, the Dubai Healthcare City site opened in 2007 and treats more than 1,500 patients annually. The trio of centers in Amman, Doha, and Dubai was founded by Dr. Khaled Sharif, who completed his residency and worked as an eye surgeon for more than 10 years in the UK before coming to the Middle East in the mid-1990s. An internationally known surgeon and researcher, he pioneered the use of LASIK procedures and laser cataract surgery in Jordan.

The clinic's leading specialties include UltraLASIK corrective procedures, cataract surgeries, implantable contact lenses, and treatment for keratoconus, a degenerative eye disorder. More than one-third of the international patients treated annually at the clinic come from the US and Canada. English is the primary language of business at the clinic, but translators are available for patients who speak Arabic, French, German, Russian, Spanish, and Tagalog.

Leading Specialties: Ophthalmology

Tawam Hospital
PO Box 15258
Al Ain, UNITED ARAB EMIRATES
Tel: +971 3 767.7444; +971 3 707.4100
Web: tawamhospital.ae/english/

Located 100 miles south of Dubai, the 477-bed Tawam Hospital delivers internationally competitive care in collaboration with the Baltimore-based Johns Hopkins Hospital.

Tawam is a full-service hospital with a wide range of specialties. The hospital's department of oncology is the official cancer referral center for the UAE and other Gulf states. Established in 2004, the 46-bed department includes hematology, radiology, and palliative care. Nearly half of the rooms are high-efficiency particulate-air filtered. Diagnostic workup is provided for both benign and malignant disorders, including all types of solid tumors and hematological disorders. The medical staff includes more than a dozen oncology specialists.

The Dental Center was one of the first dental facilities in the Gulf region to provide a complete implant dentistry service, specializing in one- and two-stage dental implant replacements. The center employs 120 people, including 16 general dentists and 14 consultants or specialists, representing every clinical dental specialty. The majority of its dentists have Western qualifications or experience.

The newest medical department at Tawam, the department of surgery, covers all sub-specialties except cardiovascular surgery. The department has six fully equipped operating rooms that support more than 4,000 inpatient and outpatient surgeries each year. The center's most common surgical procedures include arthroscopic surgery for knee and hip replacements; ear, nose, and throat surgery using endoscopes; prostatic surgery; neurosurgery; and reconstructive surgery, especially to treat burn cases.

Tawam's clinical nutrition department offers uncommon treatments for inherited metabolic diseases, such as disorders of amino acid metabolism and fatty acid oxidation.

The hospital's sizable nursing team (numbering around 900) represents 33 different nationalities.

Tawam received its first JCI accreditation in 2006 and was most recently re-accredited in 2012

Accreditation: Joint Commission International

Leading Specialties: Dentistry, neurosurgery, oncology, orthopedics, urology

DESTINATION: **UNITED STATES**

■ AT A GLANCE

Baltimore, Cleveland, Houston, New York City, Rochester

Languages	English, some Spanish
Time Zones	GMT –10, GMT –9, GMT –8, GMT –7, GMT –6, GMT –5,
Country Dialing Code	+1
Electricity	120V, plug type B
Currency	US dollar (USD)
Leading Specialties	Cardiology and heart surgery, neurology and spine surgery, oncology, ophthalmology, orthopedics, pediatrics, stem cell and regenerative therapy, transplant
Standards and Affiliations	Accreditation Association for Ambulatory Health Care; American Association for Accreditation of Ambulatory Surgery Facilities; The Joint Commission

■ TREATMENT BRIEF

Throughout most of the twentieth century, venerated US medical institutions dominated the world in research, academics, training, complex diagnosis, and technology-driven treatment. As with other sectors, the US now shares the healthcare landscape with top medical and academic institutions around the globe.

A private US hospital typically offers technologies and surgical expertise considered too expensive or too specialized for patients in many other countries. The US also offers a confidence factor: top US medical centers such as Stanford, Harvard, Cleveland Clinic, and Mt. Sinai remain the envy of the world, with unmatched high standards and rigor. Similarly, US physicians are subject to the most arduous system of ethical and legal accountability in the world.

■ TOP DOCTORS AND DIAGNOSES ATTRACT INTERNATIONAL PATIENTS

Geography may prove a secondary consideration when the vast experience of a specialty hospital or a team of sub-specialists is required.

In its 2013–2014 rankings of the best hospitals in the United States, *U.S. News & World Report* awarded its top spot for cancer care to the University of Texas MD Anderson Cancer Center in Houston, Texas. A close second was Memorial Sloan Kettering Cancer Center in New York City.

The top rankings in neurology and neurosurgery went to the Johns Hopkins Hospital in Baltimore, Maryland, and the Mayo Clinic in Rochester, Minnesota. For orthopedics, the Hospital for Special Surgery in New York City earned the top spot, with the Mayo Clinic and Cleveland Clinic close behind.

Cleveland Clinic in Ohio ranked first in heart surgery, second in gastroenterology, and second in rheumatology. International patients are finding first contacts with specialists at these and other US institutions easier with the advent of online consul-tations, which give patients—through their overseas doctors—access to the best medical advice the US has to offer, without leaving home.

THE UNITED STATES AND MEDICAL TRAVEL

Each year some 800,000 international patients visit the United States seeking excellence in specialty care—especially in complex or "last-resort" cases. US facilities and physicians are rarely able to beat the price at a JCI-accredited hospital in India, Turkey, or Thailand; however, American specialists often are called upon to treat cases considered difficult to hopeless elsewhere.

Although the US healthcare system remains largely wedded to the general hospital model, pil-lars of specialty treatment can be found in vibrant regions, where academics, research, and clinical care come together to form a powerful whole. For example, Houston's Texas Medical Center (TMC) is composed of 54 hospitals and specialty clinics, including luminaries such as MD Anderson (oncol-ogy), Methodist (orthopedics, transplants), and Texas Children's Hospital and its recently opened Women's Pavilion.

Similarly, healthcare clusters in south Florida tend to attract the Latin American and Caribbean patient, whereas Boston and New York bring in af-fluent patients from all over, including Africa, the Middle East, Western Europe, and, increasingly, Rus-sia and China.

Most leading US international hospitals have been serving cross-border patients for decades, with established international patient services that include airport pickup and drop-off, hotel shuttle, translators, and travel planning. An Intercontinental Hotel is connected to Cleveland Clinic, and the Marriott Texas Medical Center welcomes visitors, with special amenities for the TMC patient.

DOMESTIC MEDICAL TRAVEL ON THE RISE

Since the start of the twenty-first century, the trend of consumer-driven healthcare has given rise to patients traveling beyond their backyards for spe-cialty care not available close to home. The internet is finally having its impact on healthcare, and cost-conscious patients are discovering they can take advantage of wide price disparities without sacrific-ing quality, if they are willing to do the research and pack a suitcase.

Employers and insurers are responding as well. In 2010 Lowe's Corporation entered into an arrange-ment with the renowned Cleveland Clinic in Ohio to give its 40,000 employees and their covered depen-dents the option to travel to that facility for heart care. PepsiCo entered into a similar arrangement with Johns Hopkins Medicine in Baltimore for its nearly 250,000 US employees and dependents. The travel surgery benefit includes cardiac and complex joint replacement surgeries, paid travel and accom-modations, and often cash incentive for patients willing to travel.

SELECTED HOSPITALS AND CLINICS

Baptist Health South Florida
6855 Red Road
Coral Gables, Florida 33143-3632, USA
Tel: +1 786 596.2373
Email: international@baptisthealth.net
Web: baptisthealth.net/International

Baptist Health South Florida—the largest faith-based, not-for-profit healthcare organization in the region—has been serving patients outside the US since 1991. The organization's 2,000 physicians and 14,000 employees handle nearly 900,000 outpatient visits and more than 70,000 inpatients annually throughout its seven hospitals and more than a dozen medical plazas. Baptist Health physicians see about 14,000 international patients each year.

Baptist Cardiac and Vascular Institute and South Miami Heart Center at South Miami Hospital offer the services needed to diagnose and treat complex medical and surgical heart-related conditions. Both facilities emphasize a team approach, with physicians, surgeons, nurses, and technologists collaborating to provide individualized patient care. In 2011 doctors at Baptist Cardiac and Vascular Institute became the first in South Florida (and among the first in the US) to use a new MRI-safe pacemaker.

The Neuroscience Center at Baptist Hospital provides diagnosis and treatment for disorders of the brain, spine, and nervous system. The neuroscience team at Baptist Health's Doctors Hospital in Coral Gables, Florida, was the first institution in Florida—and is still one of a few facilities in the US—to offer Gamma Knife radiosurgery.

Each year Baptist Health South Florida providers treat more than 5,000 adults and children who have cancer, using sophisticated technology for early, effective diagnosis and treatment. Baptist Health is a major partner in the Tampa-based Moffitt Cancer Center's landmark study, Total Cancer Care. This five-year study is gathering data on the genetic profile of individual tumors that may lead to personalized treatments for specific types of cancer.

The Center for Orthopedics and Sports Medicine based at Doctors Hospital offers an advanced orthopedic surgery program, along with comprehensive physical and occupational therapy. Doctors Hospital orthopedic surgeons are pioneers of new techniques in knee-ligament reconstruction, shoulder and elbow injuries, and ankle reconstruction. The center's surgeons and rehabilitation therapists also serve several professional and college sports teams.

In addition to medical care coordination, Baptist Health International offers concierge services at no additional cost, such as translation; assistance with travel, transportation, and local lodging; and discounted rates at local hotels.

Special services available to the international medical community include second opinions and video conferencing. Most international patients visit Baptist Health from the Caribbean, South America, and Central America because of its proximity, ease of travel, and cultural familiarity.

Accreditation: The Joint Commission

Leading Specialties: Cardiology and heart surgery, oncology, orthopedics, spine surgery

Cancer Treatment Centers of America
CTCA Eastern Regional Medical Center
Philadelphia, Pennsylvania 19124, USA
Tel: 888 847.7410 (US toll free)
Web: cancercenter.com

Founded in 1988 by Richard J. Stephenson, CTCA sprang from personal experience. When his mother, Mary Brown Stephenson, was diagnosed with cancer, Mr. Stephenson and his family searched for the most advanced, effective treatments available. They were frustrated to find that many world-renowned cancer hospitals did not provide comprehensive care.

Following his mother's death in 1982, Mr. Stephenson vowed to create a new and better model of cancer care, ultimately developing a whole-person cancer treatment approach. His commitment to establishing a patient-centered treatment experience has been, and still is, the organization's guiding vision. Appropriately, patients receive the Mother Standard of care—that is, the way you would want your mother to be treated if she were diagnosed with cancer.

CTCA physicians treat only cancer and are experienced in complex and advanced-stage cancers. Using a personalized approach to promote healing of body, mind, and spirit, the doctors and clinicians at each of the five CTCA inpatient medical centers provide a combination of advanced cancer treatments—medical, surgical, and radiation oncology, pathology, hematology, gastroenterology, gynecology, neurosurgery, anesthesiology, and plastic/reconstructive surgery—with supportive therapies ranging from physical and nutritional therapy, pain management, chiropractic, and psychiatry to mind-body and naturopathic medicine.

Each patient at a CTCA hospital is assigned a fully integrated healthcare team. Known as Patient Empowered Care, this approach brings experts in advanced cancer treatment together with providers of supportive therapies.

On its website, CTCA publishes advanced-stage survival statistics for the 10 most prevalent cancers treated at CTCA. These are also compared to the National Cancer Institute's Surveillance, Epidemiology, and End Results (SEER) database. The CTCA and SEER figures are presented in an accessible, consumer-friendly format.

CTCA clinicians access and utilize innovative treatment approaches not available at many other facilities. These leading-edge therapies, combined with a patient-centered approach, deliver high-quality treatment for cancer patients at any stage. Cancer treatment programs at CTCA include chemotherapy, radiation therapy, gastroenterology, hormone therapy, immunotherapy, interventional pulmonology, interventional radiology, neurosurgery, orthopedic oncology, and hematologic oncology.

The CareEdge program at CTCA guarantees new patients with breast, colorectal, lung, or prostate cancer a diagnosis and treatment plan in five days or less at an all-inclusive package price. Prices range from US$10,000 to US$14,500 and cover professional and facility services, travel, and lodging in connection with the evaluation. Package pricing does not cover treatment but rather is for evaluation and treatment-plan development only.

CTCA hospitals are distributed regionally to provide convenient locations across the US. Each location is near a major US city served by direct domestic and international flights offering easy access to patients from around the world:

- Eastern Regional Medical Center in Philadelphia, Pennsylvania
- Midwestern Regional Medical Center in Zion, Illinois, near Chicago
- Southwestern Regional Medical Center in Tulsa, Oklahoma
- Western Regional Medical Center in Goodyear, Arizona, near Phoenix
- Southeastern Regional Medical Center in Newnan, Georgia, near Atlanta
- Seattle Cancer Treatment and Wellness Center, an outpatient treatment facility in Seattle, Washington

CTCA has cancer information specialists available 24 hours to discuss treatment options by telephone, online chat, or email.

Accreditation: The Joint Commission

Leading Specialties: Oncology

Cleveland Clinic
9500 Euclid Ave.
Cleveland, Ohio 44195, USA
Tel: +1 216 444.8184
Email: interna@ccf.org
Web: clevelandclinic.org

Cleveland Clinic opened its doors in March 1921, eager to implement what was then a new and untried concept: a group practice. Over the next several years, a new 240-bed hospital and research annex were built. In the 1950s, heart care became a major medical focus. At Cleveland Clinic, coronary angiography and bypass surgery were born.

Since then, Cleveland Clinic has built 15 family health and surgery centers and acquired a system of nine community hospitals. In 2002 it founded the first new medical school program in the US in 25 years. Today Cleveland Clinic has grown to become the second largest group practice in the world. Its 37,000 employees—2,000 of them physicians and scientists—work in 120 medical specialties and subspecialties.

The clinic's statistics are phenomenal, with more than three million patient visits, nearly 75,000 surgical cases, more than 50,000 inpatients, and more than 3,600 open-heart surgeries annually. Cleveland Clinic surgeons perform more heart-valve operations than any other medical facility in the United States.

The Robert and Suzanne Tomsich Department of Cardiovascular Medicine has physicians in every cardiovascular specialty working to offer the latest medications and interventional heart disease procedures. Specialty sections include cardiac electrophysiology and pacing, clinical cardiology, cardiovascular imaging, invasive cardiology, heart failure and transplantation, preventive cardiology and rehabilitation, and vascular medicine.

The department of thoracic and cardiovascular surgery is one of the largest, most experienced cardiac and thoracic surgery groups in the world. Its surgeons offer virtually every type of cardiac surgery, including elective or emergency surgery for heart-valve disease, aortic aneurysm, coronary artery disease, and arrhythmias. Surgeons of the department of vascular surgery perform more than 5,000 procedures annually, nearly a third of them for treatment of atherosclerosis.

Cleveland Clinic's Digestive Diseases Institute (DDI) offers patients advanced, safe, and proven medical and surgical treatments for disorders of the gastrointestinal tract. DDI houses the largest institutional registries for inherited colon cancer in the United States and the second largest in the world. It is the largest referral center in the US for repairing failed pelvic pouches. DDI surgeons use the latest in diagnostic and treatment options, including transanal endoscopic microsurgery and intraoperative radiotherapy. DDI colorectal surgeons avoid a permanent colostomy in approximately 80 percent of rectal cancer cases.

The Glickman Urological and Kidney Institute is a world leader in treating complex urologic and kidney conditions in adults and children. Institute physicians have pioneered medical advances, including dialysis, partial nephrectomy, laparoscopic and robotic-assisted urologic surgery, and the bioartificial kidney. Cleveland Clinic surgeons perform more than 3,000 laparoscopic partial nephrectomies annually.

The multi-disciplinary Cleveland Clinic Neurological Institute is a leader in treating and researching the most complex neurological disorders, advancing innovations such as epilepsy surgery, stereotactic spine radiosurgery, interstitial thermal therapy for brain tumors, and deep brain stimulation. Annually, the institute's staff of more than 300 specialists serve 140,000 patients and performs 7,500 surgeries.

In recent years, the clinic's footprint has become increasingly global, with such innovations as its award-winning website, podcasts, and web seminars, and the secure transmission of electronic medical records for both physicians and patients. Also, Cleveland Clinic has partnered with Mubadala Healthcare to build a full-service hospital and specialty clinic in Abu Dhabi, UAE. It also manages Sheikh Khalifa Medical City in Abu Dhabi.

Accreditation: The Joint Commission

Leading Specialties: Cardiology and heart surgery, neurology, oncology, ophthalmology, orthopedics

Johns Hopkins Hospital

600 North Wolfe Street
Baltimore, Maryland 21287, USA
Tel: +1 410 614.4629
Email: international@jhmi.edu
Web: hopkinsmedicine.org/international

Since the opening of Johns Hopkins Hospital in 1889, and the first class in its School of Medicine four years later, Johns Hopkins Hospital has been revolutionizing medical practice in the United States. By integrating patient care with the best in medical education and research, Hopkins set the benchmark for standards ranging from the rigorous training of physicians and nurses to the rapid application of research to improvements in patient care. Today patients, clinicians, and researchers come from all over the world to learn from Hopkins physicians, many renowned in their fields.

Johns Hopkins Hospital is actually part of a larger medical enterprise called Johns Hopkins Medicine, headquartered in Baltimore, Maryland. Johns Hopkins Medicine operates four academic and community hospitals, four suburban healthcare and surgery centers, and 25 primary outpatient sites. This us$5 billion non-profit conglomerate handles more than 96,000 inpatient admissions annually, as well as 263,000 emergency visits. Claiming 25 primary healthcare sites, Johns Hopkins Community Physicians provides more than 540,000 patient visits each year. With more than 30,000 employees, Johns Hopkins Medicine is among Maryland's largest private employers and the largest in the city of Baltimore.

The Sidney Kimmel Comprehensive Cancer Center at Johns Hopkins is one of only 40 cancer centers in the United States designated by the National Cancer Institute as a comprehensive cancer center. It provides a wide spectrum of specialty programs for adults and children, including the treatment of tumors of the bone marrow, brain and spinal cord, breast, colon, reproductive organs, urinary tract, lungs, and skin. The center offers complete family and patient services that include a counseling, survivors' and palliative care programs, and the Hackerman–Patz Patient and Family Pavilion for patients and their families traveling from out of town.

The department of otolaryngology–head and

neck surgery at Johns Hopkins focuses on diagnosing and treating ear, nose, and throat diseases. Specialty areas include audiology/hearing (including cochlear implants), dentistry and oral surgery, facial plastic and reconstructive surgery, minimally invasive brain and skull-base surgery, otology and neurotology, pediatric otolaryngology, rhinology and sinus surgery, snoring and sleep surgery, and motion and balance research.

Johns Hopkins has achieved an international reputation for excellence in heart and circulation treatments and surgeries—a reputation expected to expand since the new Cardiovascular and Critical Care Tower opened in 2012. In the new facility, state-of-the-art diagnostic and therapeutic services are seamlessly integrated under the Johns Hopkins Heart and Vascular Institute. Specialties include vascular medicine, aortic diseases, arrhythmias, noninvasive cardiac imaging, cardiac rehabilitation and exercise, cardiac surgery, cardiomyopathy and heart failure, congenital disorders, valve surgery, endovascular therapy, and ventricular assist devices.

The departments of neurology and neurosurgery provide patients around the world with cutting-edge care, including treatments for acoustic neuroma; aneurysms; brain tumors; cerebrovascular disease; epilepsy; glioma; hydrocephalus; meningioma; Parkinson's disease and movement disorders; skull base tumors; spinal cord injuries; spine and spinal cord tumors; trigeminal neuralgia; and other disorders of the spine, brain, peripheral nerves, and pituitary.

Specialists in the department of orthopedic surgery provide treatment in the following areas: adult reconstruction, foot and ankle, hand surgery, pediatric orthopedics, orthopedic oncology, shoulder surgery, orthopedic spine surgery, sports medicine surgery, and orthopedic trauma.

Surgeons of the Brady Urological Institute at Johns Hopkins have long been pioneers in their field and were the first to perform landmark operations, such as radical prostatectomy, nerve-sparing radical retropubic prostatectomy, and minimally invasive live donor kidney removal. Hopkins urologists have extensive expertise in surgical techniques, including urologic reconstruction; laparoscopy; microsurgery for infertility; vasectomy reversal; hypospadias

reconstruction; bladder exstrophy reconstruction; and treatment of rare stone disease, benign prostate hypertrophy, erectile dysfunction, kidney disease, and urinary incontinence.

Johns Hopkins Medicine International offers hospital management, healthcare consulting, and clinical education services through strategic alliances and affiliations in North America, Latin America, Europe, the Middle East, and Asia. Johns Hopkins Medicine serves patients from more than 100 countries annually.

Accreditation: The Joint Commission

Leading Specialties: Cardiology and heart surgery, neurology, oncology, ophthalmology, orthopedics, urology

Mayo Clinic

200 First Street SW
Rochester, Minnesota 55905, USA
Tel: +1 507 284.8884
Email: intl.mcr@mayo.edu
Web: mayoclinic.org

Mayo Clinic developed gradually from the medical practice of a pioneer doctor, Dr. William Worrall Mayo, who settled in Rochester, Minnesota, in 1863. From the beginning, Mayo doctors employed a team approach to patient care, and doctors and students have come from around the world to learn new techniques at Mayo. Patients flock there, too: Mayo Clinic is now the largest integrated, not-for-profit group practice in the world.

Today its team approach is carried out by more than 55,000 doctors, nurses, scientists, students, and allied health staff at Mayo Clinic locations in Minnesota, Arizona, and Florida. Collectively, Mayo Clinic facilities care for more than half a million outpatients and 124,000 inpatients each year. Mayo is nationally and internationally recognized for its excellence in neurology; neurosurgery; cardiology and heart surgery; orthopedics; nephrology; gastroenterology; endocrinology; urology; gynecology; rheumatology; ophthalmology; otorhinolaryngology; rehabilitative medicine; geriatric care; and the treatment of diabetes and pulmonary diseases. The Mayo Clinic Cancer Center is funded by the US National Cancer Institute as a comprehensive cancer center, in recognition of Mayo's scientific excellence and focus on cancer prevention, diagnosis, and treatment.

Mayo Clinic researchers are often at the forefront of medical research. For example, in 2009 Mayo scientists demonstrated that induced pluripotent stem (iPS) cells—stem cells converted from adult cells—can be used to treat heart disease. The researchers "re-programmed" cells that ordinarily contribute to scars after a heart attack to become stem cells that could repair heart damage. This is the first application of iPS-based technology for heart disease therapy in the world.

Mayo Clinic researchers have pioneered in many other fields, including non-invasive stool testing for the diagnosis of colorectal and gastrointestinal cancers. Mayo Clinic researchers have also completed breakthrough research on other digestive disorders ranging from celiac disease to Barrett's esophagus dysplasia and have pioneered a minimally invasive treatment for esophageal cancer. Mayo Clinic cardiology researchers have identified a peptide that helps preserve and improve kidney function during heart failure, without affecting blood pressure. Benefits of this new peptide include increasing kidney filtration rate, suppressing harmful protein production, and keeping water and salt flowing from the body.

Mayo Clinic is known for its emphasis on continuing education and professional development for its staff. In 2009 the Mayo Quality Fellows program was launched. It provides physicians, nurses, and allied health staff with advanced tools for improving the quality and safety of services to patients. MayoExpertAdvisor, an online tool for health professionals, is part of MayoExpert, a Mayo-designed software system that analyzes data from a patient's electronic medical record and alerts providers about test results that require immediate action. The alert links to another segment of the system called AskMayoExpert. It includes important medical information, which is vetted by Mayo medical experts, about the patient's disorder. The system also offers instant access to discussions with colleagues who can provide expert advice.

Each year more than 8,000 international patients from 140 countries travel to one of Mayo's locations. Mayo's international patient offices work to ensure that distance and language are not obstacles to receiving excellent care. With representative offices in Canada, Ecuador, Guatemala, and Mexico, all Mayo facilities offer interpreters in any language at no cost. Interpreters can attend appointments, translate patient education materials, and offer other assistance as needed. In addition, multi-lingual appointment, registration, and finance personnel assist patients and families before, during, and after their visit to Mayo Clinic.

International Center staff members arrange appointments, find interpreters, and answer questions about billing and insurance. Mayo's concierge service guides global patients in making travel and lodging arrangements and utilizing community services, including shopping, entertainment, banking, and worship. The center also arranges fee-based travel services, including airline and hotel reservations, and ground transportation, including shuttles, limousine service, and car rentals.

International patients can request an appointment at Mayo Clinic locations in Minnesota, Florida, or Arizona with an online form. A representative from one of Mayo's international appointment offices responds to requests within three business days. Many patients schedule their own appointments at Mayo Clinic. Patients or their physicians may also request an appointment by email, phone, or fax. eConsult is available through the patient's home physician for US$750. International patients can request an estimate of charges for services through international financial representatives who work at all three Mayo locations.

Accreditation: The Joint Commission

Leading Specialties: Cardiology and heart surgery, nephrology, neurology, oncology, ophthalmology, orthopedics

MD Anderson Cancer Center (University of Texas)
1515 Holcombe Blvd.
Houston, Texas 77030-4009, USA
Tel: +1 713 745.2300; +1 713 745.0450 (International Patients Center)
Email: international@mdanderson.org
Web: mdanderson.org

One of the world's most respected centers devoted exclusively to cancer, MD Anderson Cancer Center is on the campus of the Texas Medical Center in Houston. Since opening its doors in 1944, MD Anderson has treated 900,000 patients. In 2012 alone, more than 115,000 people—nearly one-third of them new patients—received care at MD Anderson.

Anderson has developed a network of regional care centers in Texas, New Mexico, New Jersey, and Arizona, and, notable for international patients, are the centers in Madrid, Spain, and Istanbul, Turkey.

MD Anderson surgeons and physicians treat all forms of cancer in its many specialty centers, including cancer prevention, cardiopulmonary disorders, dermasurgery, orthopedics, pain management, radiation treatment, reconstructive surgery, and stem cell transplantation.

The Children's Cancer Hospital is home to specialists in pediatric oncology. The MD Anderson Proton Therapy Center offers a precise form of proton therapy known as pencil beam scanning.

Each international patient is assigned an individual care representative fluent in the patient's own language to assist with appointments; visas; travel arrangements; airport arrival and transportation; banking and business services; and cultural, religious, and dietary needs. Housing can be arranged at the Jesse H. Jones Rotary House International on the MD Anderson campus or at nearby hotels or apartments. MD Anderson provides a comprehensive travel service, along with special discounts for patients, family members, and caregivers.

Accreditation: The Joint Commission

Leading Specialties: Oncology

Memorial Sloan Kettering Cancer Center

1275 York Avenue
New York City, New York 10065, USA
Tel: +1 212 639.4900
Email: international@mskcc.org
Web: mskcc.org

Memorial Sloan Kettering Cancer Center (MSKCC) is the world's oldest and largest private institution devoted to prevention, patient care, research, and education in cancer. MSKCC scientists and clinicians generate innovative approaches to better understand, diagnose, and treat cancer. Since its founding in 1884, MSKCC has been focused on both patient care and innovative research, making significant contributions to new and better therapies for the treatment of cancer.

Memorial Sloan Kettering Cancer Center is a consolidation of two organizations: the Sloan Kettering Institute, one of the nation's premier biomedical research organizations, and Memorial Hospital. They were unified as a single entity in 1960.

Today the center has more than 800 physicians and 11,000 employees accommodating more than a half million outpatient visits and more than 24,000 inpatient admissions each year. Services are delivered at numerous sites, which together constitute a network of community-based cancer treatment facilities. MSKCC's Breast Examination Center of Harlem, for example, provides breast and cervical cancer screening at no extra expense to the women of the Harlem community.

During the past decade, Memorial Sloan Kettering researchers have made impressive advances in understanding the causes of cancer, particularly the genetic basis of many common cancers, and in developing new approaches for prevention, early detection, and treatment. MSKCC's 23-story Zuckerman Research Center, which opened in mid-2006, houses many laboratories and research programs.

Memorial Sloan Kettering's distinctive disease management program formalizes the institution's interdisciplinary approach to care. A disease-management team brings together experts in specific types of cancer—such as breast, colorectal, and lung— as well as prevention and wellness. Teams may consist of medical oncologists, radiation oncologists, pathologists, and other health professionals, an approach that integrates the knowledge and expertise from numerous disciplines to optimize care for each patient.

The social, emotional, and psychological needs of patients and their families are at the forefront of care. The center offers a full range of programs to help patients and families throughout all phases of treatment, including support groups, genetic counseling, help managing cancer pain and symptoms, rehabilitation, and assistance in navigating life after treatment.

MSKCC also offers integrative medicine services at the Bendheim Integrative Medicine Center. This spa-like facility is open to community members as well as families and friends of Memorial Sloan Kettering patients, offering such therapies as massage, acupuncture, hypnotherapy, meditation, nutritional counseling, music therapy, and yoga.

For patients seeking refuge and respite from cancer and its treatment, the Memorial Sloan Kettering Patient Recreation Pavilion offers adult patients and their visitors a wide range of arts and crafts activities, a well-equipped library, an outdoor terrace, and regular entertainment events. Recreation therapists lead such activities as copper enameling, watercolor, woodworking, origami, and stained glass. Live performances by outside entertainers, including students from the Juilliard School, are held several times each week. Crafts and activities are also available in patients' rooms.

Patients traveling to MSKCC from outside the United States are accommodated through the Bobst International Center, which provides a comfortable place for international patients and their families to coordinate their clinical and personal needs.

Before a patient's arrival, specially trained staff members assemble the medical information physicians need to arrange for an opinion by mail, an on-site second-opinion consultation, or medical care. During a patient's stay, guest services staff serve as liaisons for planning lodging, air travel, local transport, and other services.

A limited number of private hospital rooms and suites are available for patients with special needs. One of the hospital floors offers private suites, featuring spacious rooms, baths, and sitting rooms, as well as a lounge and library for family members and companions. Upon request, interpreters can be made available to assist international patients with medical consultations as well as non-medical encounters.

Accreditation: The Joint Commission

Leading Specialties: Oncology

PART THREE

Resources and References

Additional Resources

World, Country, and City Information

The World Factbook (cia.gov). Cataloged by country, *The World Factbook*—compiled by the US Central Intelligence Agency (CIA)—is an excellent source of general up-to-date information about the geography, economy, and history of countries around the world. On the website, click on the "Library" tab, then click the "Publications" link, then click on "The World Factbook."

Wikipedia (wikipedia.org). Wikipedia has amassed reliable information on every country and city that qualifies as a medical travel destination, including information on healthcare and tourism for most entries.

Centers for Disease Control and Prevention (cdc.gov). This US government agency focuses on disease control and prevention. Its "Travel Health Notices" pages provide up-to-date alerts on disease outbreaks and required and recommended immunizations and vaccines for travelers.

Passports and Visas

Travisa (travisa.com). Dozens of online agencies offer visa services. We have found Travisa to be reliable and accessible by telephone as well. The agency offers good customer service and follow-up. Travisa's website also carries information links to immunization requirements, travel warnings, current weather, and other valuable travel information.

Currency Converter

XE Currency Converter (xe.com). This easy-to-use site is an excellent source to learn quickly how much your dollar, pound, or euro is worth in nearly every country in the world.

International Hospital Accreditation

Joint Commission International (jointcommissioninternational.org). Mentioned frequently throughout this book, JCI remains the world's leader for independent international hospital accreditation. For a current list of accredited hospitals by country, click on the "About JCI" tab; then click on "JCI-Accredited Organizations."

The Accreditation Association for Ambulatory Health Care (aaahc.org). AAAHC is the world's largest independent accrediting agency of outpatient (same-day) medical services, including clinics and medical centers specializing in dentistry, cosmetic surgery, orthopedics, fertility, and screening and testing centers. Its international arm awards accreditation to qualifying facilities around the world.

The American Association for Accreditation of Ambulatory Surgery Facilities International (aaaasfi.org). AAAASF focuses on accrediting ambulatory (outpatient) surgery centers. Its international arm, AAAASFI, has accredited dental and surgery facilities in some 16 countries, including Mexico, Costa Rica, Colombia, Switzerland, Belgium, South Africa, and Australia.

Medical Information

Often the best place to begin a diagnosis or obtain a second opinion is with your own research. Although online resources can never replace a qualified dentist, doctor, or specialist, many provide basic information. Whether you are seeking care at home or abroad, it pays to be armed with information before your consultations.

MedlinePlus (nlm.nih.gov/medlineplus). This US-government-sponsored medical site brings together a wealth of information from sources such as the National Library of Medicine (the world's largest medical library), the National Institutes of Health, *Merriam-Webster's Medical Dictionary*, and the United States Pharmacopeia.

Mayo Clinic Diseases and Conditions Center (mayoclinic.org). Click on the "Patient Care and Health Info" tab. The Mayo Clinic has amassed an impressive body of easy-to-understand information on hundreds of medical ailments.

Merriam-Webster's Medical Dictionary (merriam-webster.com/browse/medical/a. htm). Several free online medical glossaries provide more than you probably want to know on most health topics. *Merriam-Webster's Medical Dictionary* is one of the most comprehensive and highly regarded. You can also type "define <term>" in your browser bar, and you will be presented with a host of choices, including Merriam-Webster.

Other Online Resources

In a world where you can search, compare, and purchase nearly anything online—from a stock or bond to a toaster or a car—medical care is sadly and singularly lagging behind. Although change is on the horizon, hospitals and clinics rarely post rankings, ratings, or pricing, as of this writing. While we wait for medical transparency to become a reality, international health travelers can visit aggregators that provide information on facilities and doctors, and sometimes pricing. Although most focus on US-based providers, international directories are beginning to emerge, lending greater opportunity for patient choice and safety.

Healthgrades (healthgrades.com). The largest search directory of US doctors and hospitals, with some 250 million visitors annually. Healthgrades also rates doctors and facilities via patient reviews and internal research.

ZocDoc (zocdoc.com). Like Healthgrades, ZocDoc is a mostly US-based doctor finder, with robust patient reviews and an appointment-booking feature. The company is expanding to include doctors outside the US.

Dental Departures (dentaldepartures.com). The largest global search site for dentists, Dental Departures provides information on some 3,000 dentists and clinics in 30 countries. Detailed pricing is featured for each clinic, along with patient-generated reviews.

WhatClinic (whatclinic.com). Founded in 2006, WhatClinic is a global doctor and clinic finder database featuring more than 100,000 doctors and medical facilities in 100 countries. Patients seeking the highest-quality care among this vast array will need to carefully vet their choices.

MediBid (medibid.com). More than a search tool or aggregator, MediBid carries inventory for various procedures, which is auctioned to patients by price and location. Largely US-based, MediBid now offers a medical tourism component, including all-in medical/travel packages. Online registration is required. Use caution when shopping on price alone.

Publications and Periodicals

The International Medical Travel Journal (imtjonline.com). The *IMTJ* is the world's leading journal for the medical travel industry. Though geared more toward industry professionals than healthcare consumers, it does provide a free online guide for potential patients. There is a free email newsletter, too, and a paid subscription service for those who are serious about industry news.

Travel and Tourism

It is often easier, faster, and cheaper to book flights, accommodations, and even restaurant reservations yourself through a growing number of online sites, including these:

Expedia, Inc. (expedia.com)
Kayak (kayak.com)
Hotels.com (hotels.com)
Orbitz (orbitz.com)
Priceline.com (priceline.com)
Travelocity (travelocity.com)
TripAdvisor (tripadvisor.com)
Yelp (yelp.com)

International Society of Travel Medicine (istm.org). This organization was founded in 1991 to promote safe and healthy travel and to facilitate education, service, and research in travel medicine. The site offers valuable information about immunizations, infectious diseases, and other aspects of medical travel. Most useful to the health traveler is the society's searchable database of health travel practitioners.

MEDICAL GLOSSARY

Many medical terms are used in this book. The following is a list of the most commonly used terms. For further information, plase consult your doctor.

Acute care. Providing emergency services and general medical and surgical treatment for sudden severe disorders (as compared with long-term care for chronic illness).

Addiction. Occurs when a person has no control over the use of a substance, such as drugs or alcohol. Also includes addictions to food, gambling, and sex.

Aesthetics. A general term for medical treatments and surgical procedures undertaken to improve appearance. Such procedures include (but are not limited to) facelifts, tummy tucks, laser resurfacing of skin, Botox injection, cosmetic dentistry, and others.

Alzheimer's disease. A degenerative disorder of neurons in the brain that disrupts thought, perception, and behavior.

Anesthesia. Loss of physical sensation produced by sedation. Anesthesia may be given as (1) general, which affects the entire body and is accompanied by loss of consciousness; (2) regional, affecting an entire area of the body; and (3) local, which affects a limited part of the body (usually superficial).

Angiography. An x-ray procedure that uses dye injected into the coronary arteries to study circulation in the heart.

Angioplasty. A procedure that uses a tiny balloon on the end of a catheter to widen blocked or constricted arteries in the heart.

Arthroscopy or arthroscopic surgery. The use of a tubelike instrument utilizing fiber optics to examine, treat, or perform surgery on a joint.

Bariatric. Pertaining to the control and treatment of obesity and allied diseases.

Birmingham hip resurfacing (BHR). A metal-on-metal hip replacement system, surgically implanted to replace a hip joint. The BHR is called a resurfacing prosthesis because only the surface of the femoral head (ball) is removed to implant the femoral head-resurfacing component.

Bone densitometry. A method of measuring bone strength, used to diagnose osteoporosis.

Botox. A nonsurgical, physician-administered injection treatment to temporarily reduce moderate to severe wrinkles on the face.

Cardiac. Pertaining to the heart.

Cardiac catheterization. The insertion of a catheter into the arteries of the heart to diagnose heart disease. See also **angiography.**

Cardiothoracic. Of or relating to the heart and the chest.

Cardiovascular. Pertaining to the heart and blood vessels that comprise the circulatory system. See also **vascular surgery.**

Cataract. Cloudiness of the lens in the eye, which affects vision. Cataracts, which often occur in older people, can be corrected with surgery to replace the damaged lens with an artificial plastic lens known as an intraocular lens (IOL).

Colonoscopy. An examination of the interior of the colon, using a thin, lighted tube (called a colonoscope) inserted into the rectum.

Computed tomography (CT). Sometimes known as CAT scan. A noninvasive diagnostic tool that uses x-rays to provide cross-sectional images of the body. Used to detect cancer, determine heart function, and provide images of body organs. May be used in conjunction with **positron emission tomography (PET).**

Coronary artery bypass graft (CABG). Surgical procedure to create alternative paths for blood to flow around obstructions in the coronary arteries, most often using arteries or veins from other parts of the body.

Cosmetic surgery. Plastic surgery undertaken to improve appearance. See also **plastic surgery.**

Craniofacial. Relating to the head and face.

CyberKnife. A tool for radiosurgery that delivers precise, high-dose radiation to a tumor. Can be used for tumors of the pancreas, liver, and lungs.

Diabetes. A chronic disease characterized by abnormally high levels of sugar in the blood.

Discectomy. Removal of all or part of an intervertebral disc (a soft structure that acts as a shock absorber between two bones in the back).

Electrocardiogram (EKG or ECG). A diagnostic test that measures the heart's electrical activity.

Endocrinology. The branch of medicine that studies hormonal systems and treats disorders that arise when hormones are out of balance.

Endoscope. A slender, tubular optical instrument used as a viewing system for examining an inner part of the body and, with an attached instrument, for performing surgery or detecting tumors.

Extracorporeal shock wave therapy (ESWT). A noninvasive treatment that involves delivery of shock waves to a painful area.

Gamma Knife. A form of radiation therapy that focuses low-dose gamma radiation on a precise target, such as a tumor of the brain or breast.

Gastroenterology. The branch of medicine that studies and treats disorders of the digestive system.

Genetics. The study of inheritance.

Gynecology. The branch of medicine that studies and treats females, especially as related to their reproductive system.

Hematology. The study of the nature, function, and diseases of the blood and of blood-forming organs.

Hemopoietic or hematopoietic. Pertaining to the formation of blood.

Hepatitis. Inflammation of the liver caused by a virus or toxin. There are different forms of viral hepatitis. Vaccines are available for hepatitis A and B. There is no vaccine for hepatitis C.

Hepatobiliary. Relating to the bile ducts.

Hepatology. The branch of medicine that studies and treats disorders of the liver.

Holter monitor. A wearable electronic device used to obtain a continuous recording of the heart's electrical activity. See **electrocardiogram.**

Immunization. Inoculation with a vaccine to render a person resistant to a disease.

Immunology. The branch of medicine that studies and treats disorders of the body's mechanisms for fighting disease, especially infectious diseases.

Implant. *In dentistry:* a small metal pin placed inside the jawbone to mimic the root of a tooth. Dental implants can be used to help anchor a false tooth, a crown, or a bridge. *In fertility treatment:* to place an embryo in the uterus.

Intensive Care Unit (ICU). The ward in a hospital where 24-hour specialized nursing and monitoring are provided for patients who are critically ill or have undergone major surgical procedures.

International Organization for Standardization (ISO). An organization based in Geneva, Switzerland, that approves and accredits the facilities and administrations of hospitals and clinics, but not their practices, procedures, or methods.

Intracytoplasmic sperm injection (ICSI). A type of fertility treatment in which a single sperm cell is inserted into an egg using special micromanipulation equipment.

Intrauterine insemination (IUI). Introduction of prepared sperm (either the male partner's or a donor's) into the uterus to improve chances of pregnancy.

In vitro fertilization (IVF). Known as the test-tube baby technique. Eggs are fertilized outside the body, and then embryos are introduced back into the woman's uterus.

Joint Commission International (JCI). The international affiliate accreditation agency of The Joint Commission, which inspects and accredits healthcare providers worldwide using US-based standards.

Laparoscope. A thin, lighted tube used to examine and treat tissues and organs inside the abdomen.

LAP-BAND® System. An adjustable silicone band inserted laparoscopically around the upper part of the stomach, thereby reducing the food storage area of the stomach and promoting weight loss.

LASIK (laser-assisted *in situ* keratomileusis). A laser procedure to reduce dependency on eyeglasses or contact lenses by permanently changing the shape of the cornea, the clear covering of the front of the eye.

Liposuction. The surgical withdrawal of fat from under the skin, using a small incision and vacuum suctioning.

Lithotripsy. A procedure that breaks up kidney stones or gallstones using sound waves. Also called extracorporeal shock wave lithotripsy (ESWL).

Magnetic resonance imaging (MRI). A noninvasive diagnostic tool that produces clear images of the human body without the use of x-rays. MRI, which uses a large magnet, radio waves, and a computer, is used to diagnose spine and joint problems, heart disease, and cancer.

Mammography. X-ray imaging of the breast for detection of cancer.

Maxillofacial. Of or pertaining to the jaws and face.

Microsurgical epididymal sperm aspiration (MESA). Obtaining immature sperm cells from the epididymis (which joins the testicle to the vas deferens), in cases where obstruction in the genital tract leads to absence of sperm in the ejaculate. The recovered sperm can be used for intracytoplasmic sperm injection (ICSI).

Minimally invasive surgery. Any of a variety of approaches used to reduce the trauma of surgery and to speed recovery. These approaches include "keyhole" surgery, endoscopy, arthroscopy, laparoscopy, or the use of small incisions.

Myocardial infarction. Heart attack.

Neonatology. The branch of medicine specializing in the care and treatment of newborns.

Nephrology. The medical specialty that deals with the kidneys.

Neurology. The branch of medicine that studies and treats disorders of the nervous system, including the brain.

Neuro-oncology. The branch of medicine that studies and treats cancers of the nervous system.

Neuro-ophthalmology. The branch of medicine that studies and treats disorders of the nerves in the eye.

Neurosurgery. Surgery on the brain or other parts of the nervous system.

Obstetrics. The branch of medicine focusing on pregnancy and childbirth.

Oncology. The branch of medicine that studies and treats cancer.

Ophthalmology. The branch of medicine that studies and treats disorders of the eye.

Orthodontics. The branch of dentistry dealing with the prevention and correction of irregular tooth positioning, as by means of braces.

Orthopedics. The branch of medicine that studies and treats diseases and injuries of the bones and joints.

Osteoporosis. Thinning of the bones and reduction in bone mass, which increases the risk of fractures and decreases mobility, especially in the elderly.

Otolaryngology. The branch of medicine that studies and treats ear, nose, and throat disorders.

Pacemaker. An electronic device surgically implanted into a patient's chest to regulate the heartbeat.

Parkinson's disease. A movement disorder most common among the elderly.

Pathology. The branch of medicine that focuses on the laboratory-based study of disease in cells and tissues, as opposed to clinical examination of symptoms.

Pediatric. Of or pertaining to children.

Periodontics. The branch of dentistry dealing with the study and treatment of diseases of the bones, connective tissues, and gums surrounding and supporting the teeth.

Physiotherapy or physical therapy. The treatment or management of physical disability, malfunction, or pain by exercise, massage, hydrotherapy, and other techniques without the use of drugs, surgery, or radiation.

Plastic surgery. The branch of medicine focusing on corrective operations to the face, head, and body to restore function and (sometimes) to improve appearance (also called **cosmetic surgery**).

Polio (poliomyelitis). A paralyzing disease caused by a virus and characterized by inflammation of the motor neurons of the brain stem and spinal cord.

Positron emission tomography (PET). Also known as PET imaging or PET scan. A diagnostic tool that captures images of the human body by detecting positrons or tiny particles from radioactive material. Used to detect cancer and determine heart function. May be used in conjunction with **computed tomography (CT).**

Prosthodontics. The branch of dentistry that deals with replacement of missing teeth and other oral structures with artificial devices.

Proton therapy. A type of radiation treatment that treats diseased tissue in a more focused way than traditional radiation, using proton beams, and thus destroying less surrounding healthy tissue.

Psychiatry. The branch of medicine that studies and treats mental disorders.

Radiofrequency ablation. The use of electrodes to generate heat and destroy abnormal tissue.

Radiology. The branch of medicine dealing with capturing and interpreting images, such as x-rays, CT scans, and MRI scans.

Radiosurgery. The use of ionizing radiation from an external source (such as a **Gamma Knife**), to destroy cancerous or diseased tissue.

Radiotherapy. Treatment of disease with ionizing radiation, especially by targeted irradiation using external beams, implantation, or infusion.

Reconstructive surgery. The branch of surgery dealing with the repair or replacement of malformed, injured, or lost tissues of the body, chiefly by the transplant of living tissues.

Rehabilitation. The process of restoring health and improving functioning.

Renal. Relating to the kidneys.

Rheumatology. The branch of medicine that studies and treats disorders characterized by pain and stiffness afflicting the extremities or back.

Stem cell. An unspecialized or undifferentiated cell that can become specialized to perform the functions of diverse tissues in the body.

Stent. A tube inserted into a blood vessel or duct to keep it open. Stents are sometimes inserted into narrowed coronary arteries to help keep them open after balloon angioplasty.

Tertiary care. Care of a highly specialized nature.

Testicular epididymal sperm aspiration (TESA). A surgical procedure to obtain sperm from within the testicular tissue.

Transplant. *Organ transplant:* the surgical insertion of an organ from a donor (living or deceased) into a patient to replace an organ that is diseased or malfunctioning; transplants are available for heart, liver, lungs, pancreas, kidney, cornea, and some other organs. *Stem cell transplant:* a procedure in which stem cells are collected from the blood of the patient (autologous) or a matched donor (allergenic) and then reinserted into the patient to rebuild the immune system. *Bone marrow transplant:* a procedure that places healthy bone marrow from the patient (autograft) or a donor (allograft) into a patient whose bone marrow is damaged or malfunctioning.

Typhoid. An infectious, potentially fatal intestinal disease caused by bacteria and usually transmitted in food or water.

Ultrasound. The use of high-frequency sound waves in therapy or diagnostics, as in the deep-heat treatment of a joint or in the imaging of internal structures.

Urology. The branch of medicine that studies and treats disorders of the urinary system.

Vascular surgery. The branch of medicine focusing on the diagnosis and surgical treatment of disorders of the blood vessels.

Wellness. An area of preventive medicine that promotes health and well-being though various means, such as diet, exercise, yoga, tai chi, social support, and more.

X-rays. A form of electromagnetic radiation, similar to light but of shorter wavelength, which can penetrate solids; used for imaging solid structures inside the body.

Index

Hospital and clinic names are in **bold**. Specific treatments are in *italics*. Main treatment categories are indexed; specific treatments may be found in the text.

ABOUT THE AUTHOR

Josef Woodman is an outspoken advocate of affordable, high-quality medical and preventive care for healthcare consumers worldwide. He has spent eight years touring more than 200 medical facilities in 35 countries, researching and vetting international healthcare options. Co-founder of MyDailyHealth (1998) and Ventana Communications (1987), Woodman's pioneering background in publishing, healthcare, and technology has allowed him to compile a wealth of information about international health travel, telemedicine, wellness, integrative medicine, and consumer-directed healthcare.

Woodman has lectured at the UCLA School of Public Health, Harvard Medical School, Duke Fuqua School of Business, Scientific American, and the International Society for Travel Medicine. He has keynoted and moderated conferences on medical tourism and global healthcare in 20 countries. He has appeared in numerous print and broadcast media, including *The Economist, The New York Times,* CNN, ABC News, Fox News, Huffington Post, *Barron's, The Wall Street Journal,* and more.

CPSIA information can be obtained at www.ICGtesting.com
Printed in the USA
LVOW03s0950260115

424370LV00001B/1/P